Democracy
Is Awkward

Democracy Is Awkward

Grappling with Racism
inside American Grassroots
Political Organizing

Michael L. Rosino

THE UNIVERSITY OF NORTH CAROLINA PRESS

Chapel Hill

Designed by Richard Hendel
Set in Miller and The Sans
by codeMantra
Manufactured in the United States of America

Complete Library of Congress Cataloging-in-Publication Data for
this title is available at https://lccn.loc.gov/2024045000.
ISBN 978-1-4696-8562-5 (cloth; alk. paper)
ISBN 978-1-4696-8563-2 (paper; alk. paper)
ISBN 978-1-4696-8383-6 (epub)
ISBN 978-1-4696-8767-4 (pdf)

For Angelica

Contents

Democracy
Is Awkward

Introduction
Welcome to the Party

Democracy is awkward.

The United States faces a turbulent present and an uncertain future. Confronting pressing problems such as racial oppression, obscene concentrations of wealth, subversion of democracy, and the environmental crisis requires everyday people to wield political power for the greater good. Yet progressive political organizations in the United States have frequently failed to materialize real social change. At the same time, barriers such as voter ID laws, access to polling locations, gerrymandering, felon disenfranchisement, and voter roll purges continue to marginalize people of color from the political process. Given all this, how can grassroots progressive organizations build an inclusive and just multiracial democracy?

Grassroots progressive politics should, by its very nature, be accessible and inclusive. Grassroots political organizing, the development of political movements and parties that include and amplify the needs of nonelite, ordinary people, presents one of the most important tools for combating racial inequality and boosting the political voice of the disenfranchised. Addressing the challenges of creating durable, multiracial grassroots political organizations and their potential for achieving liberation from racial oppression is vital to creating a more equal, democratic, and just society.

Being troubled and curious about the paradox of democracy and oppression, and seeking to understand relevant social processes, has driven much of my work as a sociologist. I sought answers to such questions in historical archives and large datasets of digital documents. After deep analysis of contexts such as chattel slavery, Jim Crow racial terrorism, the racialized rules and expectations of daily life, contemporary racial politics, media content about the racial implications of policy, the fragile multiracial coalition of the 1960s Freedom Movement, and the ongoing struggle for the human rights of African Americans, I found myself faced with questions that I wanted to answer through direct observation and experience.

As this project became more concrete, I began observing social patterns, like those I had recognized in the context of my past research projects, in the world around me but with greater clarity, relevance, and practical insight. Two questions emerged to guide me: (1) *How* do the participants in progressive grassroots political organizations engage with racialized barriers and social inequalities? (2) Given the radical promise of grassroots democracy, *why* do these barriers and inequalities often remain intact, and *how* can they be dismantled?

I began truly grappling with these questions around 2015. They seemed to be simmering under the surface and growing with the rise of grassroots progressive movements. Going into this study, I had no idea precisely how tumultuous and chaotic this political period would be. From the election of Donald J. Trump to renewed attempts to disenfranchise people of color from democratic participation to the rise of both the "alt-right" and antiracist resistance groups, these moments in recent history exemplified many of the tensions and contradictions in our politics and society that I sought to capture and better understand. These issues also remain largely unresolved in the years since.

From 2015 to 2017, I immersed myself in a grassroots progressive political party that exemplified these challenges and contradictions. I call this organization the Grassroots Action Party (GAP). This name and those of participants, locations, regional chapters, and other organizations are pseudonyms. Some readers may be clamoring to know the "real" name of the organization. But there are important reasons for keeping it under wraps. First, this anonymity allowed people to share their thoughts and experiences. Second, perhaps more importantly, the purpose of this book is not to talk about a specific organization or person. It is something much bigger.

I discovered how people's awareness of racial inequality and daily habits and routines impact their participation in progressive grassroots politics. I learned how confronting the contradictions between an organization's goals and practices can be a catalyst for transformation and racial justice. However, without deep engagement and awareness, these contradictions can also be objects of ignorance and rationalization. Along the way, I unearthed practical insights that grassroots progressives can use to break through barriers and obstacles when creating a more racially just society.

CRASHING THE CONVENTION

I took a deep breath and entered the convention hall. I followed a sign that read "GAP Convention Downstairs" and walked through a large doorway. After years of interest in political participation beyond the ballot box, walking through this door represented a new foray into the world of grassroots democracy. The Grassroots Action Party was holding a major regional meeting. This meeting was my opportunity to understand grassroots politics from an insider perspective. After registration, I sat in the back of the main hall. Looking down, I noticed my name tag signaled that I was not a registered party member.

I was already somewhat familiar with the GAP. Their online presence and platform intrigued me. Social equity, environmentalism, human rights, and democracy stood out as animating principles. They emphasized politically empowering people of color and commitments to racial justice. There was even an event on racial oppression on the day's schedule. However, looking around the convention hall, I noticed that, at the risk of assuming people's racial backgrounds, almost all of the around sixty attendees appeared white, except for perhaps four.

This racial makeup for an organization or event may seem commonplace or unremarkable to some of us. On average, whites spend most of their time in racially homogenous spaces.[1] Encountering a sea of fellow white faces would not raise a red flag for many whites. But I was not simply a white person pursuing my political participation. I was also a sociologist in training. At its best, sociology helps us investigate the taken-for-granted and find the social dynamics behind things that feel normal.[2] So I became motivated to unravel the mystery—why a progressive grassroots political organization that professed the value of diversity and racial justice *just happened* to be disproportionately white.

As sociologist Amanda Lewis points out, "Although numerous all-white groups are not explicitly racial, their racial composition is not an accident but is a result of whites' status as members of a passive social collectivity whose lives are shaped at least in part by the racialized social system in which they live and operate."[3] Understanding how a grassroots political organization that values racial diversity and inclusion struggles to translate those goals into concrete actions can reveal profound truths about racial oppression, everyday life, and democracy in the contemporary United States. More importantly, though, it can unearth practical insights. These insights can help us strengthen participation in democracy and build durable multiracial coalitions to address interconnected crises like economic inequality, racial oppression, and environmental collapse.

The meeting began. A white, middle-aged man walked to the front of the room. Someone attempted to hand him a microphone. He bellowed, with a grin, "I don't need a microphone!" He talked about how the GAP was the most progressive political organization. He argued that it represented the politics of the future. At several points during his speech, he was interrupted and even corrected by audience members. Yet he continued, unfazed, saying, "We are an idea—we need people to see through our lens." Based on this opening speech and my experiences in the coming months, I realized that the GAP represented a set of ideals for many of its members. It was a source of group identity as much as an organization with concrete strategies and goals. Its organizational identity, the shared sense of "we" among participants, was an intrinsic aspect of how the GAP functioned and how people made decisions.[4]

Next was a talk on election rigging and electronic voting machines, followed by a short break. During the break, I talked to a young white man wearing a polo and khakis in the bathroom as we washed our hands. I noticed he was also not a registered member. I asked what he thought of the meeting so far. He told me he was just there for his brother, who "loves this stuff," as a birthday present. He explained that he agreed with what the organization was trying to do. However, he felt that the GAP could not put people in office, so he voted strategically in local elections.

I returned to my seat for a talk focusing on animal welfare issues. The speaker, a middle-aged white woman, tied the rights of animals to social justice. She brought up the concept of intersectionality and argued that violence against nonhuman species was an aspect of inequality. On the projector screen behind her, she displayed a quote from the labor activist Cesar Chavez: "Racism, economic deprival, dogfighting and cockfighting, bullfighting and rodeos are all cut from the same defective fabric: violence." She said she agreed with Chavez that we could not address social justice issues like racism without addressing violence toward animals. She stated that animal mistreatment perpetuates a "violent energy" reverberating through society.

She detailed local legislative successes around animal cruelty. During the presentation, she showed pictures of hurt and mutilated animals. These included a rabbit with burned skin and a starving dog. These images, understandably, upset the older white woman next to me. She teared up. I looked around and noticed that many people in the audience looked distressed. Their reception and reaction affirmed a sense of shared morality. It helped them express a collective identity—that they were good people horrified at the world's evil people.

The speaker moved on to animal exploitation in entertainment. The accompanying PowerPoint slide showed an image of a dog chewing on a chew toy made to look like former NFL quarterback Michael Vick. Outrage about Vick's involvement in dogfighting seemed reasonable from an animal rights perspective. However, considering the racial demographics of the audience, something felt unsettling about an effigy of a Black man being chewed by a dog as a source of comedic relief. Images of civil rights protesters in Birmingham, Alabama, being attacked by police dogs formed in my mind by association. But the audience laughed at this image.

Soon after, the speaker visually compared the conditions for egg-laying chickens in large-scale farms to the thousands of disproportionately Black victims of Hurricane Katrina who were displaced and held in harsh, dangerous, and cramped conditions in the New Orleans Superdome.[5] Her comparison was based on the principle of compassion for all living beings. Nonetheless, it was reminiscent of how "nonwhite" people have been symbolically dehumanized, materially exploited, and physically controlled through comparisons to beasts or animals throughout history.[6] As the shock of this comparison wore off, the speaker reiterated her previous point about animal rights as a social justice issue. She ended her talk to heartfelt applause.

After another session where candidates for local offices introduced themselves and their platforms, it was time for lunch. I entered the dining area of the hall and sat down at a random table. After making a plate of vegan Jamaican food, I introduced myself and began to talk to an older white woman sitting next to me named Janice. I expressed my interest in getting involved with the party. She invited me to attend an upcoming meeting for the Moosewater branch of the GAP at another member's home in a nearby city.

We exchanged contact information and talked about local food. Janice mentioned that she was part of a local food co-op. I asked her what she thought about the fact that poor people often cannot access these foods. She agreed that this was an essential issue for the local food movement but that there were significant challenges to making local food more affordable.

She then asked me about myself. I explained that I was a graduate student in sociology. I talked about a course I was teaching and mentioned that I wanted to understand how people can become more aware of and resist social inequality in their everyday lives. She looked at me and paused. She said, "It's hard."

Just then, several older white men came and sat down with us. They loudly changed the subject. The women at the table and I sat silent. These men discussed issues like communication technology and workers' rights. The tone of the conversation changed as they set the agenda and spoke over us and each other. I wondered whether this was part of a larger interactional pattern shaped by social inequalities.

Eventually there was a lull as the men at the table began to focus on the plates in front of them. I asked Janice why she decided to get involved with the GAP. She told me that despite organizational problems, she liked that anyone could get involved and impact their community. However, she also noted that it was difficult to influence state-level agendas and policies, and it was often hard to access meetings and information. These are typical political barriers to participation and influence that grassroots political parties face.[7]

Alongside those dressed in casual or business casual attire, there were also several interesting-looking characters dressed in bright and outlandish outfits. They seemed to be party fanatics. As I used the bathroom after lunch, I saw a white man in a tricorne hat, like those famously worn by early presidents and the founders of the US government in the eighteenth century, covered with various progressive political pins. He vomited in the sink. He noticed my presence and explained that he had drunk too much coffee and eaten too fast. Thinking back to Janice's words about how anyone can get involved, I wondered if that was not only a favorable attribute but also a liability. Anyone, no matter how off-putting, even a guy doing Revolutionary War cosplay, could represent the organization. I imagined that the more professional members of the organization then struggled to disprove this stigmatizing image.

I walked back to the main hall. An older white man played "Redemption Song" by Bob Marley on the ukulele. Participants stood around and chatted, taking a break from the formalities of the convention. My concentration was soon broken by someone attempting to get my attention. It was the man in the tricorne hat. He handed me a flyer about a local progressive organization. He explained that while he did not live in that city, he was moving there "in six months after my girlfriend moves there soon because I need to get a relationship with her kids first." I told him, "That makes sense." I wasn't sure what else to say, so I walked away.

Next on the meeting schedule were elections for positions within the party. Each of the candidates took turns speaking about their platform and goals. In her remarks, a middle-aged Latina woman named Nina, running for a significant role in the party, argued that she saw the party as a potential vehicle for fighting racial injustice. I realized this was the first mention of how the party could address racial oppression of the entire day. I watched as the members went through their elaborate system for choosing representatives.

I glanced down at the schedule of the events. I was especially interested in those that focused on resisting racial oppression and organizing and outreach. I was glad that the organization was centering these pragmatic and vital concerns. Next on the agenda was a workshop on anti-Black oppression in the main hall. I helped some other attendees place chairs in a circle in preparation for the discussion. As someone who had spent much time engaging with racial oppression and inequality issues, I grew curious about how the party would facilitate a critical dialog about such important, but often tense or controversial, social issues.

The local activist who was scheduled to address racial oppression never showed up. So, instead, the event organizers tapped two of the very few attendees of color at the last minute to take his place. The selection of two of the only prominent party members of color at the last minute for these roles, much like the organization's demographics, was not coincidental. It reflected broader social trends. In majority-white organizations, people of color are often positioned as ambassadors for their entire social group, facing pressures for adequate social performances to disprove dominant stereotypes.[8] They are also routinely relegated to roles in these organizations where they are tasked with "diversity work" or "urban outreach," which have more to do with their group identities than their skill sets.[9] Though these positions may be valued, they often provide little opportunity for advancement.[10]

Through no fault of their own, the newly appointed facilitators seemed unprepared for this new role. Nonetheless, they valiantly attempted to lead the workshop. One of the workshop leaders, a middle-aged Black man, started with a rambling and inaccurate background of the Black Lives Matter movement. He told us that the movement began with the book *The*

New Jim Crow by Michelle Alexander and then escalated and grew with the reaction to the shooting of Michael Brown.[11] He said that it also had links to the school-to-prison pipeline issue.

As the discussion began, people began to talk about their experiences with activism and the challenges of forming mass movements against racial inequality and police brutality. The other workshop leader, the Latina woman who previously talked about racial oppression in the pitch for her campaign, discussed her struggles to produce more racial diversity and inclusion in local political organizations. She mentioned the importance of including people of color in positions of political power. Echoing historian Ira Katznelson, she said that affirmative action was only problematic to whites when it was about helping people of color.[12] Still, there has been affirmative action for whites from the beginning. People applauded this point.

Next, the workshop leaders discussed how to frame issues of racism to reach a wider audience. They focused on strategies to have discussions that don't turn white people off. These included emphasizing that "it's not about being antipolice but against police brutality," pointing out that "mass incarceration affects white people too," and reminding them that Black Lives Matter "means Black lives matter *too*." The Latina woman mentioned that she received flak as a local political leader for marching with Black Lives Matter. But she pointed out that they received community support even though the police condemned them. This point and the tension that it entailed between respectability and direct action was something many participants navigated. The goals and strategies of activists and politicians converge and conflict in grassroots politics.

An older white woman talked about how racial violence was part of a more extensive system of violence, including violence against animals. She suggested that racial oppression was rooted in violence against animals. She said there was a similar feeling of an emotional high that someone gets from committing violence and that forms of violence carry over. This claim received a lukewarm response. It seemed that she was merely repeating talking points from the previous presentation on animal welfare.

Another younger white woman talked about how difficult it can be to educate people about privilege. She said that it was important when explaining these issues to do so that poor white people don't blame people of color. She said that they needed to understand that privilege is relative.

In her discussion, she used an awkward and mixed metaphor about the ability to dunk a basketball as an example of privilege.

Before she could finish her point, an older white man abruptly interrupted her to talk about how the police aren't independent and that the government is the root of racism. As one of the workshop leaders responded, he interrupted to say, "Can I finish?" so that he could repeat his point. This terse back-and-forth created some tension. As the leaders began getting the workshop back on track, a middle-aged white man in a Che Guevara T-shirt interrupted. He said the police are a terrorist organization occupying communities of color and can't be reformed. He argued that all this talk of reforming the police was a waste of time and funds. He proposed that arms should be taken from police and redistributed among communities. Some workshop attendees appreciated his radical thinking. Many others were put off by the interruptions and the fanaticism and harshness of his words.

Within this meeting, I noticed several instances wherein older white men silenced women, younger people, and people of color. And many of these older white men seemed to possess a sense of entitlement to assert what is true or define the overarching issue. They engaged with others in ways better described as "telling" rather than "discussing." These patterns contradicted the organization's value of deliberative democracy. These meetings aimed for people to engage in organized discussions to determine the shared interests and best practices that should guide their collective political actions.

Deliberative democracy is a robust process. Many grassroots organizations use this process in their meetings and events. However, research on deliberative democracy in practice between unequal social group members suggests that dominant social group members tend to silence, interrupt, disregard, or mischaracterize subordinate group members' contributions.[13] The pursuit of ideals of inclusion, diversity, equality, and democracy made up a substantial part of the GAP's organizational identity. However, it was clear that producing a social reality that conformed to these ideals was a work in progress.

Steering the conversation back to less contentious territory, the discussion leaders mentioned that language matters. One of the leaders, the African American man, pointed out that it was necessary to name "race" in talking about these issues after someone said, "It's about being antioppression" rather than just about racism. The white man in the polo and khakis whom I had previously spoken to in the restroom talked about his experiences working in the corporate sector. He stated that, at his job, he dealt with people on both sides of the political spectrum. In his experience, he said, it was "about having empathy and not using jargon or making things confusing but breaking it down on a basic human level" to get people to understand racism. People nodded in agreement.

These divergent concerns and definitions made for a disorganized and meandering conversation. Several party members mentioned marching with Black Lives Matter throughout the workshop to bolster their legitimacy and authenticity. They positioned themselves as activists focused on the challenges of antiracist mobilization and resistance. Some members concentrated on abstract questions like "Why is there racism?" Others talked about how to call out racist expressions from family members or acquaintances. Of course, discussions on race and racism are often marked by incoherence and contention.[14] But at the session's close, I was left wondering what we had achieved and what the original speaker would have said or done.

Next, I attended a workshop about recruiting new candidates. Due to the popularity of another talk on issues with electronic voting systems, almost no one else was there. The meeting attendees' lack of engagement was counterintuitive. Recruitment, outreach, and community engagement are crucial functions of grassroots political organizations. Yet interest in gaining knowledge about politics that would bolster members' political identities seemed to take precedence. As I talked with the workshop's leaders, two middle-aged white men who had worked on previous campaigns, I wondered how these priorities impacted the party's strategies and achievements.

Walking to my car and driving home, I grappled with all I had just witnessed. The attendees were kind, welcoming, and passionate about progressive politics despite some awkward moments. I had conflicted feelings about criticizing people who, if nothing else, were trying to get involved and make a positive difference. But I had already noticed unresolved contradictions that seemed to undermine their goals. I also wondered how my social position as a young, middle-class, white male impacted how people treated me and what I noticed that day. If nothing else, I reminded myself that this vantage point allowed me access to white-dominated spaces to pick up on the silences, implied meanings, and patterns that take place.

My initial contact with the GAP raised more questions than answers. Why were the participants so disproportionately white for an organization that placed such a high premium on racial justice and the empowerment of people of color in its agendas and statements? Why did its engagement with issues of racial justice and its connection to communities of color seem so clumsy and underdeveloped? How did the participants themselves think and feel about these events and issues? How did they attempt to practice grassroots democracy in the context of racial and political inequality? I was propelled by these queries to keep showing up, paying attention, asking questions, listening, and getting involved.

ANALYZING AWKWARDNESS

"Democracy is awkward."

Sean, a member of the Grassroots Action Party, blurted out this phrase after a particularly disordered meeting. He may have a point. The sociologist W. E. B. Du Bois explains that democracy is "a method of realizing the broadest measure of justice to all human beings."[15] However, that "method" of both practicing and obtaining democracy is complicated, to say the least, if not downright messy. Many of us recognize this messiness when we reflect on our experiences in a complex and unequal society. We can also see this messiness in the tensions and contradictions I witnessed on my first day with the GAP. However, so much of our established knowledge about political action fails to take this insight seriously.

Studies focused on politics tend to rely on large-scale surveys or the quantified characteristics of states and nations. They tell us how relatively democratic a government is or about a group of people's opinions or attitudes. Research on people's political behavior often occurs in manufactured and controlled settings using sanitized social experiments. Studies of political parties and their engagement with issues like racial injustice often focus on large-scale social and political systems or the rational choices of individual political actors.[16] But we are missing the more crucial story—the practical human challenge of working to build democracy in a racially unequal society.

We discuss political action as though it were exclusively a set of hyperrational and intentional strategies working toward big goals and abstract ideals. But more frequently, we experience it as the daily routines and habits that make up the patterns and flows of our lives. This book takes a micro- and meso-level approach to understanding the role of consciousness, comfort, and conflict in grassroots progressive racial politics. In other words, while keeping the big picture in mind (or the macro-level), it focuses on what happens in our daily interactions, organizations, and communities. This perspective helps clarify the implications of racialized political inequality in everyday life. Perhaps more importantly, we can gain practical insights for achieving greater democracy and equality through grassroots progressive organizations. We must look closely at people's lived realities to see the genuine experiences, joys, and frustrations of democratic participation. Acknowledging these dynamics is the only way to find better ways of tackling and transforming the tensions and paradoxes of a society where political power is concentrated along racial lines.

The "totality of . . . racialized social relations and practices" in society provides a social and structural context for our day-to-day lives.[17] This context can facilitate or restrict our democratic participation. Everyday social interactions in political life contribute to racial inequality via the "role of routine and repetitive practices in the making of social structures."[18] Focusing on everyday political participation reveals how people negotiate racial politics in everyday life.

Because our social, cultural, and political environments are racialized, our feelings are also racialized.[19] For example, for centuries, whites' unrealistic fears around the threat of racial "others" have maintained policies and practices that upheld racial inequality.[20] *Awkwardness* is another, albeit more subtle, way that we feel and experience the racial order of society. But our obsession with rationality in understanding politics and racial inequality ignores the profound role of such feelings in shaping our lives and actions. Our emotions help create a sense of otherness and sameness between people that orients us in the world.[21] This implicit sense of difference and social distance is part of how we engage in everyday social life, cultural production, and political enterprises. Human emotional lives have been racialized since the advent of colonialism. So, while currently living white people did not actively create the racialized structure around them whole cloth, they nonetheless inherit and adopt a sense of proximity and familiarity reflecting generations of racial domination.[22]

Sociologist Mark Carrigan explains that "awkwardness tends to be relegated to the periphery of social life when in fact, it is something constitutive of it."[23] Many of us relate to the uneasy experience of knowing that we *should* be doing something but avoiding it because we imagine it to be uncomfortable, unwieldy, or humiliating. We might even fall into a shame spiral where we feel self-conscious and uncomfortable about feeling awkward, especially about a situation that should be straightforward or comfortable.[24] However, if we do not confront them, these challenging emotions can lead us to languish in ignorance and avoidance around difficult topics like racism and political inequality. As the author James Baldwin wrote, "Not everything that is faced can be changed, but nothing can be changed until it is faced."[25]

We experience similar discomfort when we hold different understandings of a situation than those around us, leading to miscommunication and lingering tension. Situations that do not have clear rules and norms or put our social relationships, roles, and expectations at odds, like a large financial transaction between friends or seeing someone you know from one social context in another, can also feel awkward.[26] Our choices and actions are tinged with fears of shame, not meeting others' expectations of us, or embarrassment.[27] They are also shaped by the racial structures of our society. People of marginalized racial backgrounds regularly experience this awkward tension in white-dominated settings.[28] In contrast, whites more easily navigate segregated and white-dominated spaces, taking for granted that they are protected from the hazards of racial conflict and any ensuing embarrassment.[29]

So, while the conditions for racialized feelings of awkwardness are a fact of life for people of color in a white-dominated society, they are seemingly optional for white people who hold a position of dominance and normativity. Awkward feelings can lead us to either avoid social situations or address and transform them.[30] Rather than acknowledging and facing these feelings, white people may avoid moments of solidarity and connection with people of color because it can lead to shame in thinking about their own position or complicity. Feeling that certain situations or topics are awkward may simply be a projection of internal shame or embarrassment.[31]

Whites may feel anxiety about being perceived as prejudiced and anticipate that good faith attempts at vulnerability and connection across racial lines will only create space for harsh judgments around not being racially conscious enough to meet the moment.[32] However, discomfort and conflict are entrenched aspects of social change and the practice of greater inclusion in democracy. We so often derive our sense of comfort and security from the idea that we can depend upon things to remain a certain way. Nevertheless, an equitable democracy is one in which we do not turn away from any temporary discomfort, uncertainty, or even good old-fashioned awkwardness that comes from fully acknowledging and addressing the full humanity of each other.

Denying the broad human relatability of awkwardness would be difficult. It is a throughline in media representation of human social life ranging from sitcoms to reality shows and even horror films.[33] However, we often think of awkwardness as just a feeling, something ephemeral in our minds and nervous systems and less concrete and vital than a goal or a strategy. We think of it as a set of idiosyncratic quirks or underdeveloped social skills that some of us individually possess. But our feelings are social, cultural, and even political.[34] Like other emotional experiences in everyday life, "awkwardness remains a social phenomenon, and therefore the analysis of awkwardness should focus not on awkward individuals but on the entire social situation in which awkwardness makes itself felt."[35]

Racialized social settings are oriented toward specific racial groups of people. In white-dominated contexts, whites experience a feeling of being at home, whereas people of color often feel out of place.[36] Whiteness lets people comfortably occupy and travel through these settings "to inhabit the world as if it were home" and ultimately "take up more space."[37] Conversely, white discomfort, or *white racial awkwardness*, is a set of emotional habits that place racialized limitations on connection, solidarity, and understanding.[38]

In this book, I tried to capture the racialized feeling of awkwardness that pervaded the GAP. But this was not an easy task. People's desires to avoid the stigma associated with being labeled racist or expressing overtly racial views can complicate researchers' ability to capture how people approach daily actions and political activities concerning racial inequality.[39] But involved, long-term observation and participation in these spaces helped me bypass these barriers. It helps us uncover the relationship between what people say, how they think, and what they do in their political participation. And paying close attention to social patterns of omission, uneasiness, and evasiveness reveals much more than it hides about racial politics.

Everyday Exclusion and Engagement

Despite the profound influence of such vaunted ideals as fair and equal representation, political inequality remains in the United States. Political inequality describes group disparities in political power and participation that reflect other forms of social inequality.[40] In overly simplistic terms, marginalized social groups such as women, the poor, and people of color have had less representation and influence in government decisions in the US in comparison to whites, men, and the rich.[41] Beyond these basic categorical differences, complex and intersecting social inequalities also structure political engagement and political inequality.[42]

How we navigate discomfort, ambiguity, contradictions, and conflict in real life is a core feature of our political action. Unresolved contradictions lie at the heart of US politics. Accordingly, grassroots progressive politics is fraught with challenges and dilemmas at the intersection of democracy and inequality. It requires us to get outside our comfort zone, connect and interact with others, and name and address problems and issues that we might otherwise feel compelled to avoid.

Despite narratives exalting American progress and the reality of social change, these forms of exclusion continue. The state and the political realm remain white-dominated spaces in the United States. People of color face institutional barriers to influencing political processes, including voter ID laws, selective placement and closing of polling and ID-granting locations, racial gerrymandering, felon disenfranchisement, and voter roll purges.[43] These types of barriers are "top-down" impediments to democratic participation. They are imposed from above, set in place by the powerful, and impact ordinary people.

But what about "bottom-up" participation?

Opportunities for civic and political engagement in communities also often fail to produce equality and justice in their outcomes. For instance, local planning and zoning board meetings are meant to be public forums where community residents can have a voice in shaping housing policies. Nevertheless, the interests of men, older people, longtime residents, and homeowners are overrepresented in these settings.[44] Even controlling for these factors, whites are overrepresented compared to Black and Latino residents in these public meetings.[45] While these forms of political and civic participation are ostensibly open and accessible, they are laissez-faire in their approach. Things should look different when we look at grassroots progressive organizing, which is supposed to be intentional in its pursuit of remedying entrenched inequalities. But do they?

Ideally, the institutional barriers of elite-dominated political systems should matter less at the level of everyday people coming together for political organizing. Progressive political organizations operating at the grassroots level have much potential for creating radical social change. But the reality is not ideal. Forms of social inequality, such as racial oppression, nonetheless impact people's democratic engagement and political activities. This book examines how grassroots progressives in these contexts develop political strategies and engage with activism, electoral politics, racial diversity and inclusion, and outreach and organizing.

Though the GAP's stated goals included racial equity and the inclusion of people of color, and many of its members sought to advance those goals, its membership and leadership remained disproportionately white. The organization also had mixed success in prioritizing and actualizing its racial justice agenda. Through this case and its context, this book offers new ways of understanding the relationship between racial inequality, grassroots democracy, and political participation. This regional context is also noteworthy. From the nation's founding to the enduring legacy of town halls as bastions of deliberative democracy, the northeastern region of the United States holds rich mythology as a democratic laboratory.[46] Considering the particularities of this region, as we see in chapter 2, allows us to rethink the role that regional politics plays in grassroots democracy.

Grassroots politics sits on the cusp of social movements and major political parties. Grassroots political parties act as a bridge between activist and electoral politics. Recent research on racial politics demonstrates political elites' strategic use of racial meanings to gain and maintain power.[47] Academic works in cultural and political sociology examine how political parties "produce, shape, and reshape shared meanings over time" and "use symbols and cultural products to achieve political ends."[48] And studies on social movements demonstrate the potential of investigating everyday interactions and social identities for understanding the impact of racial oppression and inequality on collective action.[49] This book builds upon these bodies of knowledge to uncover the relationship between racial inequality and everyday social practices and political strategies at the grassroots level within voluntary and localized progressive political organizations.

Political research has often focused on statistical models rather than people's stories and lived experiences.[50] Political scientists employ public opinion surveys and psychological experiments to examine correlations between racial categories, party membership and support, and voting behavior.[51] But they fail to capture the consequential processes of everyday social life. People's actions and speech are not detached from their immediate real-world context.[52] As the sociologist Andrew Perrin writes,

"The key, then, to understanding individuals' political participation is understanding how individuals form and experience their political and social environments."[53] So, in contrast to public opinion or experimental approaches, this book seeks to understand racial inequality and political participation through social relations—how people make meaning amid the dilemmas and routines of daily life.

We can learn a lot by centering people's interpretations in political life. The meanings that people give to situations, others, and interactions make social life possible. For example, a crucial component for understanding political participation is understanding how people interpret their interests so that specific actions connect with ideas and become idealized.[54] As sociologist Max Weber argued, "Very frequently the 'world images' that have been created by 'ideas' have, like switchmen, determined the tracks along which action has been pushed by the dynamic of interest."[55]

I uncovered social interactions and communication patterns that were only visible up close and over time. I observed and participated in organizational meetings, informal social gatherings, political campaigns, and protests and demonstrations. I conducted interviews to capture how grassroots activists of various backgrounds interpret the opportunities, barriers, and meaning of their participation. Through interviews and informal conversations, I documented their personal histories to understand the development of their racial and political awareness and the activities and contexts that produced them. By merging these multiple data sources and themes, I bring people's awareness of racial inequality and their daily habits and routines into sharper focus as dimensions of engagement in progressive grassroots politics.

By illuminating the everyday contours of racial inequality in social and political life, this book provides insights for developing practices and policies for building more robust and empowering spaces of grassroots democratic engagement. Grassroots political action is often considered only in the conclusions of sociological texts as part of their calls to action to address the tremendous social problems of our age. In contrast, this book shines a light into these corners of American society and politics that are often idealized from afar as beacons of hope in a disenchanted and unorganized world.

Grassroots political organizations are largely voluntary associations accessible to the public for involvement, service, and running for office. Yet even at the level of grassroots organizing, the impact of centuries of racial oppression on geographic boundaries, social networks, and ways of thinking produces barriers for progressive political organizations. Racial inequality in the US political system is a major stumbling block to implementing political visions that benefit society.

In the democratic ideal, the interests and goals of the people are reflected in collective decision-making and public policies.[56] The word "democracy" derives from the ancient Greek word "demos," meaning "the people." Grassroots democracy is a method to empower people politically. Building solid and inclusive multiracial grassroots political organizations is critical to creating a more democratic, equal, and sustainable society.[57] However, achieving these goals requires rethinking not just large-scale institutions but also people's activities and understandings and how they structure organizations.

POTENTIAL AND PERIL

We proclaim our devotion to democracy, but we sadly practice the very opposite of the democratic creed.... This strange dichotomy, this agonizing gulf between the ought and the is, represents the tragic theme of man's earthly pilgrimage.—Martin Luther King Jr., 1963

Commentary pleading for a progressive grassroots organization to claim a significant role as a "third party" due to dissatisfaction with the two major parties and especially with the perceived elitism and centrism of the Democratic Party abounds in contemporary discourse.[58] A 2023 Gallup poll found that 63 percent of Americans were dissatisfied with the options available and stated that a major third party would be beneficial.[59] Another Gallup poll in 2023 found 43 percent of respondents identifying as independents, which ranked higher than each of the major parties.[60] Events such as the nomination of Hillary Clinton over Bernie Sanders in the 2016 presidential election have added to the dissatisfaction among progressives and leftists with the Democratic Party.[61] Looking into the challenges and experiences of the growing cadre of grassroots progressives in the United States provides insight into the realities involved in these trends and their consequences for racial justice.

The rise of grassroots progressives reflects the broader social and political situation in the United States. Since the early 1990s, the Democratic

Party has attempted to gain and maintain political power by combining progressive politics of recognition and symbolic inclusion with neoliberal policies such as economic deregulation and the weakening of public programs designed to help the poor and marginalized.[62] Unsurprisingly, entrenched social hierarchies and forms of exploitation have endured multiple Democratic presidencies. A growing consensus recognizes that the dominant Democratic coalition has failed to address our lives' underlying structural problems. In this context, grassroots progressives face renewed possibilities and impetus for forming and empowering coalitions for social and political change.[63] Grassroots progressive organizations offer the potential to give a political voice to the collective harms and suffering of diverse groups impacted by structural inequalities.

In the aftermath of the 2016 election, calls to transform the Democratic Party through a mix of outside pressure and internal insurgency from grassroots progressives further mounted in the age of Trump.[64] The failure of the Democratic Party to win the 2016 presidential election served as an essential catalyst. The rise in public prominence of figures like Bernie Sanders and Alexandria Ocasio-Cortez played another vital role. Pointing to the 2018 Bronx, New York, Democratic primary victory of democratic socialist Alexandria Ocasio-Cortez, British writer George Monbiot argued that the US was experiencing a political transformation reflecting "a real rootedness in community and awareness that it's got to be genuine grassroots."[65] He further articulated grassroots progressive ideals, stating, "You've got to build up strong communities, even on the nonpolitical side, but out of those—that participatory culture, you develop a politics from which people are not going to back down. You allow people to articulate the changes that they need, and then feed that up into the electoral process."[66]

For these reasons and more, a diverse slate of progressive grassroots parties and organizations has flourished. The Working Families Party expanded its presence from four states in 2013 to nineteen in 2022.[67] The Party for Socialism and Liberation saw attendance at their New York City–based meetings almost triple in the months after the 2016 election.[68] Socialist Alternative membership increased by 30 percent in 2016, while Democratic Socialists of America (DSA) reported more than doubling their membership.[69] The DSA gained over a thousand new members in a single day in 2018 after the electoral victory of Ocasio-Cortez.[70] New national grassroots progressive organizations like Our Revolution and Justice Democrats formed and took influence alongside various regional and local ones. And despite being locked out of many opportunities afforded to the two major parties, the United States Green Party garnered a million and a half votes in the 2016 election.[71]

Grassroots political organizations present unique opportunities and constraints for political and social action. Sociologist Charles Derber argues that "the progressive grassroots wave" developing in the Trump era and beyond is "fragile," but "it is the last best hope not only for social justice and human survival, but for stopping the rise of an American police state or neo-fascism."[72] It's common to hear commentary about what these organizations should do or what their rise may mean for our political system. But what about the meanings, dilemmas, choices, and habits that matter on the ground for grassroots progressives? The resurgent relevance of grassroots progressive politics begs essential questions that remain unanswered, particularly in the context of entrenched racial injustice.

Such meanings, dilemmas, choices, and habits have vital social and political consequences. As political scientist Byron Shafer points out, it is "the 'culture' of parties and partisanship, an all-embracing approach to the activities of daily life which distinguishes political actors."[73] This dimension of grassroots progressive organizations requires deeper examination to understand the relationship between grassroots progressive politics and racial inequality—particularly if we want to know how to use grassroots movements for racial justice.

Growing the Grassroots

Racial oppression is a fundamental feature of our society. However, it cannot coexist with realizing an inclusive and just multiracial democracy. For centuries, dominant group members have perpetuated social hierarchies. Within these social hierarchies, people classified as "white" continue to benefit from economic resources passed on through generations, preferential treatment in institutions and everyday social life, and control of the government in the United States.[74] These arrangements and practices comparatively disadvantage, harm, and limit the success and well-being of those classified as "nonwhite."

Racial oppression is not just an unequal relationship between groups. It is an ongoing process.[75] Through this process, whites, as a social group, practice greater control over the distribution of resources, the formation of formal and informal rules, and the life chances of other groups. Centering racial oppression means understanding unequal outcomes in dimensions of social life such as politics by looking at institutional patterns, collective action, and recurring interactions. The concentration of political power in the hands of those racialized as white, especially whites who benefit from other dominant social statuses, is a significant facilitator of racial oppression.

White elites continually use their power and resources to socially and legally categorize people of color as inferior, disenfranchising them from influencing major political processes and securing further power and resources.[76] A critical dimension of this process is that institutions ranging from families to schools and the media socialize many people, especially whites, into developing ignorant and false perceptions about the causes and consequences of racial inequality.[77] The dominant ideas and narratives that most whites use to understand the world make unequal social arrangements, such as racial oppression, appear fixed, just, or natural.[78]

Despite common perceptions of racism as something aberrant, the typical social conduct among whites maintains racial oppression and inequality. As legal scholar Daria Roithmayr points out, "Even if all people everywhere in the US were to stop intentionally discriminating tomorrow, those racial gaps would still persist because those gaps are produced by the everyday decisions that structure our social, political, and economic interactions."[79] Yet, despite its seemingly deterministic and intractable implications, this situation does not suggest that change is impossible. Instead, it implies that working towards racial equality requires a massive rise in conscious awareness of these conditions and intentional collective action to change them.

Grassroots politics ideally represents the realization of political power in its most accessible form to the average person. The hallmarks of modern states and political systems include bureaucratic administrative offices, highly organized political parties, and professional politicians who engage in political leadership as a career to make a living.[80] These features give rise to a political class of elites and barricade the masses from participation and influence. In this context, it is easy to see the promise and potential of involvement in grassroots progressive movements to empower people to work together to challenge racial oppression.

It is tempting to idealize grassroots progressive politics as a panacea for society's ills. However, it is no less bound by social reality. It is not a magical force outside of the racialized social system. It depends upon social networks, varying notions of community and public, and distributions of resources. Yet grassroots political actions also have the power to radically transform society. After all, radical social change requires "grasping things at their root," a task that is perhaps only possible through grassroots movements.[81] Despite their potential for advancing justice and equality, grassroots political activities also have the potential to form around existing social barriers and boundaries rather than reshaping or demolishing them.

Even for those with great intentions, a society built on white supremacy and systemic racism encourages practices that support the status quo. People collectively and routinely uphold racially unequal and harmful social outcomes, whether willingly or unintentionally. However, these problems are not just interesting social phenomena to map out and diagram. They are causes of brutal social suffering. They demand adequate and actionable solutions. Eliminating the human costs of racial oppression requires actual collective action. By examining the promises and pitfalls of grassroots action and organizing, this book can inform and empower people engaged in struggles for racial justice.

Civic engagement, at its best, enables people to face new situations and people that give them a new outlook on social problems and their impacts.[82] Grassroots political participation can influence people's perspectives and change their thinking about themselves, others, and the social world. Inclusive collaboration between members of varied social groups that is conscious of the impacts of power relations and social inequalities can be a fantastic catalyst for improving society. It helps us achieve mutual understanding, form alliances, and develop political strategies to achieve shared goals.[83]

It may be tempting to romanticize democratic participation in the United States or to dismiss it cynically. But to truly understand it, "one needs to look away from the centers of elite power and ask ordinary citizens what they are actually doing in their own communities to get organized, exert power, and demand accountability."[84] Understanding grassroots progressive politics as an actual social practice rather than an abstract ideal or social good means addressing some concrete questions: Who participates in our political system at this fundamental level and why? How do social inequalities influence participation and outcomes in such potentially egalitarian and liberating settings? And why do grassroots political organizations fail or succeed in achieving idealized progressive goals such as social justice, inclusion, and empowerment of oppressed groups?

Identifying Inequalities through Interactions

It is also *awkward* to point out that those who believe in racial equality (such as the participants of progressive grassroots politics) can fail to actualize it in their lives and organizations. Yet, as the sociologist Eduardo Bonilla-Silva argues, "hunting for 'racists' is the sport of choice of those who practice the 'clinical approach' to race relations—the careful separation of good and bad, tolerant and intolerant Americans," and so, like Bonilla-Silva, I seek to "uncover the collective practices . . . that help reinforce the contemporary racial order."[85] Of course, individuals hold racist attitudes and engage in practices such as discrimination and expressions of racist beliefs. However, these attitudes and practices are fundamentally social, not psychological or individual.

One benefit of an ethnographic case study like this one is that it allows us a window into how people navigate and engage in conditions of racialized political inequality. I primarily observed and participated in small social interactions (albeit many over a long period). But people's everyday social interactions "do not take place in isolation from larger social realities."[86] Seeing these often-invisible connections requires that we view the social and political world "at an awkward angle . . . in order to see it differently."[87]

This book invites us to think deeply about the patterned social interactions that form the relationships between us and racial oppression. My goal is to help you take up a unique vantage point on racial politics between "the closeness needed to hear others' voices" and "the distance needed to . . . understand."[88] From here, we can see patterns and contradictions emerge from ambiguities and randomness. As sociologists Jodi O'Brien and Peter Kollock note, the "false separation of the individual and society deters us from a comprehensive and complex understanding of the ways in which we are both products and producers of society."[89] My goal, and hopefully yours, is to identify social mechanisms and practices that maintain and challenge racial oppression in the context of grassroots progressive politics.

In this book, I uncover *how* and *why* a grassroots progressive organization fostered specific racialized outcomes, agendas, strategies, and participation patterns. This task requires that we move beyond simply depicting the *who, what, when,* and *where* of these specific events.[90] Focusing on patterns, social practices, and mechanisms allows us to apply these insights to other situations. This approach, focusing on social tensions, habits, and relationality, also avoids oversimplifying the issue of racial oppression. Racial inequality is not merely a product of our ideas, feelings, attitudes, and cognitive states. It is a product of the recurring things we do and the unequal social positions from which we perceive the world and act.

People's everyday lives, including political participation, occur within a feedback loop between racialized structures and interactions that I call the *racialized interaction order.* Focusing on the interaction order allows us to see how the broader society impacts everyday interactions. It encourages us to examine the assumptions and meanings people bring to social life and the implications for how people treat one another.[91] It highlights the relationship between racially unequal social structures and everyday life's implicit rules and dominant meanings.[92]

This feedback loop relies on two intersecting parts. Structural context, how the overall society is organized, influences the immediate social context of our everyday social interactions. The patterns of these interactions reinforce or challenge the collective meanings we give to each social encounter and its context. The social context produced by the interaction then supports or challenges the structure of society. Structural racial inequalities and racialized social interactions are intimately intertwined. The perspective afforded by this book can help us see their connection.

Awkwardness is also part of the racialized interaction order in all its ambiguities, nuisances, misunderstandings, and potential to escalate into conflict, embarrassment, or shame. Indeed, "there could be no social interaction without awkwardness because its possibility is inherent in the coming together of individuals in social situations."[93] When we navigate the racial order of everyday life, it often presents itself as something utterly incoherent. The criteria we use to racialize each other in our interactions remain inconsistent, spanning from skin tone and hair texture to religious practices and language.[94] We find ourselves arbitrarily distant or close to each other within a set of categories and institutions built up over hundreds of years of racial domination and subjugation. It is an act of creativity and agency to make sense of, let alone normalize, the racialized rules and assumptions that pervade our lives, whether we see them or not.[95] How we fill in the awkward gaps in the racial meanings and politics of our day-to-day realities can change the conditions of our future interactions, organizations, communities, and perhaps even society itself.

MAGNIFYING MICROPOLITICS

From the earliest moments of my time with the GAP, I could tell that what was happening in these spaces of deliberation, planning, and interaction reflected contradictions and obstacles inherent in grassroots progressive politics amid racial inequity. Yet these dynamics came into focus only through repeated and diverse encounters with the GAP and its participants. Throughout my time with the GAP, I paid close attention to the overlap between racial identities and inequalities, everyday social habits, and what organization theorists call *micropolitics*. The term "micropolitics" describes "activities taken within organizations to acquire, develop, and use power and other resources to obtain one's preferred outcomes in a situation in which there is uncertainty or dissent."[96] Looking up-close at this connection, which I call *racial micropolitics*, can help us understand racial inequality in organizations, impact their collective strategies and outcomes, and, armed with these insights, identify new practices for social change.

In the following chapters, I explain racial micropolitics by contextualizing, describing, and illustrating patterns and interactions among the participants in several chapters of a grassroots progressive political organization in the northeastern United States. In chapter 2, I explore and merge insights on racial oppression, grassroots democracy, and political participation. I emphasize the apparent tension between the ideal of democracy and the reality of white supremacy in the United States. I also draw connections between these tensions and the contexts and dilemmas relevant to the case study analyzed in the following chapters.

In chapter 3, I examine the features and processes of collective political identity held by grassroots progressives drawing on findings from the study. In chapter 4, I examine the relationship between white participants' level of racial consciousness, social habits, and the political strategies they take within their organization. In chapter 5, I explore the experiences, narratives, and dilemmas of participants of color within the organization's context and its qualities and dimensions as a predominantly white social space where whiteness is routinely normalized and idealized. Finally, I use this case study's findings to understand racial politics further and draw out implications for political and social praxis toward racial equality.

1

Constituted by Contradictions

Grassroots Parties and Racial Oppression

If democracy depends for its survival on what citizens do,
it could still be that citizens are not up to the task
envisioned for them.
—Jeffrey Stout, 2012

Democracy is full of contradictions (but also possibilities).

Political parties do not just represent their leaders, rank-and-file members, or voters. They also represent interests and ideas.[1] These can be seen in a party's platform, statement of values, or agendas. The GAP's goals and ideals included racial and ethnic diversity and inclusion, restitution for oppressed racial groups, social, economic, and environmental justice, and the political empowerment of women and people of color. Grassroots parties like the GAP seek to adopt positions and platforms that are, ideally, untethered to the corrupting influences of political elites. Grassroots parties can directly promote specific sets of policies and principles from their participants.[2]

This further underscores the power of conducting an ethnographic study—observing people's daily lives and participating in events. Without it, I might have missed out on a crucial component—social action. Let's imagine I had just read the meeting agendas and seen items on racial diversity and inclusion. Or perhaps I had simply asked participants through a survey whether they saw recruiting candidates and members of color as a worthwhile goal. I might have concluded from either of those approaches that the party values diversity and social justice. However, intentions and ideals by themselves present incomplete representations of reality. This conclusion would be, at best, preliminary and, at worst, misleading. People's actions can have consequences that counter achieving their goals.[3] To understand racial inequality and exclusion within a grassroots political organization, it is essential to look at both what people say they want to do and what they actually do.

Keeping both factors in mind, we can see the tensions that form in the gap between our stated intentions and practical actions. Interrogating this disconnect can be difficult without context and concepts to guide us. This chapter lays the groundwork for adding all my observations and experiences up to larger patterns. It sets the stage for understanding the speech and actions of GAP participants and what they tell us about how racial oppression relates to consciousness, community, and conflict in grassroots politics. By weaving these themes and concepts together, we can build a new framework for thinking about and doing racial politics.

IDEALS AND INTENTIONS

Focusing on good intentions can obscure issues of inequality. If we are truly interested in equity, we cannot ignore inequitable outcomes even if they are the result of well-intentioned actions.—Sarah Mayorga-Gallo, 2018

Translating goals and visions into procedures and practices is a vital but complicated, perhaps even *awkward*, process. Activists' strategies depend on external opportunities and how they interpret and react to them.[4] Yet political organizations are influenced by participants' routine actions even when they are not highly strategic or intentional toward stated goals. This point may seem obvious when we think about daily life and our reliance on rituals. But it is regularly overlooked in public discussions of politics and collective action. Paying close attention to routines and habits allows us to rethink our everyday activities in the context of entrenched racial inequalities.

Holding racial justice ideals or an antiracist identity is one thing. But engaging in everyday social practices and pursuing intentional political strategies to fight racial oppression is another. Moreover, a mismatch between our ideals and the impacts of our actions can be challenging to confront. This awareness can make us feel self-conscious, embarrassed, or averse. It is tempting to avoid those feelings. If we are part of a dominant group, we can ignore the social realities of inequality and our place in reproducing them. Or, as many white participants in the GAP did, we might attempt to reframe this disconnect as something benign, a product of social ineptitude or innate personality traits rather than a matter of power and exclusion. However, our ability to navigate discomfort, reconcile contradictions, and align our actions with our ideals has immense political and social stakes.

Awkwardness in Action

We often think of political strategies as the result of hyperrational reasoning. Consider how many contemporary public discussions fixate on political "horse races" rather than substantive issues, policies, and their impacts on communities. In election coverage, media commentators use the language of sports, games, warfare, and other forms of strategic competition. They fixate on wins and losses, public spectacle, and predicting rather than influencing or evaluating outcomes. As political scientist Thomas E. Patterson wrote of the 2016 Republican presidential primary, "Election news . . . was dominated by the competitive game—the struggle of the candidates to come out on top. Overwhelmingly, election coverage was devoted to the question of winning and losing. Poll results, election returns, delegate counts, electoral projections, fundraising success, and the like, along with the candidates' tactical and strategic maneuvering, accounted for more than half of the reporting."[5]

This overemphasis on tactics and party competition makes us more cynical about the political process and less knowledgeable about substantive policy issues.[6] It also assumes that our political action is motivated by some straightforward and clear reasoning about attaining and maintaining power. From this perspective, grassroots political organizations like the GAP are simply "instruments designed to attain specific goals."[7] But, as I came to see during my time with the GAP, the relationship between a grassroots political organization's ideals, actions, and impact is neither simple nor obvious.

Unfortunately, our public conversations continue to center on strategies for attaining power and predicting the consequences of significant events and trends. As a byproduct, we routinely think about racial politics and political participation in terms of outcomes and tactics rather than the real-life social processes that produce them. Understanding these processes means looking at what people do—the approaches they use, the stories they tell, the ways they feel, and the daily habits they engage in—as they confront the ambiguities and challenges of democracy amid inequality.

Our political activities are not simply driven by a cold and calculated quest for power and influence. More humanistic pursuits also shape them. We find motivation in our opinions about social issues, sentiments of camaraderie, sense of morality, and deeply felt affective states such as fear or hope. We find comfort in traditions and organizational routines, from which we can cultivate a sense of familiarity and security. All these influences collide in our political engagement and participation in the racialized social system.

The idea that people are motivated by a conscious and rational pursuit of explicit goals also conflicts with the maxim presented by a GAP participant in the dilemmas and flow of political life—that *democracy is awkward*. By acknowledging the *problem of awkwardness*, we can pay better attention to how racialized feelings of familiarity and discomfort and our unconscious daily routines shape our political participation. It helps us consider the often difficult-to-confront distance between a group or organization's stated goals of racial justice and the daily behaviors that uphold exclusion and inequality. This unresolved contradiction doesn't simply reflect a lack of awareness but also an unwillingness to grow our racial literacy and solidarity rather than shrinking in the face of contradictions that make us feel awkward.

Our perspectives, social positions, and upbringing influence how we see opportunities for achieving goals in the social and political sphere. Given all this, we can think of our ability to engage in strategic political actions as what sociologist Andrew Perrin calls *democratic imagination*.[8] Our democratic imagination is creative. It can enable us to develop innovative strategies that respond to opportunities. Our political actions depend on our abilities to imagine social relationships, conditions for social flourishing, and better futures.[9] However, our imagination is also limiting. It is finite. There are many things that we do not do in political life due to the simple fact that we fail to imagine them as a possibility. Or, if we do imagine possible lines of action that would lead to greater solidarity and racial equality, we may imagine them to be impractical or unpleasant. At the limits of our imaginations often lie the unfathomable and unrealized opportunities that lead to real social and political change.

During my time with the GAP, I grew increasingly fascinated by the impact that participants' taken-for-granted awareness, tastes and preferences, group customs, social networks, and social habits had on the political strategies they developed and deployed. I came to see how all these factors were not merely a product of participants' individual personality traits or idiosyncrasies. They demonstrate how racial oppression structures society and shapes our perspectives and assumptions.

Potential for Power

How we deal with these contradictions and ambiguities determines whether grassroots progressive political organizations reach their potential as instruments for redistributing power.[10] This potential is not just something we need to imagine. It is established in history. Grassroots parties preceded major parties in supporting the abolition of slavery, women's suffrage, direct election of political leaders, and a graduated income tax.[11] Racially progressive grassroots organizations have advanced issues important to marginalized communities.

They can mobilize disenfranchised group members for social and political change.[12] Grassroots organizations with ties to social movements can even be springboards for activists and community organizations to shape politics.[13] Grassroots progressive parties have played an essential role in the ongoing struggle against racial oppression throughout US history. They have been able to claim moral superiority and legitimation as the true democratic representatives of excluded groups and depict prominent party representatives as illegitimate or discriminatory.[14] They have also acted as satellite parties or independent parties that enable marginalized communities to gain recognition, positions, and influence within major parties or the government.[15]

In the 1960s and '70s, the grassroots party La Raza Unida, connected to the Chicano Movement in the Southwest, seated Mexican American activists and organizers into local political positions in Texas.[16] They successfully channeled frustrations with the exclusions and inequalities of the Democratic Party into cultural recognition and political momentum, eventually expanding to three other states.[17] The influence of La Raza Unida birthed the Hispanic Caucus of the Democratic Party, which ultimately disintegrated the party and integrated a large portion of Mexican American voters and politicians into the Democratic Party.[18]

In 1960s Mississippi, at the height of the civil rights era, a coalition of grassroots organizations formed a grassroots party known as the Mississippi Freedom Democratic Party (MFDP). They worked to resist the racist

violence and political disenfranchisement experienced by Black Mississippians.[19] The MFDP was formed in 1964 and connected to the broader
struggle for Black liberation in the American South. It came to represent
and resist how the Mississippi Democratic Party disenfranchised and
marginalized Black citizens through discriminatory practices at the local
level.

In many places in Mississippi, Black potential voters outnumbered
whites yet were denied the ability to vote through subjective measures
of "fit" and administrative discretion.[20] The ideals of representative democracy were overrun to protect the maintenance of white supremacist
power structures. The MFDP helped Black Mississippians realize their
potential political power. They organized the Freedom Vote, in which a
symbolic vote was cast to demonstrate the latent ability of potential voters
whose participation in the political system was blocked by the prevailing
system of racial discrimination.[21] MFDP representatives then traveled to
Washington to claim congressional seats as the true representatives of
Mississippi.

The MFDP ultimately failed to gain seats in the party but succeeded
in cultivating support for Black political rights from liberal Democrats
while also alienating pro-segregationists, thus influencing the political
agenda of the Democratic Party.[22] The MFDP was influential in aligning
the racial politics, major political parties, and geographical regions that
subsequently took shape. In creating a situation where the Democratic
Party in the South was held accountable for how it disenfranchised Blacks
from the political process, it shifted the political orientation of the party.[23]

The temporary alignment of northern liberals and southern Dixiecrats
was broken. Democrats became the party of a multiracial progressive/
centrist coalition, while Republicans became the party of white backlash.[24]
The actions of the broader social movement organization coalition dubbed
the Freedom Movement and the strategies and tactics of the MFDP itself
amplified political enfranchisement for Blacks in Mississippi, including
increased voter registration and Black political leadership.[25]

As these examples demonstrate, grassroots progressive parties hold
promise as vehicles for racial justice, especially in local communities.
Racialized political inequality persists even at the local level.[26] However,
grassroots parties can mobilize racial group members presently marginalized from local political processes. A party can increase the participation

of marginalized racial groups in democratic decision-making when they intentionally focus on meaningful engagement with impacted communities rather than simply gaining additional votes.[27]

Participatory Progressive Politics

Even if partial, the successes and triumphs of grassroots progressive political organizations are worth documenting and analyzing. These moments reveal that we can increase political participation and prevent social inequalities from becoming political inequalities. The sociologist Charles Tilly argues that organizations can advance democracy by facilitating the "adoption of procedural devices that insulate public politics from categorical inequalities," "formation of politically active coalitions and associations for crosscutting categorical inequality," and "wholesale increases of political participation, rights, or obligations, that cut across social categories."[28] At their best, grassroots progressive political parties do all this and help build multiracial democracy in the United States.

However, grassroots progressive organizing also faces significant obstacles. Historical inertia, the structure of the political system, the financialization of the electoral process, and the importance of public events and mass media attention for gaining votes all act as roadblocks.[29] But these organizations also offer unique functions for those of us who participate. They are essential spaces to embody, define, and practice progressive racial politics. In these spaces, we can develop and clarify our social and political identities in a group context and better understand political practices and issues.[30] They serve as "an outlet for frustrations" and provide "hope that people are not powerless."[31]

Grassroots progressive parties present openings for radical forms of participatory democracy and empowerment. Dominant liberal approaches to democracy encourage us to focus on passive expressions of our concerns and values. They narrow our civic participation to shallow forms of representation, such as voting in major elections and making economic choices in the marketplace.[32] These approaches fail to guarantee access to the necessary resources, knowledge, and skills to realize and act upon our political interests fully. In contrast, deep and direct political participation in grassroots political organizing enables "excluded classes an opportunity to discover their real interests."[33] But from these observations, a new and more fundamental question emerges: what determines whether grassroots progressive parties can effectively seize their potential as agents of racial equality and justice?

ORGANIZING AMID OPPRESSION

It is through constructing spaces (including segregated spaces) that whiteness itself can be constructed as a social collectivity, and this segregation provides fertile soil for the emergence of group thinking that rationalizes the white habitus as objective and neutral—simply the way the world is.—Ali Meghji, 2022

The importance of political organizing for social change is widely recognized, but it demands much more attention as a matter of actual practical activity.[34] For instance, in the conclusions of influential works on racial oppression and social injustice, authors routinely extol the necessity of collective action, organizing, and political mobilization that crosscuts racial boundaries and empowers politically marginalized segments of society. The question, however, is what we do to advance democracy while under the shadow of white supremacy. If democracy, at its best, is meant to be inclusive and empowering, the forms of consciousness, habitual actions, and spatial relations that position whiteness as idyllic, standard, and inherently dominant contradict these ideals. Our ability to engage in impactful grassroots progressive political organizing hinges on our willingness to challenge the unequal social relations of racial oppression.

We need to examine white supremacy to understand how progressive grassroots organizations can contribute to racial justice. The term "white" in white supremacy describes an invented racial category with abundant real-world consequences.[35] "Whiteness" refers to the multifaceted social implications of this category. They include (1) an advantaged position in society, (2) a perspective from which to view oneself and others, and (3) relevant cultural practices.[36] White supremacy is the social and political order that endows those categorized as white with a greater license to dominate others and a de facto entitlement to power and opportunity.[37] Looking at grassroots progressive politics in this context "registers a commitment to a radically different understanding of the political order, pointing us theoretically toward the centrality of racial domination and subordination."[38]

White supremacy also means people have been categorized under the broad typology of "nonwhite races" within the racialized social system. The dehumanizing and stigmatizing connotations that dominant group members attach to the diverse groups of people classified outside the bounds of "whiteness" continue to facilitate oppression, exclusion from substantive citizenship, nonrecognition of humanity, exploitation, expropriation, and genocide.[39] In this sense, whiteness came to signify social advantages and a sense of superiority accessible to some degree even to those "whites" disadvantaged in their other social or economic locations.[40]

Social hierarchies based on these racial divisions produced a sense of group interests and attitudes, often implicitly driving those endowed with "whiteness" to maintain this unjust social arrangement.[41] So, "in a racialized social system, all actors are racialized, including whites."[42] Interrogating whiteness and racial oppression helps us unpack how grassroots progressive parties, even those with strong racial justice platforms, can be dominated by white participants and fail to advance racial equality. So how does the system of white supremacy impact the practice of grassroots progressive politics? If you will forgive my overuse of alliteration, it occurs through *awareness, actions, and areas.*

Awareness (or Racial Consciousness)

We all have varied levels of awareness of our society's conditions and relationships. Economic sociologists have long examined class consciousness—understanding of the personal implications of how capitalism creates economic positions, shapes social relations, and constitutes social groups.[43] Along similar yet distinct lines, *racial consciousness* is awareness of the connection between racial oppression, the arrangements and practices that maintain it, and people's daily lives and subjective experiences.[44] Through its underlying social causes and consequences, our racial consciousness plays a vital part in larger patterns of change, conflict, and continuity.

Our racial consciousness can range from complex or heightened awareness to relative ignorance. For instance, sociologist W. E. B. Du Bois famously wrote about *double consciousness.*[45] In basic terms, members of racially oppressed groups cultivate this form of consciousness as they account for their self-awareness and social awareness of how they are viewed and treated in a white-dominated society. In contrast, whites often lack a thorough awareness and acknowledgment, at times even intentionally, of how racial oppression impacts communities and shapes their lives and the lives of people of color.[46]

The racial consciousness of the individuals involved influences the implicit rules and assumptions in each social interaction.[47] Du Bois remarked that a metaphorical *veil* separates the consciousness and perceptions of Black and white Americans.[48] The veil has multiple meanings and implications. In one sense, it represents the limiting conditions imposed on Black Americans through subjugation and lack of access to education and formal opportunities. In another, it means "the blindness of whites who from fear, foolishness, and blatant racism, refuse to step beyond it to see the powerful potentials and the sorrowful spectacle of their oppressed brothers on the other side."[49]

These two sides of the veil are knitted together by practical reality. Navigating everyday life requires that Black Americans are conscious of themselves as both members of a community with concrete values and a sense of group interests shaped by oppression and exclusion and as participants of the broader, white-dominated society.[50] Yet, particularly in white-dominated settings, whites often think of themselves as racially unmarked individuals simply striving for personal goals.[51]

The sociologist C. Wright Mills wrote that "individuals, in the welter of their daily experience, often become falsely conscious of their social positions."[52] Variations in racial consciousness shape our social actions and interactions during political participation. Consciousness is a "special sensitivity to certain features of the outside world rather than others" that shapes our "rational and emotive attention."[53] Our racial consciousness affects our attention to and interpretation of large-scale political events, the social dynamics of communities, and subtle forms of self-representation in social interactions. These differences in awareness and empathy foster whites' microaggressions, discrimination, social control, surveillance, and acts of violence against people of color.[54]

The concept of the veil enables us to see the links between everyday social interactions and larger structures of racial oppression. Sociologist Howard Winant writes that the veil "divides the human psyche and figures the human body; yet it also fissures soul and nation, collectivity, polity, history, and culture."[55] It signifies "a profound social structure that has been built up for centuries, accumulating among the infinite contradictions of race and racism as they have shaped our identities and social organization."[56] Our interpersonal social contact is entwined with systemic, historical, and institutional processes of racial oppression. We can see this connection in many implicit but dominant rules, boundaries, stereotypes, and assumptions that govern our interracial social interactions.[57] Our political lives involve these same processes of interaction and negotiating shared understandings of each other and reality.

Our differences in racial consciousness are not simply related to our alienation or social distance from one another. They are products of power relations. The veil reflects an asymmetry. Many whites go about daily life without ever having to gain a strong awareness of the social realities of people racialized as "nonwhite."[58] In contrast, Black people, and other racially othered and marginalized group members, familiarize themselves with the implicit rules and patterns of white interactional norms and social contexts for their basic survival.[59] Similar racial and power dynamics can take shape in grassroots political organizing.[60]

We are not born with innate racial consciousness. It is cultivated, strengthened, and maintained throughout our lives through social context, dialogue, and education. It is a product of both our socialization and personal agency. We bring it with us as we enter our political and civic engagement. But it is also plastic. Our experiences and choices can reshape it through our participation in grassroots progressive politics. A critical racial consciousness, for instance, requires opportunities and choices to confront the social realities of race and racism.

Other social settings, like families, provide spaces to develop, refine, and apply our understanding of racial inequity. For instance, in studying British multiracial families, sociologist France Winddance Twine found that many white mothers provided their biracial children with historical and social context and frameworks for understanding the impacts of racial oppression that they may face.[61] In contrast, in the context of the home or private settings, white children often receive indirect and overt "negative messages about racial minorities" from their parents and may internalize "negative racial stereotypes before experiencing personal contact with people of other races, which influenced the nature of their future interactions."[62]

As our racial consciousness develops and becomes refined over time, we experience diverse influences throughout our lives. These include stories and ideas articulated by others, mass media representations, and direct experiences of patterns and social barriers. Discussions of race and racism are essential. Many people of color can recall early conversations wherein family or community members informed them of the realities of discrimination, inequality, and violence they may encounter in a racist society.[63] In similar discussions, if they even occur, whites receive mixed and varying messages about racism ranging from progressive antiracist statements, racist stories and stereotypes, and color-blind platitudes to utter silence and evasion.[64]

Yet the raw materials from which we cultivate our awareness of the implications of racial oppression go beyond mere discussions. We develop our racial consciousness by observing the racial demographics and dynamics of the spaces we navigate and the actions and choices we and others make. We are active participants in the development of our racial consciousness. For instance, white children "interrupt white racial socialization all the time through their questions, their confusion, and, most of all, their own unique interpretations and refinement of the cultural ideas presented to them."[65] While the influence of our early experiences and internalized meanings is strong, our awareness of racial oppression and ability to recognize its effects on daily life is still dynamic and context dependent. Subsequent experiences provide a whole host of opportunities to refine our racial consciousness.

Racial consciousness is not simply a matter of knowledge but also spontaneous social application. It describes our ability to apply and integrate information and concepts in various contexts and interactions. Like other forms of consciousness, our racial consciousness "acts as an integrating and discerning factor of experience."[66] It describes the distinctions and connections we draw between social and material conditions produced by racial oppression and people's daily lives and subjective understandings. As the philosopher Lucius X. Outlaw points out, "Only a grasp of the whole—social structures and processes; ideas and mutually conditioning interactions—can provide such an understanding."[67] Racial consciousness manifests in how we think about social life, profoundly impacting the daily habits and routines that make up participation in grassroots progressive politics.

CONSTRAINED OR CULTIVATED CONSCIOUSNESS

Our awareness of racial oppression can be intensely cultivated or severely constrained. To further underscore the role of racial consciousness in political organizing, let us first look at variations in awareness among GAP participants. On a sunny afternoon, I sat and talked with Harry in his truck in the parking lot after the GAP meeting at a local church. Harry was a middle-aged white man in the Elkington chapter of the GAP. He exuded emotion as we talked about his life and politics, at times even becoming overwhelmed with sadness, frustration, and empathy. He told me he "was raised in a rural town in a middle-class professional family which had good basic family values and community values, but had sort of, out of lack of familiarity, sort of racial fears about Blacks and folks like that." However, he experienced a turning point in his awareness that occurred early on and helped him become cognizant of the harsh and hostile treatment of Black people by whites in the United States:

> When I was three years old, I had a serious injury and spent a number of weeks or months in a hospital away from home. And one of my early conscious experiences in life is being either three or five years old and being in a hospital ward with—there were twelve of us in the ward as I can best remember, eleven of us were white and one Black kid. And the white kids would torment the Black kid. *[He begins to get choked up.]* And I can remember saying, "This sucks. What is wrong with this picture?"—being very sad for that kid.

Harry told me that from this experience, he developed a sense of the injustice of overt racial discrimination. He recognized the unfairness that Black people faced as a moral problem and a source of empathy. But he did not necessarily develop an awareness of the historical and social contexts that facilitated these harmful interactions or their implications for contemporary society.

Many other white GAP participants grew up in contexts that shielded them from the lived experiences of people of color. They had an even more limited awareness of racial oppression.

For instance, Soren, a young white male college student in the Edgepond GAP chapter, was taking time in between classes to video chat with me from a computer lab at his college. I joked that he intentionally faced the camera so that he was in front of a whiteboard covered with writing and equations. We laughed as I quickly realized that I had done the same thing by sitting in front of a bookshelf. As the conversation switched to more serious topics, I asked Soren about his earliest memories of being aware of racism and racial inequality. He replied, "Around the time the Black Lives Matter issue took off, you know, that's when I first became aware of it. So, I guess I'm kind of ashamed to say that I kind of became conscious of racial issues in America at the same time everyone else did because, you know, when something is out of sight, it's out of mind and . . . you know, issues around police violence that was something I was really unaware of."

Soren expressed shame that he had gone through most of his life without being remotely aware of the impacts of racial oppression on his life or the lives of others. He knew that others did not lack this awareness and that his lack of understanding was a problem. However, Soren generalized these experiences. He told me everyone had woken up to the reality of racial injustice as police shootings of Black people became a prominent issue of public debate in the early to mid-2010s. Perhaps in his immediate social network or community, those events and the discussions around them became the first time many had to confront or even think seriously about the continuing existence of racism in the United States.

Racial consciousness denotes our awareness of the implications of past and ongoing racialized social arrangements for everyday social life. As the sociologist Amanda Lewis writes, "Because of their social location (as dominants), whites historically have had the luxury of racializing others without necessarily, except strategically, developing or invoking a strong racial consciousness."[68] In their everyday political activities, members demonstrated a range of perspectives, including in-depth awareness, first-hand knowledge, and ignorance concerning racial oppression. Regardless of their laudable collective intentions and goals, their actual daily routines reflected their engagement with the social fact of racial inequality. These everyday activities had latent but crucial consequences for racial distributions of political power, particularly at the local level.

In contrast, people of color in the GAP had more concrete narratives about their pathways to racial, social, and political consciousness. These pathways operated through direct experience with challenging ideas and situations. Racial injustice was not a mere abstraction or reference point for these participants. It formed part of a lived reality that they actively worked to understand, act upon, and transform. Daily experiences of struggle and tension and opportunities to integrate new ideas and insights changed their awareness of social and political inequities.

The form of awareness developed by participants of color in the GAP was akin to what sociologists Jane Mansbridge and Aldon D. Morris call *oppositional consciousness*.[69] They gained "an empowering mental state that prepares members of an oppressed group to act to undermine, reform, or overthrow a system of human domination."[70] This awareness was partially animated by "righteous anger over injustice" and "personal indignities and harms suffered through one's group membership."[71] Moreover, this mode of consciousness impacts our perspective and interpretation of the social world. By cultivating it, we can identify the impacts of systems of oppression in the macro dimension of society; the meso area of communities, groups, and organizations; and the micro arena of daily life. Accordingly, participants of color came to hold a distinct capacity to identify opportunities and propose organizational and social change strategies.

Nina grew up in a Latino working-class community in a large city. She was surrounded by urban disinvestment, decay, and poverty but also inspirational and influential community organizing by groups like the Black Panthers and Young Lords. Her father struggled with a substance use disorder and negatively influenced her mother. She said, "I remember, on one occasion, my mother being in the hospital for several months, and they told her that she was going to die." Soon after, her grandmother helped her and her mother escape by moving a thousand miles to Puerto Rico, where they struggled with poverty. Due to the history of colonialism and exploitation by US corporations and government, the people of Puerto Rico have long struggled with poverty. As of 2018, the territory had an official poverty rate of about 45 percent compared to the US national average of 13 percent.[72] Moreover, Puerto Rico and Puerto Ricans exist in a liminal state relative to the rest of the United States. As sociologist Bianca Gonzalez-Sobrino points out,

> Puerto Ricans were already migrating to the US before they were given citizenship in 1917. At the turn of the century, they were settling in the eastern states of the mainland, and, in 1902, the US Treasury Department issued immigration guidelines that categorized Puerto Ricans as foreigners. After a legal battle that went all the way to the Supreme Court, Puerto Ricans were deemed "non-citizen national" by way of being residents of a US colony. They have remained in this limbo, legally belonging yet historically unwelcomed, ever since. It's a strange social position that affects both their material and symbolic resources.[73]

Nina credited her youth in Puerto Rico for her appreciation of nature. Yet there was a dark side to her time in Puerto Rico. Alongside poverty, her mother met a new partner who was violent and abusive. After moving back to the United States, she experienced more family disruption and conflict and lived in a nearby suburb with her middle-class aunt and uncle. She then returned to live with her mother in the city, where her mother began studying journalism at a local university. However, continued instances of domestic violence led her and her mother to South Nauset. She told me, "I'm a city girl now. I'm, and you know, really used to the urban neighborhood. And we come to live in South Nauset now, which kind of seems similar to me as New York City in a way that I'm now living in an entirely, you know, Latino, Puerto Rican neighborhood, right? And a lot of the people in South Nauset were actually people who moved up here from the city. . . . So, I wasn't feeling like, you know, I was among a different, a different culture or different people. It's just that the environment was different, right?"

After a fire displaced them from their first residence, she and her mother resettled in Pine Timbers housing complex, and her life improved. "I finally moved to where I finally began making friends and having a sense of community. So, I'm beginning to feel a sense of stability, you know, going to school. [My mom] went to school, and she got a job working with the Welfare Department, and then she got another job working with a nonprofit organization, and my mother became a badass activist." Living in Pine Timbers exposed Nina to new people, ideas, and modes of community engagement. As things got better, her mother found her place in the community as a social change agent. Nina credited her mother's personal growth and evolution: "She's beginning to find herself; she's beginning to grow; she's beginning to educate herself and she became a badass activist. She helped found a community development organization. . . . She mobilized with other community activists, and they developed, from scratch, a nonprofit organization that played a major role in rehabilitating an entire community. My mom became my mentor and my role model."

Her mother's evolution and persistence had been crucial in the growth and transformation of her political consciousness. Nina continued to grow and find her political voice and vision while graduating from high school as a teen mother, working and excelling at a local community college, and eventually transferring to a prestigious liberal arts college. After graduation, she started her work with community activism.

Formal education played a role in the growth of Nina's sense of justice and political efficacy. She grew to find that she could empower herself and others by participating in her community. She further embodied this sense of community responsibility by working with youths and people entangled in the legal system. Through participating in civic life, gaining an education, and having firsthand experiences with oppression and social problems, Nina, like many participants of color, cultivated a complex racial and political consciousness through learning, reflection, and action.

Actions (or Racial Habits)

These sharp distinctions in political and racial consciousness are just one key underpinning for the larger patterns I observed. Another crucial matter is political praxis—what we actively do in political life. The next three chapters show how people's taken-for-granted racialized assumptions, rules, and daily routines shaped tangible outcomes. In other words, we must explore the *consequences of consciousness*. We must also delve into our racial practices in political participation. Interpreting and navigating a society structured by racial oppression impacts our social habits—our everyday actions without consciously thinking about them.[74] Taken-for-granted and implicit assumptions about race and racism drive our habits. They often evade our critical and conscious awareness. For instance, identifying ourselves through dominant meanings of "whiteness" produces a sense of investment in maintaining the ideas and practices that support racial inequity.[75] Hence, many white people internalize and utilize a shared racial "common sense" despite having diverse social identities.[76] Examining everyday racial practices gives us insights into the racialized logic we employ to understand ourselves, others, and the world.

All of us who live in a racialized society enact racial habits. We do not possess the mental energy to constantly be aware, vigilant, and strategic in our activities. Our racial actions involve habitual, impulsive, and strategic aspects. Consider the following example. Most white people in the United States grow up and live in contexts wherein they primarily interact with other whites.[77] This context was also true of the white folks in the GAP. This setting impacted their perceptions, tastes, and preferences. Racial segregation in the contemporary era generates patterns of interaction and community formation. For example, whites who do not have friends of color due to their racialized habits and routines often self-report such friendships, enabling them to overemphasize their interracial contact and relationships.[78]

The concept of *habitus*, developed by French sociologist Pierre Bourdieu, can help us understand the relationship between our habits and strategies during political participation.[79] Sociologist Sarah Mayorga-Gallo notes that "a person's habitus and associated tastes are often shared with those in similar social positions" and that "these shared ways of being, or dispositions, reflect not just class but also race and regionality."[80] Habitus affects what social information we notice, how we interpret this information, and what possible actions we consider and take in a social situation.[81] It shapes our implicit and unconscious sense of whether things are normal, deviant, good, bad, or even possible or impossible. Accordingly, "because the white habitus creates a space in which whites' extreme isolation is normalized, whites do not experience troubling doubts or second thoughts as to their lack of interaction with blacks."[82]

Our political engagement reflects our routine conduct and daily conventions of thought and action. Collective habits shape our political organizations and institutions' cultures, strategies, and impacts. Attention to our everyday social practices, particularly in interactive settings, is essential to understanding how grassroots progressive organizations can advance just and inclusive multiracial democracy.[83] Focusing on racial habits helps us reveal the causes and consequences of racial exclusion and inequity we miss when we assume that every political action is only motivated by rational and conscious calculation.[84] As sociologist Eduardo Bonilla-Silva writes, "The conscious, unconscious, and semiconscious on race affairs merge like chunky monkey ice cream in Whites' minds."[85]

Habits are "deeply constitutive of who a person is and therefore [are] difficult and slow (though not impossible) to change."[86] Focusing on habits helps us make observations about entrenched patterns in human experience. But we must also recognize the potential for awareness and agency. This component of life is especially vital when we do the hard work of bringing our habits and their contradictions with our goals into sharper contrast. In the spirit of developing new forms of political praxis, we can also "refine, reclaim, and refuse the habits through which we actually live our lives."[87] So, while acknowledging the difficulty of discerning the "rational" from the "irrational" or the "conscious" from the "unconscious," I take up the following call to action from sociologist W. E. B. Du Bois: "It is our duty to assess praise and blame for the rational and conscious acts of men but to regard the vast area of the subconscious and the irrational and especially of habit and convention which also produce significant action, as an area where we must apply other remedies and judgments if we would get justice and right to prevail in the world. Above all, we must survey these vague and uncharted lands and measure their limits."[88]

Social scientists often discuss racism in terms of how people rationally approach their assumed racial interests. For instance, in the contemporary era, expressing overt racism is stigmatized. Instead, whites who seek to justify racial inequality are more likely to use abstract ideas about freedom and equality to discuss racialized social issues or to avoid the topic altogether. These strategies enable them to vocally defend the benefits of whiteness but still not come off as racist in the traditional sense.[89] Rationalization, how we justify and make sense of certain actions or situations, is an essential aspect of daily life. But it does not tell us about all the other processes and practices that maintain racial inequality.[90] So, what do we miss when we only focus on "rational and conscious acts"?

In our day-to-day activities, we internalize and practice racial meanings more often than we explain and defend them. In other words, it is vital to not simply recognize the role of our interests and preferences in our political engagement or even how we justify them but also what we *do*, especially our routine and repeated social practices. Most of the actions that we take in daily life are routine and habitual. They produce a sense of continuity over time. They tend to conform to the implicit rules and expectations enacted by others in our social space, helping us build a sense of normalcy. They help us avoid feeling *awkward*.

Our racial habits are not merely cognitive; they are also social in that "they involve our interactions with and ideas about other people."[91] They "become a part of how we move about in our social lives."[92] Racial habits rely on a set of implicit rules, covert expectations about others, and unspoken assumptions about what actions are possible or ideal.[93] Through these conventions, which provide a sense of order to the messiness of our lives, we make sense of ourselves and others.[94] Like all habits, racial habits provide us with a sense of security in the patterns of everyday life.

Political actions may be purely motivated by the desire to achieve political goals. However, they may also reflect participants' collective identities and values. The political practices people take are reflections of both "identity and moral convictions" and "assessment of what strategy is most likely to result in concrete political victories."[95] Some of the most consequential features of political life, such as the types of discourse the members of a grassroots organization use, can stem from "deeply ingrained, respected customs."[96] In other words, racial habits are not just about our individual practices but also about the collective practices within an organization. Grassroots organizations can establish and then become constrained to entrenched social pathways or shared routine ways of talking, thinking, and acting.[97]

However, it need not be this way. Engaging in progressive politics through grassroots organizations can also be a dynamic endeavor. Democratic engagement can change the individuals involved and the communities they impact.[98] At the turn of the twentieth century, the influential activist, social worker, and sociologist Jane Addams emphasized that people should throw themselves into the social situations within their community that make them uncomfortable and strike them as problems causing social suffering.[99] In this way, we should connect our civic engagement to political activism that draws from firsthand wisdom and knowledge about the social needs of our community.[100] Addams argued that direct engagement with the lives of the marginalized and disenfranchised enhances the understanding of peoples' lived experiences and challenges assumptions about how the world works, enriching political participation.[101]

Once organizations form, they begin to take on a general structure or arrangement that patterns the actions and interactions of participants.[102] Organizations develop *collective habits* much in the way that individuals develop personal routines. Grassroots organizations develop norms and group expectations about who should be included or excluded, whose interests they should advance, what goals to work towards, and shared knowledge about political processes.[103] They settle on the terminology, narratives, and ideals they should employ to articulate their issues of concern, aspirations, and approaches.[104] These ways of doing things may adjust in response to new opportunities and dilemmas. However, the social and cultural patterns set down early and carried out over long periods become a set of traditions and an almost semiautonomous force.[105]

Our racial habits and racial consciousness are profoundly intertwined. Accordingly, altering our social patterns and their political impacts requires intentionality and awareness of our habits and their contexts, causes, and consequences. However, our racialized political practices are expressions of the implicit assumptions we hold about one another in our political participation and those we have about spaces of social interaction.

Areas (or Racial Spaces)

Grassroots political organizations prioritize and focus on mobilizing and engaging specific communities. Our communities, however, are also fundamentally racialized and deeply connected to feelings of belonging or exclusion. In chapters 3, 4, and 5, we'll explore how GAP participants' varying sense of racial space shaped the strategies and achievements of the party. American studies scholar George Lipsitz points out that "the lived experience of race takes place in actual spaces, while the lived experience of place draws its determining logic from overt and covert understandings of race."[106] Residential and social segregation in the United States provides a clear example of this relationship.

Despite some reductions in racial segregation over the past century, "the decline in black-white segregation is painfully slow," and "the average level of segregation still represents a sharp separation by race."[107] In the contemporary era, "whites rarely enter predominantly minority neighborhoods but they continue to leave mixed areas" while "even the most affluent black and Hispanic households still live in neighborhoods with fewer community resources than much less affluent whites."[108] Social and geographic spaces around us continue to take on racial meanings and structures. And how we integrate this fact into our political organizing will deeply determine our ability to build multiracial movements and advance racial justice.

Participants in grassroots democracy may be motivated by concerns ranging from the personal (i.e., actualizing one's "true self" or self-interest) to the communal (i.e., advancing a set of collective interests).[109] Regardless, local grassroots organizations, such as regional chapters of the GAP, are generally intended to have ties to a surrounding community. The term "community" can refer to those practicing a shared set of ideals, social networks, people who share a common place of residence, or people who share a set of interests in common. As sociologist Patricia Hill Collins put it, "The construct of community may be ideally suited for democratic aspirational projects because its effectiveness lies in its ability to wed strong feelings to projects that are designed to advance the greater good."[110]

In broad terms, the sense of community that undergirds grassroots political actions is influenced by the context of racial oppression. As the political scientist Bruce D. Haynes writes, "Racially segregated social life makes racial identity an integral part of community identity."[111] The relationship between racial identities and communities is shaped by our sense of racial demography such that "while predominantly white communities use race as an exclusionary strategy, race becomes a major defining characteristic of any sense of community for blacks."[112] In broad terms, the context of racial oppression influences the sense of community and our feelings of belonging to certain spaces that undergird grassroots political actions.

In terms of trust, friendships, and networking, whites experience and reproduce higher rates of social isolation from people of color, particularly Black people.[113] These aspects of segregation and seclusion reinforce one another and influence grassroots progressive political organizing. As the sociologists Maria Krysan and Kyle Crowder point out, "The separation of different racial and ethnic groups into distinct and qualitatively different residential spaces produces sharp racial differences in sociodemographic characteristics and life experiences that, in turn, shape profound racial differences in residential search processes and neighborhood outcomes."[114] Centuries of unyielding racial segregation in patterns of community formation, social network development, and informal social life tie social spaces to racial identities and inequalities. And these patterns profoundly shape our political engagement.

One significant consequence of all this is "white space." White space describes areas of social life where whiteness or being white becomes seen as normal or ideal by the routine occupants of that space.[115] White space can take shape in multiple bounded regions—geographic zones, institutional settings, and even social spaces formed by groups and organizations like political parties. The GAP itself functioned as a white space in this very way.

White space held disparate implications and meanings for different people in the party. For some, it was a taken-for-granted source of comfort and ease. For instance, white men often experience a heightened sense of individualism in predominantly white areas, "a distinct separation between the individual and the social world, where the person is self-governing and autonomous."[116] In contrast, participants of color more often experience hypervisibility and anticipate the judgments of others in white space.[117] All of this can lead to acts of exclusion, both subtle and overt. White spaces are often maintained through a series of practices that whites use to discern whether a person of color will conform to dominant racial norms and, if not, whether to exclude them from the space altogether.[118]

Racial habits, consciousness, and space are intricately bound in our social and political lives. Yet the pathways and processes they connect are distinct for the members of different racial groups. White people tend to have a sense of space and society that "operates non-relationally, with space understood as being comprised of discrete and bounded objects and spatio-temporal units that can be readily delineated, known and assigned 'attributes.'"[119] As the geographers Owen J. Dwyer and John Paul Jones write, "This process of categorical naturalization is the spatial correlative of whiteness's non-relational social epistemology."[120] In more accessible language, white GAP participants tended to see their own sense of space and place as natural. They did so without reflecting upon how other groups experience and understand things like community or geographic boundaries.

All of this culminates in the *racial politics of geography*—the enduring connections between racialized political contestations and power relations and our collective sense of space and community. Building cross-racial solidarity in grassroots organizing requires mutual understanding and empathy about the relationship between racial inequality, geography, and community conditions. However, in most whites' accounts of race and place, the social and spatial distances between spaces racialized as white and nonwhite are exaggerated. This move allows them to see white space as inherently standard and accessible. In contrast, they envision "nonwhite" space as something imaginary or utterly foreign. For example, sociologist Sharla Alegria noted that in a series of conversations about racial profiling, whites "referred to predominantly black areas as 'the projects,' 'drug areas,' 'low-income areas,' 'black town' and 'inner city,' while they used proper names of neighbourhoods to refer to predominantly white areas."[121] White participants were conscious and familiar with certain racialized spaces and employed a mixture of ignorance and fantasy to depict others. This dynamic reflects the broader relationship between our racial identities, social space, and inequalities as it plays out in our political lives.

Clear historical and ongoing connections exist between the conditions in predominantly "white" and "nonwhite" areas. However, this relationship is obscured by whites' sense of racial geography—producing an "easy and innocent denial of any connection between spaces of privilege and those of suffering."[122] This sense of space reflects "ways of understanding the world that make sense of racial gaps in earnings, wealth, and health such that whites do not see any connection between their gain and others' loss."[123] A deep connection to the conditions of communities and the structural forces of racial oppression are not inherent elements of the identities of all people of color. However, navigating both white and nonwhite spaces does provide more experiences that may precipitate such insights. However, the dominant white sense of space renders collective action rooted in solidarity over the conditions of racial oppression and their impacts on communities and individuals both near unimaginable and practically challenging.

TAKEN TOGETHER

It's crucial to remember what is at stake here. The collective rewards of an inclusive and equitable democracy are that giving voice to the understandings and experiences of excluded groups gives birth to a better society for everyone. As W. E. B. Du Bois points out, "The real argument for democracy is, then, that in the people we have the source of that endless life and unbounded wisdom which the rulers of men must have."[124] Yet practical barriers such as the lack of agency and human rights held by oppressed groups thwart this great potential. Political and social inequality are mutually reinforcing and act in concert to prevent democratization and social progress in the United States.

The term *politics* often recalls a set of powerful bureaucratic and hierarchical structures that enable top-down elite rule. However, grassroots progressive politics attempts to flip this notion of politics on its head by emphasizing that everyday people should grasp and exercise power. Grassroots politics is a space where "ordinary Americans become personally involved in efforts to improve our society, and they provide an important means by which nonelite Americans can have an impact on public life."[125] From this vantage point, politics is not simply about the clashing of elites with dueling interests and ideologies. It is a practice that people use to attempt to influence their communities and society. It is the localized exercise of democracy.

Grassroots political parties reveal the challenges and advantages of translating grand theories of democracy and racial oppression into concrete and embodied practices. A central component of most grassroots models of political action is deliberation or using dialogue and communication to develop strategies and goals. Through deliberation and participation, grassroots organizations emphasize "democratic legitimacy and justification."[126] They seek "democratic transformation of individuals and institutions."[127] Collective decision-making that considers a wide range of interests and active participation that enables people to clarify their individual and collective interests and aspirations are crucial and interrelated aspects of grassroots democracy. To many of us, this theoretical mode of democracy through grassroots progressive organizations sounds fantastic. But given all that we have discussed about the reality of racial oppression and its intrusion into all areas of life, it clearly remains to be realized.

Focusing on how organizations depict themselves in their official rhetoric and public-facing materials is one way of gathering evidence for whether and how these activities are taking place. However, equalizing racialized power imbalances at the level of local grassroots democracy requires more than just espousing ideals or holding good intentions. It requires active and conscious practice. And so, throughout the remainder of this book, we will look at how people's awareness, daily actions, and sense of space and community contribute to (or challenge) racial inequality in grassroots progressive politics.

2 Blue State Blues
Grassroots Progressives in the Northeast

Claiming that other people's politics are identity-based—and one's own views derive from pure reason—is the purest form of identity politics. —Victor E. Ray, Twitter, 2022

Democracy is complicated.

What does it mean to do *grassroots progressive politics*? I posed this question to Stevie, a white nonbinary member of the Edgepond chapter of the GAP in their early twenties and a student at a local college, as we sat in a small-town diner and talked over coffee and a large appetizer platter of tempura vegetables and dipping sauces. They told me,

> That's kind of the weird thing about the Grassroots Action Party. I feel like we have some overall tenants that are *extremely vague but also much focused* at the same time. . . . It's like under this ambiguous term "progress," and then just kind of motivated out into this general feeling of dissatisfaction with how things are being run in our state and the country as a whole.

A collective obligation toward social progress and political transformation tethered people to continued participation in the GAP. They felt bound by a shared political identity. But they continually renegotiated precisely what that political identity meant in various situations. They had to constantly parse out the practical implications of this obligation.

We often think about political identity as a matter of public opinion. We talk about how identification with a political party or ideology relates to attitudes, beliefs, or support for policies and politicians within a population. Public opinion provides valuable information. We can observe basic patterns—that Democrats are more supportive of government spending on science than Republicans, that liberal Democrats are more likely than moderate Democrats to support access to legal abortions, or that Democrats are more likely than Republicans to have positive attitudes toward racial diversity.[1]

However, reducing our political identities to stated beliefs and attitudes ignores the richness, complexity, and, of course, *awkwardness* of our daily lives. Our political participation is profoundly active, dynamic, and social. The decisions we make in political life—whether voting, engaging in activism, showing up at a town hall, or even campaigning for office—take place in complicated real-life situations. So, we need a different approach to political identity to understand how grassroots progressive politics can contain contradictions (like being "extremely vague but also much focused at the same time"). Understanding these tensions helps us rethink how we form and convey our political identities for doing impactful progressive grassroots politics and combating racial inequality.

PRODUCING PROGRESSIVES

Our political identity can influence things as seemingly intangible as how we feel. The more intensely we identify with major political categories such as "liberal" or "conservative," the more likely we are to fume about political issues or rage against those holding opposing partisan identities.[2] Similarly, a rise in political anxiety among the public often accompanies political transition periods and elections.[3] These emotions shape our political participation and how we respond to social problems like racial oppression.[4]

Our political identities can even have life-or-death consequences. Republicans were much more likely than Democrats to feel that the government had overreacted to the COVID-19 pandemic by instating basic public health protocols like masking and social distancing.[5] Political identity even affected people's attitudes and behaviors more than whether the pandemic had personally impacted them. We could have avoided so much suffering and death if we had all taken precautions and public health protections seriously, regardless of our political identities.

So the stakes are high. But like all identities, our political identities are not stable or fixed.[6] We actively fashion and modify them amidst life's routines and dilemmas in unwieldy and complex ways. So, our political identities matter—not just in terms of *what* they are but also *how* we express and understand them and *why*. Why and how we do things in democratic participation is especially relevant, considering the context of deeply en-trenched political and racial inequalities.

Let's return to what it means to be a "grassroots progressive." This term signifies two aspects of GAP participants' collective political identity. First, it captures their identification with a leftist, social justice–oriented, or socialist political platform (hence, progressive). Secondly, it demonstrates their commitment to bottom-up democracy (hence, grassroots). So that is the *what*. But the real key lies in understanding the *how* and *why*. GAP participants formed their grassroots progressive political identities in re-lation to regional, political, and racial categories.

Political identity is more than our support for political figures, policies, or doctrines. During my time with the GAP, I realized the more profound significance of geographic and social contexts, political and social events, and racial inequalities. As political scientist Katherine Cramer Walsh ar-gues, "To observe how it is that people interpret politics through identity-based perspectives, we need to study interaction within actual social contexts."[7] By exploring the contours of grassroots progressive identity, we can better identify activities that maintain or challenge racial inequal-ity and exclusion within the dual contexts of grassroots democracy and a racialized social system.

REGION

All politics is local politics.—Byron Price, 1932

As social psychologist Matthew Feinberg and his colleagues warned, "Assessing political identity without considering location ignores the impact of social context."[8] Our regional cultures, histories, and political contexts influence how grassroots democracy takes place. We often make meaning of ourselves via geographic boundaries.[9] Regionalization plays an important role by "manufacturing regional histories, memories, and iden-tities."[10] The regional context of the Northeast impacted GAP participants' routine practices and influenced their perceptions of the political sphere. For instance, the unique history of town meetings as spaces of democratic engagement in the Northeast provides a structure and participatory con-text for contemporary grassroots politics.[11]

The northeastern corner of the United States is often coated in a deep shade of blue by political cartographers to denote the dominance of the

Democratic Party. In 2014, political commentary website *The Hill* produced a list ranking each US state on its "blueness" or "redness" based
on the party affiliation of prominent elected officials.[12] States such as
New York, Connecticut, Rhode Island, Massachusetts, Maine, Vermont,
New Jersey, Delaware, and New Hampshire all resided firmly in the "blue"
category.[13] This trend was further validated by the results of the 2016 and
2020 elections. All of these states went to Hillary Clinton and Joe Biden
in the Electoral College.[14] All these northeastern states except New Hampshire (which went "red" in 2000) have gone to Democratic candidates in
every presidential election since 1992.

The regional dominance of the Democratic Party is ripe for critique. The
Democratic leadership in the Northeast is associated with professional-
class liberals connected to bastions of elitism like Harvard, Yale, and Wall
Street.[15] Accordingly, GAP members understood Democrats in the Northeast as out-of-touch elites. They spoke of the Machiavellian methods Democratic politicians employ to maintain entrenched and unearned positions
of power. Yet they found themselves in the *awkward* position of carving
out spaces of empowerment against overwhelmingly predominant neoliberal politics. Like many grassroots progressives, they sought to mobilize
frustration with this centrist corporatist agenda with its penchant for austerity and privatization and its inability to tackle structural injustices and
crises like climate change.

Responsibility

The term "grassroots" suggests active engagement in political life. A significant puzzle is *why* and *how*, given the myriad barriers and constraints,
everyday people engage in intensive civic engagement and political participation. Active democratic participation is exceptionally unique in a nation
like the United States that has relatively low levels of political and civic engagement. As sociologist Ruth Braunstein writes, "Active citizenship is one
choice among many, and one of the more difficult and time-consuming
choices."[16]

In my search for the *why*, I sat in a packed suburban diner with two
younger and more active GAP participants in the Whitehall chapter,
Jake and Chip, Asian American men in their early twenties. It was a late
spring day just edging over into the warmth of summer. Both donned tank
tops, shorts, and flip-flops. We idly chatted about summer plans and our

excitement to go to the beach soon. After we ordered some drinks, our conversation moved toward why they got involved in grassroots progressive politics.

Over the clatter of plates and silverware and the general din of other diners' conversations, Jake characterized the state of American democracy as "hopeless." He told me, "Um, when you start to look at how the corporate media and how, um, dirty money has infiltrated our electoral system, and you start looking into the significance of that, you begin to realize that votes don't matter." He noted that candidates now spend billions of dollars on campaigns. Jake argued that "it won't buy people's votes, but it will buy airtime—it'll buy brainwashing." Chip chimed in with agreement, stating, "I think we're in an oligarchy. I think we trend towards a strong oligarchy and money in politics and disenfranchisement of, uh, either the working class or people of color has occurred since the inception of this country. And it's, yeah, now that I see all the hurdles, even uh, behind the scenes, the bureaucratic bullshit we have to deal with to run candidates at the local level. Like, are you fucking kidding me?"

They cited examples such as the Electoral College and its impact on the political efficacy of urban areas for why American democracy fails to fulfill its promise. Chip and Jake noted that, as many political commentators have argued, the Electoral College, due to its winner-take-all structure hinging on a handful of "swing states," gives outsized influence over presidential elections to specific regions of the country regardless of their population size, thus disempowering those living in large metropolitan areas of non-swing states such as New York and California.[17]

Concern for the health of the democratic process was a source of cohesion and enthusiasm among GAP participants. On the one hand, they spoke of a responsibility to advance democracy. On the other hand, they articulated deep cynicism about the current state of democracy in the United States. Disillusionment with the political system was embodied in criticisms of the hypocrisy of the Democratic Party. It manifested in the sense of injustice and the need for radical political change that GAP members articulated.

As religious studies scholar Jeffrey Stout writes, "The question of democratic hope boils down to whether the basic concepts of our political heritage apply to the world in which we now live."[18] However, our local political participation can pressure "the state to make good on its democratic claims."[19] Through this action, "community residents sometimes create a more active, participatory concept of democracy."[20]

For many participants in the GAP, the tension between the ideal of democracy and the reality of mass disenfranchisement produced a *democratic consciousness* that contained cynicism and aspiration. This ongoing conflict—between how things are and how they should be—drove them toward approaches to political life that prioritized local democracy and attempts to empower everyday people. Chip said, "I find myself wanting to be more involved in activist and protest efforts because I want to circumvent the system as best I can while still working within it." He emphasized the role of both protest and electoral politics: "It has me like fed up and thinking that we just need to gather the people and kind of force politicians' hands."

Nina, whom I introduced in chapter 1 and who is an extremely active participant in the Maple Leaf chapter of the GAP, also recognized barriers to change within the system and the organization's internal shortcomings. Nonetheless, she found herself driven by an obligation to contest social and political inequality. She told me, "I really have this feeling that there's going to come a time where we are going to be the party of the future. . . . We just have to make sure that . . . the elements and the conditions are right for that. And that onus is upon us to do that. That responsibility is upon us. . . . I'm only one person, but I know that ethically and morally, I wouldn't be able to live with myself if I was just sitting around not doing anything and pretending that these issues don't exist, you know?"

This political outlook could be described as "pessoptimism," a paradoxical portmanteau of optimism and pessimism. A similar concept was well expressed by the Italian political theorist Antonio Gramsci. As Gramsci explained in a personal letter from an Italian jail cell, "I'm a pessimist because of intelligence, but an optimist because of will."[21] Participants' interactions with local political systems and Democratic elites often only brought more knowledge of this tension.

Radicalism

During an informal conversation, Soren, a member of the Edgepond chapter, told me, "I think it's difficult for a lot of grassroots progressives to reconcile the difference between our morals and the Democratic Party's actions." Similarly, in a separate conversation, Nina stated, "I love what the GAP stands for and its ideals. I don't believe that I could be part of a Democratic or Republican Party because they're corrupt. The donations and the dark money that's really dictating what happens with those parties. . . . Personally, it just doesn't sit well with me. I just wouldn't be able to sleep at night, contributing to these corrupt parties."

We tend to arrive at our political identity by considering how our practices, group memberships, and issue stances compare to regional norms. GAP members sought to embody a more progressive mode of politics. As GAP participants positioned themselves to the left of the political spectrum, Democratic politicians, particularly those with ties to corporations and elites, provided an obvious foil. We make sense of political events and our positions on them in everyday interactions with others in our communities.[22] In fact, we are more likely to base our political identities on the dominant politics in our region than even our support for specific policies.[23]

Reference groups play a significant role here. Many conservatives see the Democratic Party and its supporters as extreme leftists, to the point of employing McCarthyist rhetoric and imagery. The depiction of former president Barack Obama, one of the most outspokenly politically centrist political leaders in recent decades, as signaling the rise of communism in the United States among conservatives is well documented.[24] In contrast, from the vantage point of grassroots progressives, Democrats are a centrist, center-right, or even conservative political force. For instance, Roy, a middle-aged white male member of the New Easton chapter of the GAP, stated, "The Democrats and the Republicans are just different branches of the same tree. So, I decided to find another tree to climb."

On a rainy afternoon in the early summer, after a GAP meeting at a local library, I sat and talked with Megan, a white female member of the Edgepond chapter of the party in her early twenties. Megan was early in her career in a major regional industry after college, but many of her friends in the chapter were still finishing their degrees. The other, mostly college-aged, participants headed out and we stayed behind so I could get her story and perspective. In our conversation, she emphatically took the Democratic Party to task for supporting educational policies which, now that they were associated with the Trump administration, Democrats seemed to oppose:

> I didn't even know this before I really looked into it and the way
> that charter schools are moving in and how that was supported by

President Obama. And now Betsy DeVos is like charter queen, and the Democrats won't have it. Very interesting. I mean, the ESSA [Every Student Succeeds Act] is just twenty-first-century segregation, uh, that's been capitalized. . . . So, it's really, all of New Orleans is on a charter system, Detroit, Chicago is moving that way. Inner city, predominantly minority communities are essentially being sold to charter school systems, for their data, for their parents' money. It's pretty disgusting, but somehow, nobody cared about that when Obama was president, but everybody cares now.

Megan's statement indicates a broader theme I had discerned—a deep reservoir of knowledge about the national political scene and the political goings-on in the Northeast was a common attribute of participants. They spoke with near-encyclopedic knowledge of obscure or local policies, budgets, offices, acronyms, politicians, and issues.

These forms of political knowledge, particularly about local issues, operated as a resource for GAP members. They capitalized on this knowledge to acquire influence and opportunities in three primary ways.[25] First, as a political resource, it enabled participants to interpret and navigate the political system to gain power. Second, it functioned as a social resource. It allowed them to attain group cohesion and access wider progressive social networks. Finally, it provided a symbolic resource for building their regionalized political identities and developing a positive sense of self.

However, it also acted as a source of exclusion. Meetings of each regional chapter were often filled with assumptions of this knowledge as a prerequisite. More experienced participants constantly used acronyms for local organizations, government bodies, and policies. Newer participants risked appearing as a novice or an impediment to the flow of the conversation by asking for clarification. Instead, newcomers often simply stared in confusion. Reflecting on my notes from a spring 2016 meeting of the Moosewater chapter, I realized I witnessed near-constant use of jargon, acronyms, and discussion of the inner workings of specific organizations in local politics. I had seen almost no discussion of political and social issues besides comments that insinuated a preexisting consensus. At the meeting, I counted the usage of six distinct acronyms by various participants, often pronounced as words rather than a series of letters, adding further confusion to the uninitiated. At no point did anyone pause to explain their meaning or give context.

Potential new members showed up excited to talk about national politics or big picture strategizing with likeminded folks but often left disappointed. Virginia, an older white participant, had noted something similar: "The business part of the meeting can be, like, deadly. . . . When I first showed up, it was like all about the business, and it seemed like there was nothing going on. It was my initial experience. . . . I think that people come with a hopeful feeling, but, you know, we are an organization. That is more important than being a party." The idea that the business of the organization was more important than the issues and the grand goals and tactics of the party also helped participants explain the lack of growth and diverse engagement. At the end of a meeting held by the Moosewater chapter at the rural home of a participant, we discussed a recent GAP-sponsored event:

> Jacqueline: What were your thoughts on the Thanksgiving weekend
> event?
> Anne: It was good. I learned a lot. I didn't understand why there
> weren't more young people.
> Joyce: They are probably in final exams. It's the end of the semester.
> Roger: Young people don't want to do meetings. Our generation
> knew that to get things done you had to go to meetings. It's not
> glamorous.

Knowledge of local political dysfunction was crucial to how GAP members distinguished themselves from both unserious newcomers and centrist Democrats. While at the diner, Jake and Chip had highlighted a recent story about Democratic legislators drinking on the job in a northeastern state government to highlight their awareness of elite corruption:

> Jake: There's a lot of corruption, um . . . I know probably nationwide
> as well, but they are known as like a really corrupt state. Um, the
> state house is just full of, I mean, they had FBI raids on their state
> house, and it's just insane. Um.
> Chip: Apparently, they have copious alcohol abuse going around in
> the state house.
> Jake: Did you see that article?
> Me: No, I did not hear about that.
> Jake: One of the Reps, she basically said there was like liquor,
> cabinets full of liquor in the state house.

Chip: Filing cabinets full of liquor and they were—what did she say?

Jake: I don't know the exact wording.

Chip: Some of the language was "they're in the bag"?

Jake: They're "half in the bag" while voting, while legislating. Like the
    local paper wrote an article.

Participants also bemoaned that aligning with the dominant Democratic gatekeepers in their area increased the likelihood of a candidate's
success at the local level. Localized barriers to engagement for grassroots
progressives became a similar source of identity. Thinking about these
barriers allowed them to see themselves as underdogs undermined by regional political elites and bureaucrats.

In an email to the Moosewater GAP chapter, Frank, an older white
man in the chapter, described his experiences submitting paperwork for
statewide candidacy at an elections office. He recounted that while he had
made sure to turn in the paperwork by the deadline, the workers at the
office claimed that his paperwork was past the deadline. They refused to
accept it. He wrote that he eventually clarified and emphasized the details
of his situation, and they accepted the forms. He connected this trouble
at the election office to other accounts from GAP members of receiving
false information, being given incorrect forms, and being turned away
when attempting to register, vote, or run for office. He closed the email by
emphasizing that everyone should be assertive and careful when dealing
with local election officials.

Relationships

The nature of people's relationship with the party ranged from em-
phatic to strained and from strategic to idealistic. Megan said that while
she does identify with the party, "I just kind of do this because my friends
are involved in it, [but] I do like the ideas." She also pointed out that "it
gives me some credibility when I'm trying to stifle partisan debates" and
"a lot of flexibility and leeway in what I do politically, so um, in that way,
it's been beneficial."

Similarly, Chip pointed out that he and Jake see the party "as a vehicle."
Elaborating on this idea, Jake said,

We said this from the beginning. We said this to everybody. "Look,
if . . . a party or another group that has our values comes up and just

starts sweeping house, we'll jump ship. You're probably going to lose us. And you'll probably lose everybody." I mean, realistically, what are our goals? Our goals are to get whatever legislation we want passed and change the country for the good with our progressive values. That's what our goal is. So, if another group does it, I don't give a shit if it's the Grassroots Progressives, or the Democrats, or Working Families, or the Greens, or the Socialists, or whatever the hell.

Identification with the GAP also played out in more subtle ways. At a local public library meeting room, an African American man in his early thirties, Rafael, was among the two newcomers who wanted to check out the chapter. He was a longtime grassroots progressive who had recently become disillusioned with other left-leaning political parties in the area. As they spoke about potential changes in the organization and recruitment strategies, Rafael weighed in with his own experience—"I was having trouble trying to find out about this chapter of the GAP. . . . *We, you guys* need to reach out to other groups like younger people. Millennials don't have time to look into it. Not everyone is as diligent as I am."

As sociologist Darnel Hunt notes, "Pronoun usage may serve as an insightful indicator of the solidarity social actors share with important ingroups and their distance from certain outgroups."[26] Pronouns of solidarity construct a sense of "we" or "us" and pronouns of distance include "me," "they," or "you." Rafael had previously used the pronouns "I," "them," or "you" throughout the meeting. His temporary slippage into "we" suggested a moment of possible identification, but in the correction to "you guys" he ultimately resisted the seduction of collective identification.

Our decisions to participate in specific local political practices and join organizations have significant ripple effects within broader political systems and in developing who we are over time. Whether new members see themselves as part of the "we" can make or break their continued participation in a regional political organization and determine whether parties grow or shrink in size and influence. The features of our early contact with localized or regional organizations help us form our sense of attachment to or alienation from political parties. And entrenched ideas of "we" within a party, or in other words, its organizational identity, also provide obstacles to organizational change.[27] Yet parties also face the dynamic challenge of reacting to new contexts, events, and issues as they unfold in the political landscape.

REACTIONS

*The first casualty of the Trump era is truth, the second is moral responsibility,
the third is any vestige of justice, and the fourth is a massive increase in
human misery and suffering for millions.*—Henry Giroux, 2018

In January 2017, the American Psychological Association noted that
"more than half of Americans (57 percent) report that the current political climate is a very or somewhat significant source of stress" and that
"two-thirds (66 percent) say the same about the future of our nation, and
nearly half (49 percent) report that the outcome of the election is a very
or somewhat significant source of stress."[28] While "post-election stress disorder" gripped the nation, a common sentiment among progressives was
one of being attacked on all fronts.[29] News of Trump's policy decisions and
appointments signaled the erosion of social progress, the empowerment of
right-wing activists, and the weakening of public safeguards and cherished
institutions.[30] Virginia clearly articulated this sense of dread and loss as
we sat in her living room, eating cookies, drinking tea, and discussing the
election. A somber mood hung over our conversation as she stated her
takeaway—"A lot of people will die."

The choppy wake of the contentious 2016 election left many of us
scrambling for answers. Commentators and researchers highlighted the
role of racist attitudes and beliefs, a staple variable influencing whites' voting habits. For instance, political scientists Marc Hooghe and Ruth Dassonville found that "indicators of racist resentment and anti-immigrant
sentiments proved to be important determinants of a Trump vote."[31] Studies similarly determined how economic, racial, gendered, and religious
attitudes and demographics influenced voting in the 2016 presidential
election.[32] But beyond these explanations and voter trends, this moment
was particularly impactful for those passionate about progressive politics
and grassroots organizing.

Recalibrating our self-perception and politics in the face of new events
can be an uneasy and uncomfortable process. Participants' reactions to the
turbulent 2016 presidential campaign and the election of Donald J. Trump
demonstrated their active attempts to try to make sense of a chaotic political world. Important events like elections, policy changes, or political
scandals provide opportunities for building and altering our political identities.[33] As participants struggled to make meaning of the election results

for their daily lives and political activities, three reactions unfolded: *rationalization*, *reinvestment*, and *reconsideration*.

Rationalization

As we sat outside at a small ice cream shop on a sunny summer afternoon, Jennifer, another member of the Edgepond chapter, a middle-class white woman in her early twenties, tried to make sense of the election. She argued that it was unrealistic to expect an ideal president in the current political system: "I told myself that I didn't care who won because either one of them would be terrible. I told myself I wouldn't be more disappointed by one than the other. . . . You know, you can try to say which one's worse or which one is not as terrible, but that's not the point because you're going to get stuck with a terrible president." Yet she admitted that in the aftermath of the election she felt differently. She "was appalled" and conceded that she "did want Hillary." She joked that she "would have been cool with World War 3," riffing on critiques of Clinton's hawkishness, if it meant that her liberal feminist platform was enacted.

For many of us, the outcome of the 2016 election and the events that led up to it were utterly disorienting. However, many integrated this new reality into their critical worldviews on US politics. For instance, the idea that Donald J. Trump was equally treacherous or immoral as Hillary Clinton (if not more so) enabled some participants to downplay the implications of his presidency. Megan from the Edgepond chapter found a silver lining in the results:

> I don't think Donald Trump was the worst thing to happen to us in the election. I would have rather had Donald Trump any day over Hillary Clinton. . . . Hillary Clinton, I think to myself, is very obviously, pathologically trying to be important. Um, she would want to do something drastic to get her name etched into history besides being the first female president. That wouldn't be enough for her and good for her; I mean, if I were to be the first female president, that's not how I would want to be remembered. I wouldn't want my gender to be my main signifier. Good for her. Except for she's a fucking war criminal.

In my conversation with Jennifer at the ice cream shop, she pointed out that the election "caused people to get involved and so many more young people as well, and it's gotta be good." And although she had previously admitted a preference for Clinton, she ultimately resigned herself to the idea that "you're not going to get a not terrible president, so just kinda . . . detach from that whole idea."

By positioning themselves as outside of the two-party binary, some participants in the GAP distanced themselves from the implications of Trump's election, even if it held grave consequences for causes that they championed. Younger participants who saw themselves as pragmatic political actors rather than pie-in-the-sky activists were more capable of this form of rationalization. They were quick to distance themselves from the idealists of their party. Jake pointed out that rather than focusing on elections, "they're activists. That's what they've always been." Chip followed up with an example, noting that a former leader was "unwavering he just, he's not into marketing, he's not into politics." Jake and Chip contrasted their pragmatic and strategic approach with idealistic members with a history of activism:

Jake: One word: burnout. That's how all these guys ended up.
Chip: Yeah, these guys, these guys are too involved in the intellectual or emotional aspect sometimes but not enough treating it like an organization that has to rally people and market to the people. And I think that's kind of our role. Or at least it's what we have— personality where maybe they don't.

In a later conversation, Megan made a similar claim by emphasizing the need to corral resources:

Um, they think we should be spending that time protesting, which is all well and good and all but, you know, how far does that really get you? When campaign time comes around, the people who are actually going to be changing the issues that you're protesting against need to get elected and they can't get elected unless they have strong support from their party. Their party can't support them without money. As much as the party denounces capitalism in their platform, the fact of the matter is this is a capitalist country, and this is how our politics and our society works. You gotta feed the pig so to speak.

Another form of rationalization came from using the 2016 election to diagnose problems in American democracy: major-party duopoly, financialization, the sensationalism and agenda-setting role of mass media, and the lack of political education or will held by the average citizen. Chip argued, "Most people couldn't tell you why they voted for Trump, why they voted for Clinton. They have no clue." Jake responded that people might explain their voting choices by saying, "I was told to because the media said it or whatever it might be." Critical, even cynical, awareness of social and political problems provided valuable tools in this process. Many participants insulated themselves from the shock of this turbulent political period by understanding it as symptomatic of an already dysfunctional political system.

Reinvestment

At a January 2017 meeting of the Moosewater chapter, the reality of Trump's election and its ecological, social, and political impact weighed heavily on members' minds. Despite the dour feeling about the state of the nation, there was also a celebratory tone. The meeting was held on Jacqueline's birthday at a participant's rural home surrounded by woods. I walked through the kitchen to greet everyone. After sitting at the dining room table, we sang "Happy Birthday" and passed around slices of birthday cake.

Once the birthday excitement died down and the meeting began, we resumed grappling with the despair of the political moment. Jacqueline suggested the meeting begin with each of us discussing what issues we will tackle in 2017. She began, "The new action for 2017 is recovering democracy—locally to nationally. I am attending an upcoming meeting on this, and I'm really surprised that there is something like that going on in my town. Especially something that I didn't organize." She laughed.

Participants went around the room and shared their focus, whether it was climate change, ranked-choice voting, local democracy and civic engagement, or racial justice work. Many shared their disgust about Trump's racial prejudice, dishonesty, and corruption. Paul, an older white participant who was normally quiet and reserved, became choked up and almost on the verge of tears. He said, "I have been thinking about the hatred and bigotry toward minority groups. I want to work broadly to let Muslims and Mexicans know that I care about them. I'm less concerned about policy right now, and some things are just really putrid to me. . . . I can't think clearly because there is so much smothering any long-term or policy goals."

In another instance, as he finished sharing his plans, Walter, an older white man who was also generally soft spoken, stated sternly, "Also, I think we need to get Donald Trump impeached! We need to push to get rid of that bozo! He'll probably mess up so bad that his party will lose a lot of seats in Congress. I don't mean to suggest other means." The room lit up with chuckles at this answer, and Roger joked, "Make sure that's in the minutes!"

It also became a space to hash out collective strategies and find consensus out of conflict. Virginia took her turn by mentioning, "I have been going door to door talking to people about the pipeline. And I don't even say climate change. I talk about other things." Her answer sparked a short back-and-forth around the benefits of different strategies and forms of framing issues. Frank asked, "What do you say? Property values?" She responded, "Well, I talk about safety and other issues like that. Some of them don't care once I tell them where the pipeline is going, and it's not their backyards." He said, "Without solidarity, we won't get anywhere," She replied, "Well, I really try to get people to like me and get to know me, trust and respect me." Frank, acknowledging the pragmatism of her point, conceded, "Yeah, I tend to get too preachy." Jacqueline eased the tension by joking, "I think a lot of us struggle with that one." Everyone laughed.

At each turn around the table, and especially Paul's emotional plea, other members nodded empathetically. These concerns were prescient. The meeting had been in the wake of not only the election but an immediate surge in bias incidents, hate crimes, and racial harassment targeting groups that Trump had singled out on the campaign trail with promises to build a wall on the US-Mexican border and institute a ban on Muslims entering the country. Moreover, the general sentiment that the racial climate in the wake of the election had become intense and toxic was common. Most Americans thought that Trump's election had led to worse race relations in the United States.[34] However, the discussion of racial conditions lasted only a short time. After a short pause, Roger stated, somewhat dismissively, "You know, we care about all these things, but all it takes is one hot war, and all we will care about is survival. I hate to say it." Jacqueline then wrapped up, "Thanks for sharing. I think we should focus on clustering around specific issues. If everyone picked one or two issues to focus on, we can really change things."

Jacqueline began to summarize the activity—"So the purpose of this was basically to get out our ideas about what we can do"—but someone pointed out that I and a few others hadn't yet responded. Attention turned to me. I mentioned that I was writing a book on racial justice and drug policy and that I planned to address how the new administration would impact drug laws and mass incarceration by working with organizations.[35]

The new participant, an older white man named Jeff, said, "I have been thinking lately about why mainstream and alternative media got it wrong. I see what's happening as a corporate coup—a corporate takeover of the government. There is a lack of critical mass on the left because it's so fragmented. I am also exploring the possibilities for coalitions." One participant replied, "Well, that's our party. We have the ideals, and we are the coalition." Another struck a more cautious note: "But the problem is that we don't want to lose our identity as a party." Another participant retorted, "These people are part of the Grassroots Action Party, and they just don't know it." Tensions rose as someone pointed out they were not alone in seeing themselves as the vanguard of progressive politics: "Well, they could just say the grassroots are really socialist or Democrats or Green, and they don't know it." Jacqueline again used humor to breach the disagreement, stating, "I agree with all of that" and laughing.

By sharing and verbally reaffirming their commitments to progressive principles and actions, GAP participants attempted to transform their disgust and fear into a sense of solidarity and deeper motivation for civic engagement. As sociologist Kai Heidemann notes, "As people work collaboratively to conquer fears and uncertainties in times of crisis, they undertake discursive processes of interpersonal reflection and deliberation that allow them to locate and understand the macrostructural sources of their suffering."[36] While the commentary members provided on each other's answers exposed potential rifts, it also emphasized shared concerns and commitments.

Reconsideration

While some rationalized and some reflected and redoubled their efforts, there was yet a third response to the election results: *reconsideration*. About a week after the election, we sat around Janice and Frank's dining room table for a Moosewater chapter meeting. Their home was highly decorated with rustic and local artwork collected over their long lives. I sat and took it all in, thinking that each piece must have a fascinating story behind it. About halfway through the meeting, Roger announced that, in light of Trump's election to president, he had resigned from several high-level positions in the party. We applauded and thanked him for his service.

After the meeting, Roger handed me a printed copy of his resignation letter, mentioning that it might have some relevance to my project. In thoughtful and detailed prose, his letter stated that while he remains committed to the ideals of the party, in the aftermath of Trump's election and other discouraging election results, he was stepping down from those positions to dedicate his energy to supporting liberal Democrats in upcoming key electoral races. Later that month, we sat and talked in a small coffee shop. He explained, "I was kind of starting to go down this path of . . . now we're in the common front antifascist universe where it doesn't matter where you are. If you are anywhere on the spectrum other than in the fascist party, you have to work together to try to curtail the abuse of power that otherwise could come about. That's a terrible flip to go through in a week, but that's the state of mind I was in."

After political boundaries had been dramatically redrawn overnight, staving off a rapidly consolidating and intensifying right-wing agenda through a smaller independent party seemed increasingly quixotic. He said, "I feel as though I've crossed over an interesting threshold in my experience of American politics from a time when it made more sense to work through a grassroots organization to attempt to convince those who have some power to implement the kinds of things that I want to have happen."

These reactions were characterized by disappointment but also potential and energy. Alongside the election of a questionable real estate mogul turned reality television star as president, the 2016 election also featured another salient political shift in the meteoric rise of democratic socialist Bernie Sanders as a major contender in the Democratic primary. The Sanders campaign held a populist tone and grassroots appeal, inspiring previously disillusioned progressives and centrists alike. Rafael mentioned that despite his criticisms of Democrats and his support for grassroots progressive organizations, the Sanders campaign motivated him to become involved with the Democratic Party:

I thought that the party would realize that that was the direction of
a large majority of its constituents within the Democratic Party were
leaning heavily more left of center than they were towards the centrist

politics of Democrats. . . . I was in Alabama at the time. I went to a
rally, and . . . in the biggest arena in the biggest city in Alabama, in
Birmingham, Bernie Sanders sold it out. And it was so many people
that it was literally thousands of people that couldn't get in that were
just in the streets. And I thought to myself, I said wow, maybe we are
developing as a country. In the heart of the South, here's this guy, this
democratic socialist guy with this completely radical philosophy in
comparison to what dominated major politics at the time, and he's
got a crowd like this in Alabama. You couldn't even get mainstream
Democrats to get a crowd like that in Alabama. So, the energy,
the excitement, the hope that we were going this direction, I was
completely, so I was in, you know? I was in. I was donating, I was at
Bernie rallies, I was, anything that I could do to be involved. And my
hope in the Democratic Party was restored until they took it from me.
You know, until they took it, until he conceded.

The disillusionment that accompanied Clinton's clenching of the Democratic nomination among progressives and socialists pushed many of them
back into grassroots organizations despite being temporarily brought back
into the Democratic fold. New participants showed up with similar back-
stories at chapter meetings and even larger regional meetings and events
months after the nomination announcement. They had been Bernie Sanders supporters. In the wake of his primary loss, they were looking for a
political organization aligned with the values that made them enthralled
with his campaign. On paper, at least, the GAP was that organization.

RACIALIZATION

*Racialization is the process of constructing racial meaning, including
the creation of racial categories and the signification of these categories
in relation to people, objects, and ideas.*—Matthew Clair and
Jeffrey F. Denis, 2015

Racial meanings, how we make sense of ourselves, others, and the world
around us in racial terms, are inextricable from political life. Political contestations form and transform racial categories, their meanings, and the
social structures surrounding them. Racial politics are not just large-scale
macro dynamics. They play out at the micro- and meso-levels, in the civil
and political spheres, communities and organizations, and everyday life.[37]

Racial meanings serve as a driving force influencing political actions and the formation of political identities. They impact how we interpret and react to the racialized structure of society and our place within it.

It is unsurprising that racial meanings play an indispensable role in how we position ourselves as political actors. Positioning reflects "how people use words (and discourse of all types) to locate themselves and others."[38] We engage in positioning when we talk about the categories that we and others occupy and the relationships between these categories in everyday social life. Creating distinctions between categories is a crucial aspect of social cognition in everyday political life. It is also routinely laden with racial meanings.

The role of racial meanings in political life is exceptionally well understood concerning Democrats and Republicans. Consider the following two statements by political scientists Donald Kinder and Lynn M. Sanders: "The strategic problem for Democratic candidates is to maintain the loyalty and enthusiasm of black voters without alienating conservative whites: for Democratic campaigns, the temptation on matters of race is silence and evasion." "The strategic problem of Republican candidates is to draw the support of white conservatives without appearing to make racist appeals: the Republican temptation is racial codewords."[39] But what about the racialization of grassroots progressives and their relationship to ideals, strategies, and habits? Are grassroots progressives necessarily racial progressives? How do their racial worldviews and political identities collide and interact?

Rifts

Daren, a middle-aged white man and long-standing and active member of the Moosewater chapter passionate about environmental activism, explained that the overwhelming white demographics of the party seemed connected to the established ties within the region between the interests and political practices in what he described as "diverse" communities and establishment Democratic Party candidates: "Maybe a lot of that diversity might be in the Democratic Party but I think it's because *they're* locked and held in there. Given that, you know, given that that's the option. You go in *there* and that's who's going to solve your problems."

GAP members often struggled to make sense of their racial attitudes and demographics. Exploring the coexistence of their ideals about racial justice and the makeup and actions of their organization was one way that

GAP members used racial meanings to bolster their political identities. For instance, when asked to explain why the racial justice support held by grassroots progressives did not translate into greater racial diversity and inclusion within the GAP, many respondents argued that they had difficulty competing with established political organizations.

Democrats tend to emphasize centrist racial politics, while Republicans push conservative racial politics.[40] This arrangement presents an opening for grassroots progressives to engage with racially progressive platforms and strategies. In this case, the strategies and platforms advanced by the GAP (at least on paper) include solidarity with racial justice organizations and marginalized groups such as undocumented migrants and support for policies aimed at empowering oppressed groups and producing a more racially equal and just society. Yet participants' relationships to racial issues and policies were much more complex in daily speech and practice. These relationships depended upon a host of factors, including their social positions, racial literacy, and interpretations of the goals of their political engagement.

Similarly, Megan described a quandary presented by the Democratic National Committee's (DNC) assumed monopoly on communities of color:

It's really hard because Democrats do have their fists or like their claws like very, very tightly around minority groups. And I think a lot of that is just lack of education. It's very—that's what angers me a lot about the Democratic Party, they're very paternalistic where [it's] "Don't, don't worry about it, honey. We'll take care of you, just—those guys are scary. Just vote for us. We'll take care of you. Don't, don't worry about it. Don't ask too many questions just know we'll take care of you," and we should try harder to educate those populations with how mainstream Democratic platforms have actually been harming them instead of helping them.

In a follow-up interview, I asked her to further elucidate on the racial politics of the Democratic Party and how it related to her preference for a grassroots progressive organization:

One of my big hardships with the Democratic Party itself is that it has forever been extremely paternalistic where it is, um, you know, "Don't worry about it, don't think about it, we'll take care of it for you, just vote for us," and of course again and again, they don't deliver. And often times they use these populations as leverage for them to do something else. I don't know. It gets me just really just upset.

I pivoted to asking about the racial politics of Republicans. As I had seen with other GAP members, it became clear that distinction from the Democratic Party was a more crucial aspect of her political identity. Her answer to this question was replete with tangents about the hypocrisy of Democrats:

> [*sighs*] So I think, I think a lot of what, uh, the Republicans' issue on that, that matter is not necessarily that you know they don't care about urban issues, or they don't care about minorities or that they're racists, even though a lot of them totally are. Um, but I think a lot of it is that the Republicans. When you talk to them about policies, [*takes deep breath*] At least on a person-to-person level, it's, a lot of it is just very, uh, I guess [*takes deep breath*] . . . Um, but the Republicans, I think, actually have a lot of integrity in that, in that way where they're not going to lie to you when they're saying "Yeah, we're going to decrease taxes and it's going to benefit the wealthy." I mean, they may lie to your face when they say it will trickle down and it'll benefit you in the end, but I think in a lot of ways, uh, the Republicans, they have a lot more integrity. . . . Republicans have been—they get a bad rap for it because that's not their central focus, they don't care about making things better for one specific ethnic group, they just want to make things better as a whole, so, their big picture seem to be, of course [*sighs*] their policy ideas, they help rich old white men. . . . Their main objective isn't necessarily adding diversity to their party.

The notion that elite Democrats do not have a real connection or concern for the ordinary person (in this case, people of color) was a central aspect of grassroots progressive identity. Moreover, the hypocrisy of the Democratic Party in representing the interests of people of color played a more prominent motivating role in Megan's assessment of the mainstream parties than the racial politics of the Republican Party. Participants sought to capitalize on their claim of fighting for racial justice and a racially progressive vision. However, many expressed frustrations at being outmatched by the resources and capacity of the establishment

Democratic Party. Some white members even went so far as to ascribe a lack of knowledge on the part of communities of color as a primary driver of their support for mainstream Democrats.

Recruitment

Others in the GAP emphasized that progressive racial politics could be a strategic advantage in bringing more people of color into the organization. However, participants who engaged with this line of thought also acknowledged that they struggled to fully take advantage of the appeal of their politics to the economic, social, and political interests of communities of color for various reasons. Jake and Chip talked at length with me one afternoon about how having a racial justice orientation might produce positive relationships between the organization and local communities of color.

> Jake: The party platform of the GAP is very for people of color compared to any of the other parties in the United States.
> Chip: But they might show up with different ideas even. You know what I mean?
> Jake: I don't know. We can talk, but we can say, "Here's the platform. What do you not like about it?" And that's how you have to go about it. If they came in and said, "Oh, I want this, this, and we should get reparations," that's great, and that's what we agree on. And that's even the case with other members. I mean, we have members that we don't agree with. Great, well, you're allowed to, and you can present a logical, like, well-thought-out argument for whatever view you don't like, propose it. You know? Give it to our committee, and let us vote on it, and we'll see where it takes it. You know? There's this idea of openness.
> Chip: . . . Inclusiveness means being open to change of even maybe long-held ideas.

Jake and Chip thus emphasized that the GAP would benefit not from attracting new voters and supporters but from the collective input of new communities. In a sense, they drew on the appeal of grassroots democracy and its ability to transform the organization for the better. They did not want their organization to simply attain power but also to advance political empowerment, inclusion, and equity.

They also emphasized the racial justice ideals of the GAP as a motivating factor for themselves as people of color to join and remain active within the party:

> Chip: I read their platform, their extended platform, and um, it was their platform on social justice that really um swayed me and um, to a large extent Jake. They actually have written into their platform programs of support for restitution for the negative impacts of oppression against Native Americans and African Americans, which I think, just from my political leanings, that's crucial. That should happen. That should have happened. You know what I mean?

Moreover, they suggested that even the most left-leaning members of the Democratic Party would likely not offer this stance and obligation to address the impacts of systemic racism intentionally. Similarly, in articulating why he maintained his alliance with the GAP, Terrance, an older African American man and a member of the New Easton chapter, said during a state-level party meeting, "I started from a racial justice organization that connected with the GAP. The party took a stand for Palestinian rights. We took a stand on Black Lives Matter. We take good stands. We stand for diversity, and we stand for antiracism. We will take the fight and the honest fight, and that's why I'm still here after all these years; we may not always win, but we fight an honest fight on the things we care about."

That the party takes highly progressive positions on racial justice issues was seen by people of color as an opening for transformation in terms of the racial politics of the party and surrounding communities. However, this position did not directly translate to overarching actions and patterns conducive to the inclusion and empowerment of people of color. Much like the tension of democratic disillusionment and commitment, the conflict of ideals and reality regarding racial justice and support for people of color is vital to the racial meanings that suffuse grassroots progressive political identity.

Virginia made a similar yet distinct point as I sat with her in her living room over coffee, and we chatted informally about the party's demographics. She pointed out, "If the GAP's message could get out to more Black communities, Latino communities, you know, I mean, it's an obvious fit. ... It's a perfect opening." She noted that she and the party as a whole value and appreciate having people of color on board: "When I see the email exchanges [between members], there are quite a number of Hispanic names, which is good, very good. And one of the people who ran, who was a candidate to be the candidate and he's been a member for many years, is African American." However, she also acknowledged that there was still a long way to go for the party to live up to its ideals: "That's a good thing, but we need more diversity, yes. Locally."

A major distinction that related to outreach and inclusion of people of color to the organization hinged upon whether or not the party should engage in targeting participants of color or take a more color-blind approach. For instance, Roger mentioned the following proposal during our conversation at a small coffee shop:

> One of the central candidates that ran this year, she said the GAP should just run people of color for office. Stop running any white men. And stop running white women . . . because the party won't grow unless it gets these people, these constituencies engaged and the most visible way to do that would be to step aside and promote and, I, you know, that would not have been my answer or thought, earlier, you know, I would have thought, "No, run the best candidate wherever you can run candidates," but I see this is a strategy that could be taken and it wouldn't be a stupid strategy. Uh, time will tell whether it works.

On one hand, centering on people of color appeared to be a potent and clear strategy for strengthening the GAP's relationships with communities of color and offsetting the historical whiteness of the party and its leadership. Yet, as Roger acknowledged, there was also a sense among many white participants that this strategy clashed with a general sense of meritocracy, whereby candidates are fielded based on their perceived political skills and fit rather than demographic characteristics. He further distinguished that many participants supported the ideal behind running candidates of color but struggled with its practical implications:

> Well, everybody is on board with it in the, uh, ideal. In other words, nobody would object to getting strong candidates who are people of color and any candidates who will use the, uh, social injustices as the lever of, um, you know, advancing our agenda. But you're still going to get white males of talent who are going to want to be the star of their little show and I don't know how on board all of them will be to taking

a back seat. . . . But being proactive about it, um, I think there'd be a lot of support if we could figure out how to do that.

He pointed out that due to the constraints of operating a grassroots political organization in an era of big money politics and gatekeeping, they did not often have many viable options when it came to running candidates of color who also fit the exact description of an ideal GAP candidate:

> We have so few candidates that it's not like we have multiple people more like we have one. It's just not an issue, right? . . . Where you'll hear it is "Is this person actually going to be a strong candidate?" And what does that take? We've run some very feeble candidates. So, our standards are, I think, they're not enough. In other words, we pick, we pick people who speak well and that's their only like—they're not organized. They don't get to where they need to get to. You don't have a strong candidate unless you can hire. Like, part of it is we don't have this like money answer to that. Like other parties put up poorly qualified candidates and they buy their way through all of the hurdles. But we can't . . . We want to run strong candidates who both embody our values and can be effective if they could be elected. Right? We want all of that. And that's a tall order.

How grassroots progressives in GAP accounted for progress in actualizing a racial justice and inclusivity agenda, as well as the lack thereof, was a further dimension of how racial meanings impacted political identity.

Roadblocks

The barriers to achieving political influence and electoral success for a grassroots party were often a topic of discussion among GAP members. However, people of color within the party often articulated that the barriers that they faced personally and as a part of a larger community were not only political or bureaucratic in nature but also racialized. The technical and policy barriers to political participation disfavored people of color and tended to favor whites. Additionally, local political elites were overwhelmingly white, even in racially diverse communities. A minority of the party members that I spoke with could clearly interpret and understand how these dynamics, which for many GAP members were racially neutral or lacked a racial character, were shaped by issues of racial oppression.

I met up with Nina at a large bookstore to talk about her experiences in grassroots democracy as a woman of color. Looking for a place to sit and chat, we ended up sitting in the children's section due to a lack of seating elsewhere. We both joked and laughed as we resigned ourselves to sitting on stools painted to look like tree stumps in an area designed to look like a magical forest. She recalled the following:

> I remember going up in October to the State House to testify. There was an electoral reform bill up at the State House, and I went up there to testify on behalf of ranked-choice voting. I got to speak, and so I went, and I spoke about my own experience and how difficult it was for me to run for office and be successful because I was running against a legacy. It was funny because the people on the committee . . . I said you may be aware of who this individual is . . . , and some of the committee members were nodding their heads, "Yep, we know who that is," so you know he is a legend himself in the halls of the state house. It was a cathartic moment for me because I talked about that as an individual, I have done everything right in my life. I became educated. I worked in the community. I'm a leader in my political party. I've done grassroots work in the community. I've worked for twenty-five years, you know, in the same profession. I've led a moral and ethical life. And despite all of that, sometimes there are still challenges to get into office because of gerrymandering, the demographics, racism, and the issues in the city where I live.

Racial meanings, the cultural systems used to analyze events and issues in racial terms, played a significant role in constructing, negotiating, and achieving grassroots progressive identity among GAP members. Moreover, to the extent that participants recognized structural racism and its impacts, their interpretations varied widely.

In contrast to Nina's clear articulation of the structural impacts of racial oppression on political participation for herself as a person of color, Virginia focused more on emphasizing the positives of how the party had tried to deal with these issues. She suggested that the GAP had been somewhat effective at overcoming racialized barriers to outreach and inclusion. However, she argued that their successes were not well publicized, and so she also did not know whether the party's efforts had any real and long-standing impact in communities of color. Virginia said, "Of course, this didn't get a lot of media attention, but when some of our leaders would go to the inner cities of the big cities, they were greeted very enthusiastically. We don't hear about it, and I don't know if people in those inner cities are forming GAP chapters, you know? I don't know."

Given the tremendous influence of racial meanings on political life in the United States in general, that there exist racialized dimensions of grassroots progressives' political identities is not surprising. Much like other dimensions of political identity, the racialized dimension which connected racial meanings to grassroots progressives' sense of political self was expressed in a variety of different narratives, sets of idealized actions and strategies, and ways of thinking about political life. These variations are meaningful. They shape how the organization engaged with the broader issues of import to racial equality in society: practices of racial inclusion or exclusion, awareness of racial oppression and racial justice, and the overall political empowerment and mobilization of people of color.

COMMUNITIES, CONFLICT, AND COMFORT COLLIDE

We need to move beyond thinking that our political identities (and the strategies and actions they motivate) are just the outcomes of identification with partisan labels or are merely activated while making decisions in the voting booth. They are constructed through all the relationships we form in daily social life. These relationships shape our engagement with narratives, memories, vocabularies, and ideas. Our political identities are something we accomplish in moments marked with ambiguity and contradictions. They become defined and refined as we negotiate the context of families, institutions, communities, and organizations.

Our regional culture, politics, and social conditions create a unique situation from which we accomplish our identity. The fact that Democrats were the dominant political juggernaut influenced how GAP participants formed a distinct and contrasted sense of self as progressives and participants in grassroots democracy. Pointing to corruption, power concentration, and disenfranchisement in regional politics among Democratic elites, GAP members described themselves as more faithful to the ideals of democracy and social, economic, and environmental justice.

Their political identities also became refined and clarified as they engaged with and reacted to major political events such as national elections. In the wake of a political stressor such as the 2016 election, grassroots progressives had an opportunity to process what their political identity

meant under new and terrifying conditions. Some found ways to rationalize the outcome as equally bad as the alternatives, a net positive for
spurring grassroots democratic engagement, or verification of preexisting
critiques of the political system. Others who saw themselves as activists
motivated by a cause or ideal used the existential crisis that ensued to re-
invest and develop a sense of the importance of continuing their commitment to progressive grassroots politics. Finally, a few began to question the
pragmatism of operating from a more obscure and idealistic organization
as the battle lines were drawn more dramatically between overt fascism
and a loose coalition of leftists and liberals.

Motivated by the counterintuitive mix of white-dominated demographics, a robust antiracist party platform, and incoherent strategies of antiracist action, much of this book centers on how the participants of the GAP
engage with the reality of racial oppression. Exploring grassroots progressive identity reveals how some essential pieces of this puzzle fit together.
Racial meanings and their connections to social structures and people's
identities increasingly appeared as a fault line along which the shared
political identity of grassroots progressives formed and fractured. Distinct
narratives emerged about the racial politics of the GAP in comparison to
other parties, the promises and pitfalls of taking action to create a more
inclusive and diverse party, and even underlying assumptions about why
racial justice and equality matter. As the sociologist Charles Derber writes,
"Political parties can unify movements for transformative change. Political
parties in the United States rarely carry out this crucial movement work,
but this is one such potential moment."[41] These fractures have heavy implications for social and political change. They matter for future possibilities
of achieving racial justice and greater political and social equality.

The following chapters aid in further examining such stark disparities
in how GAP members employed racial meanings to navigate the racial
structure and achieve political, organizational, and personal goals. These
aspects of grassroots progressive identity formation further suggest the
power of examining grassroots democracy, up close in people's daily lives,
as both a practice and an ideal in a racially unjust society. While keeping
the overall context of what it means to be a grassroots progressive in mind,
analyzing how members engage in racialized ways of thinking, acting, and
being can help us understand the racial demographics and practical priorities of grassroots progressive political organizations.

3

Consequences
of Consciousness
How White Racial Habits
Shape Grassroots Political
Strategies

The present attitude and action of the white world
is not based solely upon rational, deliberate intent. It
is a matter of conditioned reflexes; of long followed
habits, customs and folkways; of subconscious trains
of reasoning and unconscious nervous reflexes.
—W. E. B. Du Bois, 1940

Democracy is habitual.

Bathed in the glow of fluorescent lights and surrounded by aging off-white painted walls, we sat around a table in the activity room of a small nondenominational church. Stacks of paper, alongside paper plates, cups, pastries, snacks, and coffee, covered the table. As this meeting of the Moosewater chapter of the Grassroots Action Party began, we passed around copies of that day's agenda. According to the agenda, the chapter was "seeking especially people of color, women, new Americans, people with disabilities, low-income, LGBTQ."

I looked around at the all-white attendees. They were diverse in gender, sexual orientation, and socioeconomic status. But I pondered how the participants would recruit outside of their racial demographics. They often expressed the importance of recruiting a racially diverse slate of candidates. As the meeting proceeded, I wondered how this conversation would unfold. About halfway through, the item finally came up for discussion.

Jacqueline: Who is in the news and organizing or getting good press?
Joyce: There is a woman, her name is Amy Logan, who is taking on
    Democratic local committees. She seems interested in the GAP. She
    is an interesting person. She does stuff with puppetry.
Roger: Oh, that is a familiar name.

Joyce: She is peripherally involved in the Armenian community, and I know that because my nephew is half-Armenian.

Joan: Her mom was known as a theatre person and a private school teacher.

Roger: There is also a woman named Sara Jones who tried to run for a state-level office. She is a progressive Democrat. In our small-town setting, she is too far left for the local Democratic Party. She and her husband attended a GAP event and that was about four years ago. We should reach out to her.

Despite the text in the agenda item, the silence around their racial backgrounds suggested that these proposed recruits were racialized as white. After a pause, the following interaction led to the group moving on to the next agenda item.

Jacqueline: Well, think about your network and especially our list of "underrepresenteds."

Roger: Well, maybe this has been asked, but does Nina [*an active Latina GAP member*] want to run for office?

Jacqueline: I think she is already running for something. I'll ask her though.

Two months later, I walked into a small Mediterranean restaurant on a cool spring evening for another Moosewater chapter meeting. A medley of fragrance from cardamom, cumin, za'atar, and other delicious spices wafted my way from the buffet table. I was glad that they decided to hold their meeting somewhere where dinner, not just snacks, was included. I quickly grabbed a plate of food and walked over to the group to greet them. All the participants sat together in the center of the restaurant in a row of tables. I sat down, and someone handed me a copy of the meeting agenda. This time, the item on recruitment targeting underrepresented groups was at the top of the agenda. After the meeting started, Jacqueline asked, "Do we have any suggestions for people who want to run as GAP-endorsed candidates at the local level? We set a goal of six."

A silence ensued. Attendees glanced at each other, waiting for someone to speak. Finally, Jacqueline answered her own question, saying, "At a recent event for recruiting progressive candidates, I met a young woman. She did her senior thesis at Sunnydale Community College on millennials, boomers, and gen-Xers and their support for different political positions.

It was fantastic, really great work. She is young . . . African heritage, I'm trying to get them before the centrist Democrats can. Her and her dad. He is a businessman. International business. She was asking questions at the event, and she was apologizing for asking questions, and I was like 'Don't apologize' [*laughs*]." After Jacqueline's story, the meeting participants moved on to another item. The likelihood that the chapter would recruit and run more candidates of color in upcoming campaigns dwindled. The unnamed woman and her father were never mentioned again in conversations or meetings.

Examining the GAP's racial demographics and political strategies, given its platform of racial inclusion and empowering people of color, would be impossible without seeing how these actions reflect the broader social context of racial oppression. Grassroots political activity in the United States takes place within a racialized social system. It is shaped by "the placement of actors in racial categories or races."[1] The social world members navigated in their political lives was influenced by centuries of racial segregation, discrimination, and exploitation. GAP members necessarily had to work against "the weight of history and institutional arrangements" to advance racial equality.[2] Unfortunately, racial inequality had structured not only their social world but also their everyday social patterns. Their routines reflected a durable feedback loop between their isolation in racially segregated communities and their ongoing racial ignorance.

As a result, the organization was a *white space*. It was a social space where most inhabitants considered being "white" standard.[3] Its demographics and social norms told the story. However, as reflected in my initial bafflement at the sea of white faces I encountered at my first-ever party event, it can be difficult to discern why exactly it is that white participants dominated the GAP and steered its agenda. As sociologist Amanda Lewis points out, "The racial composition of all-white settings can result from self-conscious exclusive policies . . . , can be just one of many outcomes from exclusive policies at a different level . . . , or can be an outcome of long histories of racial exclusion, even if those discriminatory policies are not pursued actively or aggressively today."[4]

The processes that maintain the whiteness of many grassroots progressive political organizations are multifaceted and somewhat counterintuitive. The GAP does not espouse discriminatory policies and practices. Quite the opposite. The inclusion and empowerment of people of color remain significant principles of the party and crucial aspects of its identity.

In this chapter, I uncover patterns in how white participants in grass-roots progressive politics deliberate, act, and interact that exclude people of color from influence and participation in grassroots democracy. I focus on white GAP members' experiences and perspectives related to race and racism, their decisions to pursue political strategies and daily activities, and how they perceive their organization's demographics, goals, and ideals. White members' racial consciousness, habits, and relations to groups and spaces help explain the disconnect between the organization's stated intentions and ongoing outcomes concerning racial justice.

PERCEPTIONS OF POSSIBILITY

Imagination must be considered here neither as flight of fancy, nor disregard of reality; imagination cannot be reduced to representation. The power of imagination is a synthetic power of creation and of reconstruction—an ability to combine the uncombinable, to surpass binaries without merely collapsing them, to fashion something new.—Samuel A. Chambers, 2005

One evening, I called up Daren from the Moosewater chapter. I had met up with him a few times before in person, but he had been busy with work and family, so we decided this would be easier. He sat in his garage to get away from the noise and distraction of his young kids and we talked about environmentalism, local politics, and our pathways to getting involved in grassroots politics. Partway through our conversation, we came upon the topic of inequality. Noting the party's racial demographics, I asked about the need to recruit and engage people of color. He told me, "It's interesting because it's like, I know they want to do that, but it's like how do you do that? Like, uh, I wouldn't even know. It's almost like—it must be that the word isn't out and sometimes that takes money and, and, uh, I think, I think that maybe the point would be that the Grassroots Action Party doesn't always reflect as much diversity as its platform states it has and why is that?"

As exemplified in Daren's response, the strategies and habits enacted by white GAP members often steered around the racialized boundaries and barriers that protected their organization's predominant and normative whiteness rather than confronting and obliterating them. Activities that would break down these obstacles were often met with discomfort or impeded by an inability to imagine possibilities.

Daren valued diversity in the abstract, but he did not identify with the necessary responsibilities. Instead, he threw the question back at me. He was not the only member to ask me to analyze and solve the party's "diversity issue." In a way, it made sense. I had been an active member for over a year at this point. Moreover, I was an ideal candidate given my knowledge and racially diverse social networks. Yet this delegation still struck me as odd. Despite his long-running and active presence in grassroots progressive politics, Daren struggled to imagine how the organization could include, if not empower, the racially oppressed. I followed up on why he thought the party lacked racial diversity. He replied, "Uh, that's a tough one. I don't even know where to begin. How would you do that? It's hard enough to get new members nonetheless focusing on getting new members, uhh, in any type of diversity or any type of uh, yeah, and I'm not sure what strategies we even have to do that."

After some encouragement, Daren eventually named a concrete strategy. He mentioned that sometimes meetings were held in more urban locations. But he was not able to articulate how this strategy, on its own, would produce an impact—"I know that Jacqueline has tried to keep some meetings in Loudenburrow [a small city with a higher degree of racial diversity] for like location proximity. Like, I think she was saying, if we're having meetings in a proximity where it's less diverse to begin with and they can't get there or don't live there then they don't." Without developing substantial relationships and networks with people of color in their own communities, the idea seemed unrealistic. Similarly, Roger, during a conversation I had with him in a small coffee shop after a GAP meeting about how to include more new participants from diverse backgrounds, stated, "If *we* build it, will *they* come? I don't know."

Despite being a central plank of the party platform, responses from white members during conversations about racial equity and political empowerment demonstrated a lack of prior reflection. Ambivalence and uncertainty were common themes in discussions about building a more racially inclusive organization. Isolation from people of color in their neighborhoods, workplaces, and all levels of schooling hindered their awareness and imagination. They even saw this racial isolation as unremarkable, unproblematic, and possibly nonracial. However, this inability to envision alternative ways of doing racial politics was neither incidental nor autonomous. It required actively rejecting consciousness and engaging in intentional and creative acts of aversion and avoidance.

Geography and Generalizations

So, how did participants make sense of the overwhelming whiteness of their organizations, communities, and social networks? On a humid August afternoon, I talked with Soren. I asked about the demographics of his friends, coworkers, and family. After mentioning gender, sexuality, and social class diversity among his friends, he acknowledged, "There's not any racial diversity or not a tremendous amount." Realizing that his own whiteness was reflected in his social networks, he offered an explanation: "Um, I don't necessarily think that, you know, as some would say, we are all subconscious racists. I think that's more just geographically where we live."

Soren posed a dichotomy. Either the chapter members were racially prejudiced, or it was the random happenstance of geography. However, he ignored the deeper story of why, in his words, "geographically where we live," an upper-middle-class suburban neighborhood, was overwhelmingly white. The community where most Edgepond chapter members resided was on the whiter and wealthier side of one of the most segregated district boundaries in the northeastern United States. As legal scholar Daria Roithmayr points out,

> Much like a predatory monopolist, whites formed racial cartels during slavery and Jim Crow to gain monopoly access to key markets. Homeowners associations worked together with real estate boards to keep blacks out of housing markets. School boards worked together with local growers to keep Mexicans out of public schools. Working-class farmers worked together with elite planters to disenfranchise blacks and eliminate their political power. These racial cartels used many of the same anticompetitive strategies—economic boycotts and violence, for example—to unfairly drive their competitors out of the market. This unfair advantage, acquired early in our nation's history has now become self-reinforcing and cumulative. A number of institutional feedback loops parlay earlier advantage into continuing advantage.[5]

To most whites, this ongoing process—whereby they hoard opportunities to attain wealth, jobs, education, and housing—seems to mainly consist of them going about their normal routines. It does not require making any intentional, personal efforts to discriminate against people of color. By ignoring the social and institutional forces that created these boundaries, white GAP participants found themselves, as the writer James Baldwin wrote, "trapped in a history which they do not understand."[6]

I also noticed that Soren and other Edgepond chapter members routinely described their town as "white," "95 percent white," or "99 percent white." According to official figures, whites comprised about 80 percent of their town's residents. They routinely exaggerated the town's white population, but I was unsure why. White respondents routinely overestimate the demographics of people of color and immigrants in the United States.[7] This distorted sense of demographics feeds into narratives of racial threat and the loss of majority status. So, why were they misrecognizing their town's racial demographics in the opposite direction? Perhaps they were simply being hyperbolic. Maybe it allowed them to rationalize the racial demographics of their social networks and organization. Regardless, in practical terms, it rendered the people of color within their community invisible. After hearing this assertion several times, I wondered what would happen if I presented the actual figure.

And so, I did. I sat down in a rural diner talking to Stevie and Stan, two participants in the Edgepond chapter. We greeted each other and ordered. The waitress brought us our food, and we bantered and joked a bit. As the conversation gravitated toward their experiences in the GAP, I asked for their thoughts on the party's demographics. Without reflection, they agreed that the party lacked racial diversity because their town was "super white," "like 99 percent white." Seizing the moment, I replied, "I thought the town was about 80 percent white; that means 20 percent of the population is not." Stan interrupted me to question that statistic's accuracy. I pulled out my phone to show them the most recent census data, and the conversation hit a speed bump. My correction disrupted the previous flow of agreement and understanding. My desire to avoid confrontation and conflict crept in. I did not want to risk alienating them or disrupting our rapport. So, I put my phone away, allowed them to save face, and changed the topic.[8]

The idea that their town was a white space was a product of creativity rather than obliviousness.[9] Inaccurate racialized representations of their community helped justify exclusion and avoid accountability. Other narratives also served this purpose. Later in the conversation, Stan contrasted himself with his estranged racist, reactionary, and regressive father, who listened to Rush Limbaugh and used racial slurs. For many white participants, racism was not about systems of oppression and how they shape communities. It was about the explicit racial hatred of older conservatives. These ideas bolstered their organizational identity as a racially progressive but *coincidentally* white collective.

These explanations and stories reflect the *racial politics of geography*. They illuminate the role of racialized contestations over physical places and social boundaries in political life. In the context of grassroots political organizing, notions of community and locality are particularly relevant. How we imagine our community plays a role in our strategies of legitimacy, representation, and inclusion. Within whites' narratives about social and geographic space, "landscape and the experience of it [are] racially structured—whether those narratives seem to be marked by the presence or the absence of people of color."[10] In this case, the narratives of participants were marked by the absence of people of color, whether they were present in their town and community or not. Soren had put it another way: "You know, the people that are around us just aren't particularly diverse."

Estrangement and Evasion

The flip side to normalizing white space was that many white members seemed unable to fathom building familiarity with "nonwhite" spaces. When confronting this topic, they expressed a sense of estrangement. I sat at a table in a café-themed chain restaurant and talked to Frank, an older white male member of the Moosewater chapter, over coffee and bagels. Explaining the lack of Black members, he said, "There is some kind of cultural barrier or whatever that is. . . . I don't know how to operate in their social circles and world, and so, probably if a Black person is trying to organize something, they'd go right away, 'Oh yeah, we can call this church' or 'We can do that thing,' whatever. I don't know how that works."

Many white GAP members could not fathom how their chapters of the organization came to be all or disproportionately white. They could not imagine alternatives without feeling disoriented or overwhelmed. The mere thought of it brought up awkwardness and embarrassment. Meanwhile, racial segregation safeguarded them from challenging perspectives. They lacked ongoing and sustained firsthand engagement with issues of racial oppression in their daily lives and political organizing.

In my search for answers, I talked to Gregory of the New Easton chapter, a middle-class, older white man who held a position responsible for outreach, diversity, and inclusion at a regional level. I hoped he could offer concrete thoughts and strategies given this position. I asked what the organization does to include people of color and other marginalized social groups. He responded:

> The diversity component is something that I don't know how to deal with how to do—and I haven't really done. So, there hasn't been, uh— There's been efforts. There were efforts to set this up but currently, I'm not doing much with it and I don't really know. I haven't really thought about it. I haven't really thought through how I, um,—there, there are individual people who have been approached uh, so in terms of ethnic diversity, there's, there is talk about it and emphasis on some [*long pause*] um, in terms of selecting people for leadership, there is some effort, um, but I've really fallen down on the realm of reaching to diverse audiences.

The frequent "ums" and "uhs" that sputtered out of respondents' mouths in response to these types of questions were not just individual idiosyncrasies. In conversations on other topics, they were some of the most articulate and confident people I had ever met.

This incoherence may stem from a lack of experience discussing these issues or fears of being perceived as racist.[11] White GAP members who were otherwise well-spoken became tongue-tied when asked to articulate their views on the party's relationship with people of color or their positions on racial issues. It was not just a matter of linguistics. It had significant implications for their ability to actualize diversity, inclusion, and justice ideals in their organization and political work. The inability to communicate in coherent, straightforward, resilient, and thoughtful ways about race and racism, especially concerning one's own political actions, means an inability to process and reflect on these issues collectively.

Racial inequality and its impacts on the organization were only articulable in a foreign language that these participants had never learned to speak fluently. I was forcing them to speak a non-native tongue. In response, several white GAP members expressed exasperation or defensiveness. Questions about racial inequality, the organization's demographics, or outreach strategies to communities of color brought out discomfort and a desire to actively steer the conversation toward a language they spoke with greater ease. For instance, at the end of his response, Gregory pivoted to redefine the terms of diversity, telling me, "Uh, respect for diversity um, can be thought to include diversity of opinions, perspectives, and um, so separate from ethnic diversity, um, and I think that is really um, — paints a role as a big tent organization, as in not with a strict doctrine, not enforcing a strict doctrine and, um, being a loose coalition of somewhat allied groups. Um, that's it."

I routinely felt pressured to drop the line of questioning altogether. The tone of conversations changed as though I had broken an implicit rule. I wondered if the overt language of race and racism made respondents uncomfortable rather than more roundabout discussions of "diversity." While a vague and malleable concept, the idea of diversity often elicits a positive connotation as a social good.[12] Yet when I used terms such as "diversity," "inclusion," or even "community outreach," white participants redefined these terms in race-neutral ways.

For example, Roger from the Moosewater chapter pointed out that the party has a diversity of personalities: "We are predominantly white, well educated, and all over the map in terms of personalities and personal styles, but I think that just has to do with the law of small numbers, right? Individual difference is noticeable in a smaller group." Their shared social characteristics had become so taken for granted that other forms of differentiation became more noticeable. These clumsy efforts to reframe the issue signaled that diversity was valued as an abstract principle, even if the GAP failed to include people of color in practice.

Storylines and Strategies

Asking participants about their responsibilities and lives helped me better understand the paradoxical relationship between the party's goals and its members' activities. Many suggested that, as white people, it was not their obligation to include and empower people of color. For instance, Roger jokingly implied that it was the responsibility of people from underrepresented groups to show up, saying, "Um, we don't have a lot of people of color. We don't have a lot of people from inner-city, uh, population centers in this state. Our chapter is very rural. [*Laughs*] . . . Nevertheless, uh, we're all coming. We're old. We don't have enough young people. Right? So, there's, you know, there's a lot of skewing in the GAP. Um, I don't have an, I don't know the answer. Um, I come from all the groups that are, uh, well-represented. So, I've done my part [*laughs*]." Like in other organizations, people of color were seen by their white colleagues in the GAP as uniquely responsible for initiatives involving racial equity.[13]

How white GAP members thought about their own way into the party reflected a further extension of this logic. White GAP members routinely conveyed a concurrent journey of self-discovery and discovery of the organization. Particularly in suburban spaces, grassroots democratic participation is often motivated by a drive to feel personally fulfilled by our political actions rather than efforts at uplifting and bettering a specific community.[14]

As we sat in her living room on a chilly fall day and sipped tea, Lori, an older white woman who was a longtime member of the GAP, explained her backstory as follows:

> Okay, well, first of all, I had never, never heard of the Grassroots Action Party. I was actively engaged in our local historical society, and I was attending a craft fair. I was actually selling calendars at the craft fair and [I saw] Joyce. I had a table, and she was distributing different literature. Part of that pile of literature was on the Grassroots Action Party and I know Joyce, so I walked over and asked her what she had on her table, and she told me about the organization, and I was looking to the lit and I looked at the platform and I said "This is fabulous, I love this." I said, "Do you have meetings?" and she told me about the Moosewater group.

Lori happened upon the party through luck and curiosity. She immediately felt a resonance between the party's ideals and her own. These stories helped motivate sustained and meaningful participation. However, they also devalued conscious outreach and intentional connections with communities.

The styles of political conversion espoused by GAP members mirrored types of religious conversion.[15] *Orthodox political conversion* involves people uncovering the organization and its ideas as resonant with their "true selves." Participants serendipitously discover the organization. They are then drawn toward further engagement by its alignment with their values. In contrast, *evangelical political conversion* happens when people are transformed through contact with the organization and its ideas. In this case, the organization discovers and incorporates participants through purposeful outreach. The orthodox political engagement style dominated most white members' habits and strategies. Yet many newer members and members of color favored some version of the evangelical style. As the dominant group, however, the white consensus about outreach and ideal pathways into the party shaped the party's overarching strategy.

The tensions between these strategies were, at times, palpable. In the spring of 2016, the Moosewater chapter hosted a region-wide event at the meeting house of a local ecovillage. To their delight, many potential new members arrived. A smaller meeting room was set up for them while a committee meeting took place elsewhere. Longtime member Walter, a middle-aged white man, gave the new participants an informal overview of the party. One of the newcomers, Alhaadi, a middle-class African American man in his midthirties, expressed a strong interest in getting involved.

Alhaadi asked Walter how he could start a new chapter in his area and begin presenting to community groups. He wanted to learn about the party's efforts to grow and engage with surrounding communities. Walter appeared perplexed and merely stated the name of someone else in the party to contact, suggesting that this concern was not under his purview. After the meeting, I spoke with Alhaadi, and I could tell that his initial enthusiasm had melted. He exclaimed to me rhetorically, "Does anyone even do outreach?"

SILENCE SPEAKS

Indeed, on the question of questions—the Negro problem—he hears so little that there almost seems to be a conspiracy of silence; the morning papers seldom mention it, and then usually in a far-fetched academic way, and indeed almost everyone seems to forget and ignore the darker half of the land, until the astonished visitor is inclined to ask if after all there IS any problem here.—W. E. B. Du Bois, 1909

White participants' refusal to identify and articulate the consequences of racial oppression presented a major stumbling block. However, whites are not intrinsically destined to be ignorant of racial oppression and its implications. People categorized as white, if socialized in certain contexts, exposed to the lived experiences of racially oppressed groups, or through intentional choices to grow and access their full humanity, may develop a critical awareness of racism and racial inequality.[16] They may achieve racial literacy. Racial literacy describes our ability and willingness to comprehend and articulate the relationship between racial oppression, social positions, and people's lived experiences.[17] Attaining racial literacy is not simply a matter of learning new information. It is also about shifting the perspective from which we perceive situations and act.

Indeed, a few white members did discuss historical and structural factors of racial inequality. Austin, a white male member of the Whitehall chapter in his midtwenties, connected the historical legacy of redlining practices to the party's demographics. Throughout the past century, banks and the government defined majority-Black neighborhoods as a financial risk and denied their residents loans, services, and resources.[18] Austin pointed out the ignorance of GAP members in the predominantly white suburbs about these events: "One of the things that's also fascinating is redlining, uh, of neighborhoods and suburbs. . . . You have very good progressive thinking, uh, like liberal types who live in the suburbs and think they're very good, very decent human beings, and then as you move towards the, uh, urban core you see the amount of degradation of the poor. You see the way that austerity is, uh, implemented against people of color . . . and that person in the outer reaches of the suburbs is totally, uh, unaware of the existence of this situation."

Austin was not the only white person willing to recognize the relationship between the party's demographics and the habits and assumptions of its white participants. Tammy, a white trans woman who, while not an active participant, had attended several events hosted by her local GAP and considered joining, noted something similar. Remarking on the absence of people of color at these events, she told me,

> And though the Grassroots Action Party platform is supposed to be very diverse . . . it was pretty much all white people. Rare exceptions—There were some Black people there who showed up to talk about Black Lives Matter and asked some of the party leaders questions, which I think was good. I think that they handled the questions kind of awkwardly. . . . And I think a lot of white people are kind of, I don't want to say willfully ignorant, but there's sort of this like "It's not my problem" when it's a problem you're creating, thing. . . . I think that affects the demographics a lot. I think, I don't want to say people of color don't feel welcome, but—actually, I think that's exactly what I want to say.

Despite these anomalies, an overall pattern emerged—*racial silence*. The habitual avoidance of discussing racial oppression and its impacts and particularly its relation to the strategies and values of the organization had become a matter of collective expectation. This norm was not a matter of personal beliefs but rather more reliant "on a general social accountability drawn from an impression of legitimacy and consensus."[19] Even for those participants who individually sought to oppose racism, racial silence remained an implicit covenant.

Racial Reticence

In discussions with white women about race and racism, American studies scholar Ruth Frankenberg identified two major patterns: color evasiveness, which meant not acknowledging ways that racial categories and identities influence people's everyday lives, and power evasiveness, which meant not accepting that racial groups wield disparate resources and power.[20] Research over the past three decades has continued to demonstrate that white people engage in avoidance or evasion of talking about race and racism in their everyday social interactions.[21] They routinely act as silent bystanders if they witness racist actions or speech.[22]

Even if they had some awareness of racial oppression, many white participants of the GAP were uncomfortable violating the custom of racial silence. I noticed uneasiness, circumvention, and muteness in meetings and informal conversations. I also had opportunities in one-on-one discussions with GAP members to explore their underlying motivations. In a conversation with Walter from the Moosewater chapter at a local coffee shop, I asked about the social issues he found most concerning. He mentioned a budding interest in understanding systemic racism:

> Well . . . lately I've been reading the *New Jim Crow* by Michelle Alexander. It's really kind of an eye-opener about the horribly inequitable way the criminal justice system tends to work in this country and how it really tends to target, especially young men of color. And uh, you know uh, catch them in the uh in the, in the mass incarceration net. That, that does an enormous amount of harm to them and to their families and to their communities as well. Um, and typically, you know, that how that law enforcement isn't really all that equitable in this country. Uh, considering that uh, you know, who tends to get targeted for things like, stop and frisk, and uh, you know uh, highway stops, and that ultimately lead to searches that ultimately might turn up small amounts of drugs and get somebody caught up in the criminal justice system. . . . And you know disparities

in economics and uh economic well-being, and social well-being is another concern. . . . And disparities in educational opportunities . . . Um, it's uh, you know uh, plus I mean just this society, in general, seems to be torn apart you know, by race every bit as much as it was forty or fifty years ago. And of course, there's also, you know, the killings of African Americans by police. Um, you know, and that the cops just seem to get away with it constantly.

I was surprised by his answer. I had never gleaned that Walter was so aware of how forms of racial oppression operate and interact. It may have stemmed from his recent reading choice. Yet in the whole time that I had interacted with him, well over a year, he had never mentioned these concerns, especially with such directness. I wondered why he did not often talk about them.

> Me: Given that you are aware, it seems like you read about these issues, do you feel comfortable talking about this stuff? Like with friends, family members? Is it something that you discuss with other people?
>
> Walter: Not so much with my family because my family tends to be pretty conservative. And they would not tune in to anything that I might have to say about this subject in particular. Um, with friends, that's, that's tricky too because uh, you know, there's a, because just about everybody I know is white. The subject doesn't come up very much. You know it doesn't come up very much at all. So, you know it's not something that uh gets talked about, I guess . . . There's um, there is this, this kind of, oh wow, *a kind of invisible etiquette*, that you have to know. And if, and it's not always easy too, to, to figure that out or to, to, uh say things in a way that um will, uh, so that the thing you want to say will get heard. And uh you won't wind up, uh offending somebody, or, you know, making somebody tune out or dismiss you, or something like that, you know.

He seemed to be grasping this social reality for the very first time as we spoke (hence, "oh wow"). This aspect of Walter's everyday life had been masquerading as an unquestioned and unspoken truth. We temporarily breached the wall of racial silence.

As my conversation with Walter demonstrates, whites may, upon reflection, even recognize this subjective experience of discomfort and aversion.

As the white philosopher Terrance MacMullen notes, "Even after years of speaking about race in public and private environments, I still have to fight the habits that make me want to change the subject."[23] This *invisible etiquette*, as Walter so succinctly put it, is comprised of the implicit rules of the racialized interaction order.[24] In this context, maintaining white comfort and civility trumps the pursuit of racial justice. Whites feel so compelled to avoid overt recognition of racial issues that a collective assumption takes hold in white spaces; they lack any explicit, relevant, and distinct sense of racial identity.[25]

Racial silence is not just a product of how white people avoid the seeming rudeness or awkwardness of talking about contentious topics like racism. This silence can also be produced by a lack of knowledge or even deliberate ignorance.[26] My conversation with Jennifer from the Edgepond chapter further demonstrated the norm of racial silence. As we sat on picnic benches on a warm summer day outside a small ice cream shop, the conversation had otherwise been relaxed. But she quickly grew uncomfortable talking about racial inequality.

I asked if she ever talked about issues of race or racial inequality with family or friends. She responded, "Um, I don't remember talking about racial issues with my parents. I'm not sure that they would agree also. They don't always agree about things. They don't always agree with my sister and me." I pushed for further clarification on these sources of disagreement, and she became increasingly uneasy. After a long pause, she said, "My God, it's so hard to think when that thing is on," referring to my audio recorder. I told her I would hide it and placed the audio recorder behind my open laptop so that it was no longer in her line of sight. Jennifer laughed uncomfortably as I assured her it had a pretty good range.

It could easily have been the case that the audio recorder was making her uncomfortable. However, this pattern aligns with previous research on evasion, racial silence, and strategic avoidance.[27] Jennifer became particularly aware of her words being recorded during that question. It had not made her self-conscious about discussing other topics, even controversial or political ones.

Once we resolved the issue with the audio recorder, she clarified that her parents were "certainly not racist" and suggested she did not want to explore the question further. She said, "You were pointing it right at me. Um, like a lot of people that are their age, it's easy to look at inequalities and think there must be some reason based on the people. I wouldn't be surprised to hear my mom say something like, 'Oh, they don't work as hard' or whatever, but at the same time, it's—this isn't an issue that we've talked about all that much. I can't remember any specific times we've talked about it. They're certainly not racist. That's what I, *that's all I have.*" By mentioning that her mother might have explained racial inequality by looking for fault in members of oppressed racial groups, Jennifer indicated that her mother utilized ways of making sense of inequality that help maintain racial oppression. Yet she also realized that racism was morally unacceptable.

This unwieldy and defensive response was an outlier in our conversation. Jennifer did not avoid contested social issues in general or lack the ability to articulate her beliefs and knowledge. By comparison, her discussion of gender socialization and identity was extensive, detailed, and thoughtful, and she even demonstrated comfort with tension and ambiguity:

> I am female, and my sister is female, and no brothers, so it's hard to look around and see if there's any differences in how they raised us, but I know that I take on feminine-like female gender roles, and my sister did as well. This bothers me actually. I can't think of any times in particular that I can discern whether or not they did anything in particular to influence me. . . . I know that at one point, my mom and I had kind of a mild disagreement. . . . I was saying how I saw pictures of a woman's new baby, and she was dressed in like fur and like a red frilly dress and all this stuff, and I was like, "Yeah, it's sad. They're doing it already. This baby is like just a little baby," and my mom's point was "Well when they're young they can't choose anyway so the parents may as well choose. And when they get older, then let them choose, and then they can choose then," and it made me wonder when my mom did let me choose what to wear like the same thing, what caused me to choose feminine clothing if I really wasn't raised in like a box.

After our interview, I turned off the recorder. The tenor of our interactions changed accordingly. We reverted to having a casual conversation and eating ice cream. Chatting informally, we had a substantial and intricate conversation around issues such as cultural appropriation. Jennifer articulated her opinions on this issue frankly and clearly. She discussed her personal experiences and her ambivalence as to whether the concept helped address racism or if it was an alienating aspect of "call-out culture."

The contrast from her earlier apprehension to discuss issues of racism was stark. It suggested she felt, similarly to other white participants, that public conversations that overtly dealt with race and racism were inherently taxing, tense, and treacherous.

Stressful Situations

At a local racial justice protest, members of the Whitehall chapter of the GAP were in attendance. They set up a table to advertise the party and recruit new members. At the rally, Eric, a middle-aged white man from the chapter, got into a heated discussion about the 2016 election with an African American woman. The woman argued that he was coming from a place of white privilege by not supporting Hillary Clinton, whose policies would have had a less detrimental impact on communities of color.

The relationship between people's social positions and their willingness to vote for what many regarded as the lesser of two evils to prevent a Trump presidency was a common topic of political conversation. Throughout 2016, op-ed headlines such as "Privilege Is What Allows Sanders Supporters to Say They'll 'Never' Vote for Clinton," "Third Party Voting Is the Height of White Privilege," and "Bernie Sanders or Bust? That's a Stance Based on Privilege" routinely graced news pages.[28] Given this ongoing public debate, Eric's response to this woman's claims about politics and privilege could have led to a nuanced and compelling conversation. It could have provided a fruitful dialogue and perhaps even resulted in deeper engagement. However, recalling the interaction, Jake from the Whitehall chapter described Eric's reaction as follows: "He said, 'Well do you have Black privilege?' and then he just froze up."

This defensive and aggressive response suggested discomfort.[29] Whites engage in a range of behaviors, even hurtful or controlling ones, to regain control and disrupt the distress brought about by the awareness of conflict connected to racial oppression. Eric's passive-aggressive comment and subsequent withdrawal in that moment negatively impacted the organization's ability to form alliances with people of color or even open a dialogue about racial politics. Reflecting on this interaction, Austin identified it as reflecting his fellow white GAP members' lack of understanding of the role of racial oppression throughout US history:

> You need to tell a white middle-class guy like Eric, look, it's not your fault, but here's what happened. When the guys got back from World War II, they got the GI Bill of Rights. They got free college. They got

low-interest, uh, high-quality mortgages. They got a rocket launch . . .
from the working class to the middle class, except if you were Black.
That was the big difference that has rippled across generations. And
so, the level of generational wealth expanding outwards from just the
GI Bill of Rights. I mean, I'm not even going—acknowledging and
talking about things like reconstruction and the end of slavery and
all that stuff, just going back to the social contract of the twentieth
century and the end of World War II. . . . You know, people do not
have the mental capacity it seems to recognize that there was this
massive cheating of African Americans just after World War II.

Austin expressed weariness at how his racial literacy was often met with
accusations of being divisive. He said, "Articulating that, it sometimes feels
like I'm banging my head against the wall. Because, you know, uh, there's
this desire to say 'Aren't we all Americans, and, you know, we're all Americans. Damn it, let's just all be Americans but be proud to be Americans.'
It—it gets frustrating."

Other white participants described the potential for race-based stress
to crop up in interactions with people of color. During interviews, I used
a vignette to encourage discussion about why white people might avoid
talking about racial issues with people of color. In response to the vignette,
Jacqueline told me a story about a difficult moment with a friend:

I had a dear friend, and I still consider her a friend, but I haven't
talked to her in many years. We just hit it off, you know, and had a
wonderful friendship, and she was having some struggles at a certain
point, and we were in a phone conversation, and it just kind of went
down this road where, you know, she was really upset, and she just
got more and more upset and she ended up screaming at me, which,
I mean, she is one of the sweetest people I know [but] she just
screamed "Fuck you" at me and hung up. . . . I was kind of like, wow,
what happened and what is going on, and I couldn't, I sort of, it is
like, do I call her back or do I not? . . . She called me back, and she
was really upset, and she is like, "You know, I am really sorry," and I
am like, "It is not a problem, it is really not a problem."

Jacqueline told me that if she could talk to her estranged friend now,
she would say, "I love you. You are one of the people that I have been clos-
est to in my life, and I know I am a white person with stupid white person
stuff, and I am sorry, you know, and, you know, I am responsible for my

behavior at the same time, but there is a way that nobody is to blame for growing up, you know, being born into a racist society. . . . My guess is that she was angry or, you know, she knew, and you know, knows that I have privilege as a white person, as a middle-class person."

Jacqueline expressed regret that she had acted out of, as she put it, "stupid white person stuff." In telling the story, she also connected that memory of conflict with why whites might avoid conversations about racial oppression with people of color. Because racialized issues and interactions felt fraught with potential peril, white participants tried to find other ways to symbolize commitments to antiracism.

Symbols and Strategies

In their explanation of symbolic racism, a prominent theory of how racial attitudes impact political behavior, political scientists David O. Sears and P.J. Henry wrote, "The term *symbolic* highlights both symbolic racism's targeting Blacks as an abstract collectivity rather than specific Black individuals and its presumed roots in abstract moral values rather than concrete self-interest or personal experience."[30] Similarly, antiracism can also be symbolic. Antiracist orientation among many white participants of the GAP was an abstract belief in the immorality of racism and, hence, a form of *symbolic antiracism*. However, this belief was combined with social networks, habits, and ways of thinking that delimited the possibility for antiracism as a set of concrete and pragmatic practices. "People of color," "Blacks," or even "diversity" were simply points of reference.

While white participants recognized the value of opposing racial prejudice, they lacked a set of practices to manifest these beliefs into changes in their immediate social reality. They also lacked regular personal and humanizing experiences and interactions with people of color. Thus, when outreach was consciously aimed toward people of color, it occurred through formal institutions and organizations. Yet white participants tended to connect and reach out to other whites through informal social networks. When they did consider their racial isolation, many described impenetrable barriers that inhibited entering "nonwhite" spaces or even comprehending the lived experiences of their inhabitants. Frank, an older white man in the Moosewater chapter, recounted his reaction to a television program about young Black men: "Now we were just talking about something, I think we were watching something, and this kid was saying . . . 'Yeah, I had my friend, and he took me to so-and-so barbershop and look, I just had my hair cut.' I'm looking and thinking, 'He looks exactly like he did before,' and so, Janice mentioned, 'You're so white.' I mean, there is some kind of a cultural difference, but I don't know how you bridge it."

Frank was clearly trying to articulate the sense of "otherness" he felt towards communities of color. However, it was unclear how identifying and understanding cultural norms around haircuts was necessary for cross-racial solidarity and organizing. Solidarity requires people of various backgrounds to humanize one another while recognizing the unique impacts of social inequalities. It means finding points of connection and mutual support and practical ways to improve community conditions. However, for many white participants, like Frank, going beyond merely holding antiracist beliefs to engaging in actual practices seemed burdensome and unworkable. Moreover, he had referred to something he had seen on television rather than a real-life experience. For racially isolated white people, mass media images are a prime source of knowledge about people of color.[31]

Commitment to antiracism was also expressed as a literal symbol. Jacqueline always wore her Black Lives Matter button while on the campaign trail. However, her commitment to representing racial justice goals, even in such a symbolic fashion, was up for question. At a meeting, she worried about how constituents might react to the button, saying, "I am trying to represent an all-white district, so maybe the Black Lives Matter button is a bit contentious to wear." Two participants expressed support for the pin. One pointed out that it distinguished her from other candidates. However, Roger responded, "Maybe you could wear a local food button [instead]. . . . People love local food in that district. It's very popular."

These symbolic commitments also manifested in white participants' social networks. I asked Meghan from the Whitehall chapter about the demographics of her network. She mentioned several friends, her husband, and her colleagues before pausing and noting:

> I mean, so far, everyone I've been talking about is white. I know you asked about the ethnicity. Everyone is white um, so, um, um— actually, that's not true. I, uh, I was pretty friendly with, uh, Ben Caine. He was twenty when he was elected as a representative. Um, he was one of the youngest to ever be elected, and he's half Black, so, but he, uh, he actually said—well, he trends more towards libertarian, but people who have spoken to him more than I, or at least know more

about his political views, say he could very well run as a Grassroots Action Party candidate. However, knowing him, he's very smarmy, and he'll just tell you what you want to hear.

Meghan only mentioned their racial identities as an afterthought, suggesting that whiteness was unremarkable.[32] Her strained attempt to demonstrate any ethnic diversity displayed a related desire to emphasize proximity to people of color as a way of making up for this sense of emptiness.[33]

I asked her to speculate on why she could only name one person. She answered, "I really have no diversity in my, uh, in my political circles, and I think a lot of that has to do with coming from a very white suburb." She was baffled by the prospect of altering this situation: "I really don't know how to expand diversity because I don't know, it's not like—almost it's one of those things where, you think, you're thinking of it and like how could there be such a lack of diversity?" But rather than pursuing this question, she came up with a tenuous social connection that she once held with someone who wasn't white—"Even, well I was—okay, so, I know pretty well, um, I'm pretty friendly with a representative of another party, and he's, um, Latino—John Perez. We did a fundraiser together at a, um, an LGBTQ bar, and we did a fundraiser for Orlando right after the shooting occurred. Um, so I know him. . . . So, there you go. *There's one.*"

The phrase "there's one" suggested she was now off the hook from acknowledging and interrogating the whiteness of her social circle. Her need to articulate this connection to me as evidence of her character suggested she was following the "one friend rule."[34] Whites often use the fact that they know or have spent social time with a person of color (at times, exaggerating the intimacy or depth of these relationships) as evidence that they do not engage in discrimination.[35] As the sociologist Christopher W. Munn writes, "As long as the impetus for change remains at the individual level and majority members employ micro-level mechanisms like the one friend rule, the systems of racial stratification and inequality will persist."[36] The consequences are dire in the context of a political organization that depends upon social networks to maintain its membership. Racial disparities in access to social and political resources and opportunities are ultimately untouched by these gestures.

A related phenomenon to symbolic antiracism was *instrumental diversity*. Including marginalized groups was not seen as valuable for its potential to redistribute political power to their communities. Instead, it was seen as a strategy to advance the party's quest for political power and influence. For instance, the following conversation took place at the end of a meeting of the Moosewater chapter as participants prepared to do some voter registration work for an upcoming election:

> Jacqueline: A lot of people are registering people to vote. I have preregistration forms, and some are in Spanish.
> James: I'll take some of both English and Spanish.
> Frank: In Loudenville, you will use them!
> Gregor: In the state campaign in Loudenville, one of our volunteers is Hispanic background.
> Others: Well! Put it to good use!

The "it" referred to in the conversation was Spanish, not the person. This unnamed volunteer was merely a means to an end—an instrument to advance the party. Among white participants, the organization's relation to communities of color related much more to political tactics and symbols of social progressivism than combating racial oppression. The collective rituals and routines of the organization told a similar story.

REPRODUCING RACIALIZED ROUTINES

As long as the routines of everyday life continue without interruption they are apprehended as unproblematic.—Peter L. Berger and Thomas Luckmann, 1966

Through observing and participating with GAP participants for over a year and a half, I could see patterns. The organization's taken-for-granted routines were often based on implicit assumptions. They reflected ideas about who lived in their town or community, who was a likely voter or ideal member, who should be in a leadership role, which people and places they should connect with, what issues they should address, and what factors mattered in planning strategies. These patterns and routines were not race-neutral.

None of these practices were blatantly exclusionary or aggressively discriminatory. No one expressed that they did not want people of color in their organization or that they wanted to maintain barriers to their participation. Everything they told me suggested the opposite, even if they struggled to actualize inclusion and equality pragmatically. However, as the democratic theorist Marion Young points out, it is impossible to "promote inclusion simply by forbidding active and explicit exclusion."[37] The collective habits of the GAP maintained "the 'passive' exclusions that often occur in contemporary democracies."[38] At the same time, these routine and predictable ways of interacting with one another and engaging the political sphere did have a function. They were a source of sustained involvement for long-standing and deeply invested members.

The Reliability of Rituals

An oft-cited reason for white members to maintain involvement in the organization was to be around others with whom they felt a sense of familiarity, agreeableness, and comfort. Many held politically diverse social networks. In contrast, the party represented a set of reliably progressive friends. They knew they would share common cultural references, sentiments, and reactions to political and social issues at GAP events and meetings. Yet because this sense of collective identity took root in a disproportionately white organization and, in some cases, all-white chapters, it also maintained the racial norms and demographics of the organization.

For example, the Moosewater chapter developed a seemingly innocuous routine with substantial consequences. During each meeting, they discussed where and when to hold the next meeting. The participants saw this tradition as either inconsequential or practical. Yet it ensured that the locations and schedule conformed to several factors: places with which the white members were already familiar, places that fit easily into their social patterns, and dates and times they found convenient. These primarily middle-class, older, white members had unique access to spaces and free time. White participants' collective routines, such as "the timing, location, and structure" of meetings and opportunities, limited the presence and participation of marginalized groups.[39]

Scheduling meetings was just one of many ways that white participants' sense of familiarity led to exclusion. While "pounding the pavement" for a local campaign, I joined several members in door-knocking suburban, middle to high-income neighborhoods with disproportionately older, white residents. I had not pictured outreach to a rural suburban bedroom community being as impactful as outreach to nearby dense and urbanized areas. The neighborhood was composed entirely of single-unit houses that appeared to have come out of the same cookie-cutter mold. As we walked through the neighborhood, the houses seemed to go on and on forever, and almost everyone in the community was over sixty-five. The community was almost all white. There was only one Black resident during our entire door-knocking excursion. I later asked about the reasoning behind choosing these areas for outreach. I learned that it was selected because of long-standing members' familiarity with the location and the idea that, due to their demographics, they were reliable voters. I was taken aback by the intentional homogeneity of this neighborhood, but the others saw it as their target population. These racial habits reflected a desire for familiarity. They also reflected a desire for a sense of continuity and control.

Cultural Continuity

White participants contended that the composition of their organizations reflected "our friends," people who are a "good fit," or people "we want." In a Moosewater chapter meeting, members discussed the influx of new participants at a recent event. They noticed people driven to the party by disaffection with the political status quo. These new participants reflected previously unengaged demographics and presented new opportunities for growth. Yet the participants focused on protecting the existing culture of the organization. They feared that if new people showed up, they might bring new strategies and visions to the fore. They wanted to avoid rapid membership growth from "outsiders," even if it would have allowed them to embody their stated goals of empowering people of color.

These types of conversations helped maintain a sense of group identity through "positioning." Positioning refers to how we express the social relationship between ourselves and others. These are often moral relationships, such as "some person or group being located as 'trusted' or 'distrusted,' 'with us' or 'against us,' 'to be saved' or 'to be wiped out.'"[40] Through positioning, we assign groups and individuals with clusters of characteristics relating to *rights* and *duties*.[41] Newer members, in this narrative, did not have the *right* to influence and shape the party and its practices. Veterans of the organization exclusively held this right. Instead, incoming participants held a *duty* to internalize the dominant beliefs and habits of the party to prove themselves an appropriate fit.

In a smaller meeting of only longtime members, the all-white participants agreed that people should be tested and should prove themselves before joining the party. For new members to be desirable, they needed to be converted to the organization's established styles of interaction and strategy. The group also decided that new participants had to share the same goals and hold the kind of knowledge about local politics they valued. Ideal new members would conform to extant norms and, on some level, buy into the established microculture of the group. During the conversation, Roger stated:

> Well, we have to strike a balance here between too much purity and opening up the gates to newcomers who don't share our ideals. We need to have some policies that make it so that people become acculturated in the party before they take on responsibilities. . . . So, there is potential for growth because of political disaffection, but we need to make sure we're not just *opening the store and letting the looters come in.*

The metaphor of newcomers as potential looters fleeing an unfolding political disaster was striking. In this view, people interested in the party were not simply fleeing from the devastating dysfunction of modern major party politics and seeking political refuge in the GAP. The metaphor distinguishes between "acculturated" members as legitimate political actors and newcomers as illegitimate. It implies that new members might pillage the organization of unearned opportunities and resources and undermine its cherished ideals.

Most participants at the meeting seemed to hold this fear of losing the party's established culture to outsiders. Later in the discussion, Jacqueline discussed disaffected former Democrats flooding in who didn't have progressive enough ideals. She mentioned that one of the things she learned by studying organizational behavior was, "as soon as you have more than 50 percent new people, you have a new group." Ironically, it would be a resounding measure of success for a political party to double in size and incorporate a diverse membership passionate about its causes. However, this fear of losing "their" group thwarted good faith attempts at inclusion and growth that would help the organization foster racial justice.

Asserting Authority

White participants' desire for ownership and authority extended beyond their feelings about the party. It also permeated their encounters with new information and opportunities. In the fall of 2016, I attended a major regional GAP meeting. In the afternoon, scores of the predominantly white membership packed a convention hall for a workshop on environmental racism and climate justice. The workshop featured a presentation from Dr. Janice Pierson, an African American woman. She was an expert in environmental justice and a prominent racial justice activist from a national organization. A discussion would follow the presentation. Thus far, the conversations about race and racism I witnessed routinely petered out, resulted in avoidance, and failed to produce concrete strategies. I pondered whether this one would go any differently.

Dr. Pierson pointed out that the environmental crisis was deeply intertwined with the problem of democracy. She illustrated the human costs of environmental racism, whereby communities of color are disproportionately impacted by pollution and toxic waste. She told the story of a predominantly Black neighborhood where "people fought back and worked to get a trash incinerator out of their community." She emphasized how racial justice activists have been "active in struggles over climate issues and engaged in protest and . . . transnational solidarity with Afro-descendant people globally." She ended her talk with a set of ongoing initiatives that the GAP could support. These included green schools, transitioning to recycling from waste burning, equity-based transportation, multi-family housing, emotional healing, green jobs, and community clean-ups.

Given its relevance to the GAP platform, this event provided an opportunity for a lively discussion about strategies, mutual learning, and collaborations. However, when it was time to ask this seasoned activist and topical expert questions, the audience failed to seize the opportunity. An older white man raised his hand. She called on him. He said, "Have you seen *Taken for a Ride*? It's a documentary about how trolleys and public transportation were replaced by cars. I thought about that film as you were talking, and if anyone hasn't seen it, they should check it out." It was not really a question, so she moved on.

Shortly after, another middle-aged white man raised his hand. When acknowledged, he asked, "Have you read *Don't Think of an Elephant* or *The Political Mind*?" and described these books by linguist George Lakoff.[42] He then gave his thoughts on how to frame climate change to appeal to mainstream politicians. Ignoring the seemingly hypothetical question about these books, she instead pivoted to how to talk about environmental issues. She pointed out that focusing on the concrete effects of pollution on communities was more effective than discussing climate change in the abstract. After these two "questions," it became clear that the audience's engagement was not centered on identifying effective practical solutions or areas of alignment. Instead, they saw it as a means for expressing their own topical knowledge. They had reduced this pressing social problem to trivia or even a kind of progressive cultural capital.[43] They steered the discussion away from the environmental consequences of racial oppression toward more "universal" and familiar topics.

This interaction mirrored so many patterns I noticed during my time with the GAP. White, and particularly older, participants were driven by their ideals. They used meetings and events to display the knowledge base of their political identities. Because of their lived experiences and choices, other participants held a more practical awareness of the implications of social and political problems. In contrast, the dominant white participants understood issues such as environmental racism that was much more discursive. It was just something to talk about. This approach made these problems much more challenging to act on in a strategic way that resulted in any real transformations.

CONCLUSIONS ON CONSCIOUSNESS AND COMFORT

Despite its pervasiveness, a few of the white members seemed to recognize the shortcomings of their need for familiarity. During a conversation with Walter, I asked if he thought the party's lack of racial diversity impacted their strategies and platform. He told me,

> Because of the makeup of the party, because you know, it really isn't all that diverse a group even though we like to, uh, say that it is. That, uh, you know, there are a lot of people that we don't connect with all that effectively, I think, because we're an overwhelmingly white group of people, you know. Um, so, you know, we've got to figure out how to, how to fix that, and how to get more effective at doing outreach to diverse groups of people.

I asked him to describe the connection between the demographics and practices a bit more, and he said:

> Ah well, I think that the um, the, I think one of the, the drawbacks to not having more diversity is that, you know, there are a lot of people whom I suspect would probably be very much ah open to progressive ideas and progressive politics who just aren't there because *we're not very good at doing diversity*. Um, I think the, the benefits, of course, would be that uh, you know, we would get more people in with, with

a wider range of viewpoints uh being, and figure out how to be much more relevant and effective.

I then asked for specific examples, and he pointed out how it was a seeming self-perpetuating cycle:

> I mean, well, just consider the issues that we work on. I mean they're—it tends to be very heavily weighted towards uh . . . issues that tend to affect people in suburban and rural communities more than in uh the inner cities. So, you know, I think that, that definitely has an impact on the kinds of uh issues that we deal with. And of course, it's like this, you know uh, cycle that if those are the only issues we deal with, then there's no way we can, you know uh, get more, a more diverse membership because to people outside those circles, most, a lot of what we do isn't going to seem all that relevant.

Walter's response demonstrates the feedback loop between the racial consciousness and habits of white GAP members and the political strategies they encouraged. These strategies undermined the organization's goals of advancing social justice. As sociologists Michael Omi and Howard Winant argue, racial justice can be advanced by organizations that "question whether the dominant racial ideology properly applies to the collective experience of its members."[44]

If they face this tension between lived reality and "common sense," grassroots political organizations like the GAP can engage in *rearticulation*.[45] In other words, they can express and act upon critiques of the existing dominant consensus. Through rearticulation, grassroots progressive parties can produce new understandings, identities, habits, and even ways of organizing. They can foster new coalitions and form new political groups with shared goals and interests.[46] Rearticulation could unlock the potential for robust multiracial coalitions to achieve progressive social change. However, by normalizing white racial habits, the participants obscured the tension and dissonance from which new forms of collective action could emerge.

In daily life, we often avoid conflict rather than face it. Conflict can produce negative feelings like discomfort, fear, or tension. It can seem difficult or even impossible to resolve. The underlying causes and issues may seem overly complicated. Yet conflict is an inevitable aspect of working to end racial oppression. Active inclusion in the democratic process means negotiating differences in perspective and interest. It can bring to light underlying tensions to prevent domination or resentment. If effectively dealt with, conflict can produce novel solutions to community problems and get more people and organizations on board in addressing a shared problem. It can help us develop a better understanding of the perspectives and experiences of others and a better way of communicating.

When we avoid facing such difficult realities merely because they make us feel *awkward*, it results in the reproduction of the status quo. Producing meaningful social and organizational change is not just about dismantling existing racial meanings or norms. It also requires that we create new ways of being and acting that combat racial injustice. However, the racial politics of most white GAP members became a means of defining themselves as progressive, antiracist, or committed to the party's platform. But they did not creatively and productively face and process the tensions between their intentions and outcomes, which might result in changes to their racial consciousness and habits. As a result, the barriers and practices that upheld racial exclusion and inequality remained intact.

4 Contesting the Consensus

People of Color in Grassroots Progressive Politics

The quickest way to bring the reason of the world face to face with this major problem of human progress is to listen to the complaint of those human beings today who are suffering most from white attitudes, from white habits, from the conscious and unconscious wrongs which white folk are today inflicting on their victims.
—W. E. B. Du Bois, 1940

Democracy is a struggle.

On a lovely late spring day, I sat in a suburban diner with Jake and Chip, two Asian American men in their midtwenties active in their local Grassroots Action Party chapter. As we discussed the challenges facing grassroots progressive politics, Jake pointed out that "in progressive politics, it seems like there's a *white people problem*. It's white people in the majority." As an example, he described a progressive organization that formed in response to the growth of far-right movements in the US and the 2016 Trump campaign: "There's a group here called the Defiance Collective. I don't know if you've heard of them at all, but they're a huge group, and they draw hundreds of people to their meetings. Um, and their idea obviously is to combat hatred and division . . . , and they have like workshops. . . . The problem is, though, you go to their meetings, and it's literally like 99.5 percent white. Um, yeah, you know, it's really interesting because I try to figure out why that's the case, and I haven't come to the exact conclusion yet." Through his own direct experiences as a person of color in a grassroots progressive organization, Jake had come to ponder the very questions that motivate this book.

As we saw in the previous chapter, the shared ways white participants made sense of racial inequality determined the party's collective strategies and organizational identity. Many participants of color perceived this sense of agreement as a *white consensus* that guided the party toward white concerns and comfort and bred patterns of exclusion and inequality. But despite constituting a white space, the GAP was not an all-white party.

Participants of color consistently emphasized one driving factor that motivated their political participation: they hoped to advance the party as a vehicle for racial justice. For instance, later in our conversation, Chip told me, "It was their platform on racial justice that really swayed us" to join the party. This priority clashed sharply with the silence and discomfort around racial justice among white participants.

Despite coming from different backgrounds and living in varied contexts, the experiences of participants of color in the GAP shared features of marginality and contestation. These experiences allow us to put white participants' normative assumptions and habits in grassroots progressive politics in unambiguous contrast. The stories and ideas held by participants of color closely mirrored the perspectives and explanations that white participants felt so *awkward* about that they avoided recognizing and integrating them into their worldviews.

Such counternarratives challenge the definitions of reality constructed by dominant groups to naturalize their social positions and affirm their identities.[1] Counternarratives can rupture existing dominant narratives, produce new visions of reality, and reveal new potentials for transformation. As argued by legal scholar Richard Delgado, engaging with these stories "can show us the way out of the trap of unjustified exclusion" and "help us understand when it is time to reallocate power."[2] They are part of the long-standing practice of counter-framing that people of color in the United States use to identify the causes and impacts of racial oppression in the struggle for racial equality.[3]

Despite the organization being predominantly (and disproportionately) white, I interacted with and interviewed 10 participants who were Latinx, Asian American, or African American.[4] I relied heavily on informal extended conversations to tap into their experiences and concerns. I was fortunate to develop a rapport and a sense of openness in many of these conversations and encounters, which helped participants share their experiences, concerns, and struggles. The persistent marginalization and bias caused by the party's white consensus shaped their experiences—often as a source of frustration.

CONFLICT CONCEALED BY CONSENSUS

Shared assumptions about political life and racial inequality helped maintain the overwhelming whiteness of the organization's demographics. But grassroots democracy is meaningless if it is not inclusive of groups otherwise excluded from political processes. Political equality requires actively interrogating whose claims and perspectives are prioritized or excluded in democratic engagement. We must investigate how "the appearance of consensus" can be a result of "underlying conflicts, which provide a basis for understanding instability and change."[5] Looking at the dominant consensus and sources of conflict in tandem reveals underlying tensions and the potential for transformation.

Despite its often-negative connotation, conflict is not inherently harmful. Conflict is necessary for institutional change and efforts for social liberation when employed effectively. It can be a productive social force. Collaboration is essential in organizations. But collaboration always holds the potential for conflict.[6] Racial conflict within organizations can produce shifts in organizational routines and the allocation of resources, which can, in turn, lead to transformations in the larger racial structure of society.[7] Organizations like political parties are drivers of political and social conflicts over racial meanings and structures.[8]

Productive conflict occurs when we maintain our well-being and move toward resolution in the form of new solutions that reflect a greater understanding of the interests and experiences of others.[9] However, destructive conflict occurs when the people involved are harmed, and the sense of unfairness, patterns of exclusion, or opposition in goals, strategies, and routines becomes more pronounced and severe.[10] Conflict can be a resource for creative tension. Creative tension helps us identify the bigger picture of social relations and inequality.[11] It opens a space where we can understand why our experiences and interests are different from one another yet are produced by the same underlying social arrangements. Taking seriously the conflict inherent in a predominantly white political party that espouses racial justice and the political empowerment of people of color can help us understand how a social system like structural racism simultaneously impacts white people and people of color in distinct ways.

For instance, several participants discussed proposals to run only candidates of color. Many older white participants saw the proposal as controversial or even adversarial. While they did not implement this strategy during my time in the field, the recommendations promoted awareness of the optics and limitations of a normatively white organization. They sparked conversations and even collective action at the regional and national levels around racial inequality and representation. Rather than avoiding awkward and uncomfortable realities, bringing these existing tensions to the surface can create a new equilibrium.

Instances of destructive conflict were nonetheless also evident. Some participants of color became frustrated by the white consensus and decided to pare back their engagement. Others explicitly took on a role within their chapters where they could facilitate change, bring conflicts to the surface, and help the party adapt to reach its full potential as a vehicle for racial justice and democracy. But this role was also fraught with pressure and opposition.

One participant of color who took this approach was Nina, a longtime Latina participant in the GAP in her midforties. When I asked about her role in the party and how she felt about these problems, Nina told me she used her position "to highlight those issues to people." But she also faced resistance. She said, "Does everybody want to hear that? No. Ask me if I care. No, because, really, it's not about me. You know, I want it to be about us."

Nina stressed the importance of actively confronting problematic behavior, even if it meant acknowledging conflicts and contradictions. She said, "Even within a progressive party and an independent party, you still have the old guard . . . or people power-mongering and power struggling to keep things a certain way." Despite the value placed on maintaining the party's existing consensus by white GAP participants, participants of color regularly highlighted that productive conflict could transform the party.

Like other participants of color, Nina occupied a unique position. She was a woman of color who grew up poor. She was also a regional leader who, in her words, was "able to analyze the party from an upper view." She could apply the insights from her experiences with multiple forms of oppression to produce new understandings and act from a more holistic perspective. In the words of sociologist Patricia Hill Collins, Nina was an "outsider within."[12] She had an *outsider* status but found herself *within* positions of influence in institutions and organizations.

In academia, the outsider within can transform knowledge production.[13] In the context of a grassroots political organization, they can change political praxis. Nina recognized that from her vantage point, she could "give a good critique and analysis of what I'm seeing that's not working within the party." Despite the radical racial justice language in the party's platform, racialized organizations like the GAP "often decouple formal commitments to equity, access, and inclusion from policies and practices that reinforce, or at least do not challenge, existing racial hierarchies."[14] For instance, during a conversation with Nina, I pointed out this disconnect between the party's formal goals and its inner workings. She retorted that the platform was "racially progressive, but still, we have a very far way to go to strip those issues that come with white privilege and oppression."

There was no denying the lack of racial diversity in the party, even among white participants. Nina told me that while "many of the people in the party recognize that diversity or lack of diversity in representation within the party is a major problem," white participants acted as though "they can't effectively do anything about it." Furthermore, the white consensus undermined the party's impression among people of color whose interests and politics would otherwise align perfectly with the organization. As a Black short-lived GAP participant named Rafael lamented during our conversation, the most influential and visible organizations that advocate for the redistribution of power and resources and the groups who would most benefit often fail to connect and work together.

The white consensus produced an internal set of norms and expectations and an image among outsiders of the party as a white space. This reputation, and the failure of efforts to substantively change it, helped maintain the exclusion of people of color. The themes of racism, conflict, and consensus also emerged as I sat and talked to Jake and Chip about local politics in that small local diner. They also held unique vantage points as light-skinned Asian Americans. They had experienced racial discrimination. At the same time, both men recognized that they simultaneously benefitted from their status as "honorary whites" in the US racial hierarchy.[15] They joked about the complexities of their racial identities in white spaces:

Jake: Well, I have a white-sounding last name, so I'll come off as a white guy. Um . . .
Chip: Like I said, this is April. We're good right now. Come like—
Jake: Mid-July or even June . . . we'll be dark. Really dark.
Chip: Yeah, we get like—I always make the joke. I know I'm getting like tan when I'm getting pulled over more. That's actually true.

Like other GAP participants of color, Chip and Jake had distinct experiences in daily life that they could clearly connect to racial oppression.
The habits and norms in predominantly white organizations often fail to
resonate with people of color. Assumptions about the nature and stakes
of racial oppression shape an organization's engagement with potential
participants. Jake's discussion of another local organization demonstrated
this dynamic. He said, "It's a predominantly white racial justice organization. . . . White people teaching white people about what Black people are
going through. . . . One complaint that people who attended their events
say is there are too many niceties. What people of color and Latinos are
going through . . . is not niceties." Despite the desire for change, participants of color were not interested in simply producing fragmentation.
They did not want to engage in an overt power struggle that only created
conflict and division. Through confronting conflicts, they hoped to produce a new consensus that centered on racial justice practices and mutual
respect.

Coalitions and Community Conditions

When we first met to talk over coffee at a local bookstore, Nina had been
an active Grassroots Action Party participant for six years. She had been a
political activist for even longer. Her connection to the GAP boiled down
to a singular event—the planned demolition of a housing complex. Nina
was a longtime resident of the small city of South Nauset. After being displaced from their first apartment, her family moved into the low-income
housing complex—Pine Timbers.

The city planned to demolish the complex, home to primarily Latino
residents almost a decade ago. She found out about an emergency meeting
to discuss these pending plans. She said, "They had this assessment, this
environmental study that they had done prior to making that decision, and
they came to the conclusion that demolishing it would have no environmental impact. And I'm thinking, what about the people that are there?"
At the meeting, the residents of the building were in unambiguous opposition to the destruction of their homes. However, she noted that "nobody
really was hearing them. Nobody was talking *to them or with them*. They
were talking *about them*. . . . Latino residents were sitting in this big room
with all these officials, and all community residents who came to support
them, and a lot of them have these interpreter devices on. They're hearing

what's being said about them, but they're not participating in the discussion." Public meetings involve interactions between people of varying social positions, roles, and resources. Those who feel more comfortable engaging with authorities and entitled to having a voice are more likely to influence the process. As Nina observed, these procedures too often involve political and social elites talking *about* marginalized community members rather than *with them* or even *to them*.

Regardless of these exclusions, public deliberations help maintain the image of community involvement. City and town meetings can provide the policy goals of dominant groups with an aura of consensus without directly engaging the concerns of the communities most likely to face the consequences. Building a sense of shared agreement about social issues and ideas is part of what makes social and political life possible. However, as the sociologist Martin Lipset writes, "a system of stratification requires consensus about the legitimacy of inequality, while at the same time, inequality stimulates protest, revolt, and class consciousness among the underprivileged."[16] Nina saw that the emerging consensus about Pine Timbers resulted from suppressing the conflicting concerns of community members. She told me she felt that "these people need a voice," and she vowed to work so that the community members could "participate in their own circumstances" and "have influence."

This story tells us about more than just Nina; it also tells us about the GAP and its white consensus. Her connection with the GAP hadn't come about because the party consciously reached out to her or her or her community. She just happened to hear about them from some activist friends when she was developing a plan to save the complex from demolition. In that sense, Nina reached out to the party to advance the material conditions of the community, not just her personal values. She showed up at their next meeting and explained the situation and its importance to the community. GAP participants helped provide access to legal resources and support. Nina's efforts to bring together a sizeable progressive coalition were crucial in preventing the demolition of Pine Timbers.

However, she clarified that "the GAP didn't have a major role in the sense that they were boots to the ground, but that one thing of saying 'How can we help?' and that one pivotal thing that kind of swung the pendulum the other way. And ever since, I've been dedicated and committed to the party." Participants of color saw their connection to the party as a jointly valuable relationship. But it was also one laden with conflict. Much as the appearance of a consensus can be a product of inequality and exclusion in other engagement spaces like public meetings, the GAP's political strategies around forming coalitions reflected the white consensus. Many participants of color felt that they had to transform the party to change society. They pushed back against the assumptions and norms held by white participants to make the party more effective in achieving racial justice.

Participants of color in the GAP measured their sense of success in terms of their impact on the conditions in their communities, not just electoral victories or continuity of the party status quo. For instance, Nina told me about a friend who tagged her in a Facebook photo of a Pine Timbers tenant smiling and giving a thumbs-up. Behind the tenant was active construction to improve the building. In the post, her friend expressed gratitude for her leadership and its value to the tenant. Nina told me, "That's what it was all about."

By contrasting such personally held goals and strategies to those of the party writ large, participants of color identified the white consensus. They saw how it devalued intentional outreach to marginalized communities. When white participants imagined or experienced moments of potential connection with these communities, they could not imagine offering the organization as a source of mutual support and solidarity. They sought control of the situation. They sought comfort in collective routines and narrow conceptions of political success.

REVEALING RACIALIZED ROUTINES

Personal accounts of the lived experience prove most illuminating in telling what everyday racism is about: injustices occurring so often that they are taken for granted, nagging, annoying, debilitating, seemingly small, injustices one comes to expect.—Philomena Essed, 2002

Everyday racism reflects the "role of routine and repetitive practices in the making of social structure."[17] Sociologist Philomena Essed points out that everyday racism can manifest in several different ways.[18] *Marginalization* occurs when whites exclude people of color and disregard their experiences, concerns, and contributions. *Problematization* happens when whites define people of color or their actions as problematic and thereby responsible for problems and conflict. A third form is *containment,* whereby whites engage in discursive and social practices that enable them to deny the existence of discrimination or exclusion. These same processes showed up in the everyday routines of GAP participants.

Everyday racism tends to be invisible to its perpetrators. Whites often deny the experiences of people of color as valid or understandable.[19] In the previous chapter we saw this dynamic in white GAP members' daily habits and underlying common sense. In contrast, centering participants of color reveals thwarted potential and ongoing consequences.

Priorities and Participation

Participation in the GAP among Asian American, Latinx, and African American participants fell on a broad spectrum. Some were longtime active members. Others attended one or two events but lost interest. Rafael, a middle-class African American man in his thirties, attended one meeting of the Moosewater chapter of the GAP but did not return. His initial reaction to the chapter was that it was "too white and too old." Chapter participants also failed to follow up with him after his first meeting via phone or email. They had not invited him to subsequent events. When I asked about him about a month later, the participants I spoke to seemed embarrassed to admit that they had dropped the ball.

Rafael had a long history of progressive grassroots activism through several organizations and political parties. These experiences gave him an insightful perspective on politics and racial oppression as a Black man in predominantly white leftist spaces. After his first meeting, we exchanged information to meet up and talk. I met up with him in the lobby of a hotel where he was staying for work in a nearby town. Rafael shared a story of a recent conversation that he had with a young white college student: "He was like a young white guy, goes to Mackenzie College, and . . . he's talking about how every time . . . really progressive groups align themselves with the neoliberals . . . it ends up that the old liberals end up taking over the movement and taking it into a different direction and nothing ever really gets accomplished."

Rafael found a striking parallel in this narrative to the impact of racial oppression on multiracial social movement organizations:

> I said, "Well, then, you know, that sounds like every time Black people hook up with white people, right?" And he looks at me. And I said "No . . . let's think about it. . . . We're going to use that line of thought

that you just gave, saying that historically that, when one group of people have tried to work with another group of people, that the larger, more powerful group of people's interests became the direction of the movement. . . . Black people could say well, that's the reason why I'm not going to join this organization or political party. . . . Every time we get up with you all, this is what happens, and our interests and, our causes, and our problems become second to the interests of white people."

As his recounting of this conversation made clear, white grassroots progressives held a strong class consciousness or critical awareness of capitalism and how that produced concrete and distinct interests from (neo) liberals. Yet they could not imagine how racial oppression, much like capitalism, had produced substantial and divergent interests and concerns for Black people in the United States.

He noted that egalitarian and low-stratification societies, such as the Mbuti in Africa, existed long before the development of Europe, the birth of Karl Marx, and even the coining of the term "socialism." Moreover, he touched on a more profound point. As African American studies scholar Keeanga-Yamahtta Taylor notes, "Racism, capitalism, and class rule have always been tangled together in such a way that it is impossible to imagine one without the other."[20] Yet the most influential nineteenth- and twentieth-century European critiques of capitalism failed to illuminate this relationship.[21] Racial oppression was, and remains, an intrinsic element of the very economic exploitation and political inequality at the heart of capitalism that white leftists critique.[22]

Afterwards, I remembered an earlier interview I had with a white participant, Roger, who mentioned that one way that the party might increase its racial diversity would be to "go into those communities of people of color, immigrants, and you know, like missionary mode [*laughs*]. They probably wouldn't like that, but you know what I mean." It was as if many of the white GAP participants who held influence could only imagine entering communities of color for "conversion" to the party's values, identity, and platform via "missionary mode." Growing the party without altering its organizational identity, strategies, and ideology took precedence over developing authentic, mutual, and pragmatic relationships with marginalized communities. The party's ideals and interests, refracted through its white consensus, necessarily overrode the objectives and interests of local marginalized racial and ethnic community members. In this way, *marginalization* of the life experiences and wisdom of people of color took place through the everyday practices of the organization.

Many participants of color grew exasperated with how their white colleagues privileged ideas over the conditions of communities. Rafael distinguished between the kind of political consciousness that comes from directly experiencing oppression and having it shape your material interests and encountering abstract radical ideas. He pointed out that in grassroots progressive politics, combating racial oppression was often sidelined for other goals: "I think it's important for Black people to demand that . . . when we're in these organizations that we're going to be heard. And we're going to be leaders in this organization and fairly represented throughout the leadership of this leadership core of these groups, and that our issues are going to remain on the forefront of priorities within these organizations."

Rafael echoed activist Stokely Carmichael and political scientist Charles V. Hamilton's warning of "meaningless coalitions . . . which do not and cannot speak to the real needs of the black people."[23] However, he emphasized, "not working with left white groups because historically when we've done that, you know, the causes that I have become second to another group of causes, is backward." Addressing these issues head-on and working to develop a large-scale, equitable, and diverse coalition was crucial to his vision of grassroots democracy.

Intentional Inclusion

Our racial consciousness, particularly in terms of practical knowledge and awareness, influences our political action and its rationality. This relationship between our awareness and actions shows up in our preferred strategies for engagement and inclusion. Predominantly white social movement organizations, grassroots political parties, and activist collectives have had fraught and complicated relationships with communities of color—even when they have held a position as sanctioned allies in the struggle for racial justice.

Much of this conflict has hinged upon core questions around mobilizing communities: What is the purpose of grassroots progressive organizations becoming engaged and embedded in communities of color? Is it for progressives to advance to political power, grow their ranks, and convert new members to their ideology? Is it to actualize the commitment to solidarity with marginalized communities, empowering people of color, and fighting racial oppression?

Many white participants suggested that people who embodied or believed in the ideals and goals of the organization would naturally encounter them and join. Yet their counterparts of color within the GAP instead emphasized dialogue, mutual support, and intentionally forming coalitions around the causes of concern in communities. Rafael mentioned that telling people what to think rather than asking people what they think was common among grassroots progressive organizations: "When we're out at a meeting, at a rally, or are tabling, and people are walking by and, very seldom are we asking the people their opinions. How do you feel about what's going on? What issues are important to you? As a party that represents the people what would you, what do you expect from us? What do you want from us? How can we better serve the communities? It was more of 'We got all the answers. Listen to us, read this paper, adopt our line.' You see what I'm saying?"

Similarly, Chip critiqued white participants he described as "intellectuals" who "understand the nuances of the platforms in ways that I may never actually understand." He mentioned that they habitually got into technical details and local specifics. This tactic created barriers to entry that outsiders found alienating. It also lacked the urgency and clarity that would help those directly harmed by racial oppression envision the party as a vehicle for empowerment. In contrast, Chip suggested they "have an easily digestible platform that speaks to people's common populist interest." Looking around, he stated, "When it comes to, like, things that will literally affect the people that are sitting in this restaurant right now, you need to talk on their level. . . . The party has never done that."

The dominant approach also mirrors power relations forged in centuries of racial oppression. Rafael argued that whites, even when acting from a place of concern, routinely end up seeking to control people of color: "And that particularly doesn't work well in Black neighborhoods. . . . What I don't think a lot of white grassroots progressives understand is that the reason why they haven't made a good connection with Black people is because. . . . they continue to use the model that reinforces or at least comes off as the same dynamics of a relationship that Black people have had with white people all the time. You come into our neighborhood; you don't *ask* us what we think; you *tell* us what we should think."

Nina also pointed out this dynamic:

> One of the areas that I really want to target is New Easton because New Easton has a very, very strong African American population. And that is a community that needs to be on board with us. And we need to be on board with them. . . . We need to change the thinking, and we need to reach out to them when we need to be more of a support to them. It's kind of hard to do that when . . . the majority of people that are in the party are whites. And so, you know, it's like, you know, whites coming in and infiltrating a Black neighborhood . . . like the white savior mentality.

White paternalism and the idea of white saviors uniquely capable of heroically rescuing people of color from their troubles saturate US society past and present. It permeates depictions of race relations in films, literature, journalism, and television.[24] And it remains a dominant mode of engagement within racialized industries, initiatives, and organizations like volunteer tourism, humanitarian efforts, community service programs, and activism.[25] This idea minimizes the agency of people of color by depicting them as needing dominant white leaders to control the situation rather than empathy, support, and resources. It was a form of *containment* that sought to hold communities of color in an inferior position. It was an aspect of the white consensus that barricaded the party from advancing multiracial coalitions and actualizing racial justice.

Empowerment vs. Extraction

Participants of color regularly tried to position themselves as bridge builders to their communities. They focused on the practical advancement of community conditions and building long-lasting relationships. Nina pointed out prominent Black and Latinx activists and political figures who, through relationships with the GAP, helped normalize the image that the party was racially diverse but argued it had not been enough. The party had not taken the initiative to make these endeavors a significant focus. Nina's frustrations reiterated Rafael's sentiment about the importance of engagement as an expression of solidarity rather than recruitment. Explaining her disagreements over outreach with whites in the party, she stated, "Because it's not about you, it's about the issues in Black and Latino communities. . . . You just need to show up and be there and be a support.

In any way that you can help further the cause, then you do it, right? Um, but nine times out of ten, they always want to like rip something out of it, which really like drives me crazy." When parties actively mobilize, encourage, engage, and support marginalized groups, it drastically increases their democratic participation.[26] However, most political parties do not value increased participation and engagement among people of color as a goal in and of itself.[27]

Tensions arose between *extraction* and *empowerment* as forms of engagement. In the extraction approach, engagement hinged upon questions such as: "What's in it for the party or me to engage with this community; how can we use this event or encounter to advance electoral or partisan goals immediately?" The *extraction* approach included notions that other middle-class whites are "ideal" political constituents. As a result, "some members of the population are more likely to be targeted than others," with "profound implications for the distribution of political participation."[28]

Communities with a history of rightful distrust stemming from dominant group members treating them as political objects or instruments would necessarily need a different approach than extraction to collaborate with the party. The *empowerment* approach highlighted forming relationships and working to support people of color, cultivate trust and a positive image, and build alliances. It focused on developing reciprocity and social connection networks as a catalyst for increasing political engagement.[29] Nina affirmed the importance of authentic forms of engagement: "And it almost seems opportunistic, right? And people in the hood, people in communities of color, and those frontline communities know when people are infiltrating and coming into their communities and whether or not they're doing it with their own, uh, underlying motives and agenda."

During the planning phases of new initiatives, instrumental or extractive logic often crept into efforts at building coalitions. In these deliberations, their white counterparts' reasoning and actions were oriented towards personal goals like attaining political influence rather than a sense of connection to communities. In contrast, her perspective as a woman of color with important insights about connecting to communities was *problematized*. Nina provided the following example: "There was a proposal for a lawsuit to support a mobile strike initiative. And that we were going to designate any resources that we have to support that effort, right? It's kind of like coalition building with the impacted communities. So, it's not about the GAP, right? It's about the movement. . . . I was really excited to see this, right, because we haven't been seeing these kinds of proposals. That is kind of revolutionary."

However, white participants often resisted proposals to provide support and solidarity to communities. They argued that these efforts might not yield immediate electoral returns or obligations from community members. Nina noted, "So, we have this one woman who's been in the party for a very long time and said, 'Well, um, I kind of like this, but I'm not going to support it unless there's something in there about us being able to target our candidates from this process.'"

In response, Nina articulated the value of collaborative engagement and solidarity during the meeting. She told me, "She's not thinking about that the intent here is to engage communities, work with other organizations, progressive organizations, and left organizations, um, in this movement. She's thinking about how can we, you know, get people to run for office out of this effort. I said, 'This isn't about candidates.' . . . It doesn't always have to be, you know, how do you say, the two don't have to always go together, right? They can be two separate efforts, right?" GAP participants of color experienced frustration with the inability of others in their party to understand the importance of issue alignment, coalition formation, and community solidarity. Nina summarized this tension by stating, "One of the key roles or tactics that I've tried to explain to the GAP is that I'll go in, and I'll organize based on the issue, not the party, right?"

GAP participants of color saw it as hypocritical to espouse a belief in racial justice while advancing strategies that relied upon the existing political power of white communities or excluded communities of color. Participants such as Nina, Rafael, Jake, and Chip saw an entirely distinct pathway for goal attainment. According to this vision, the party should engage in practical activities that support and empower otherwise marginalized ethnic communities. They recognized that the byproducts of these efforts, while not the primary motivation, would include increased social capital and trust among these communities and the wisdom and insight of their members.

STRATEGIES AND SOLIDARITIES

We . . . went into the valley knowing that the people are in the valley,
knowing that our plight is the same plight as the people in the valley,
knowing that our enemies are on the mountain, our friends are in the valley,

*and even though it's nice to be on the mountaintop, we're going back to the
valley. Because we understand that there's work to be done in the valley, and
when we get through with this work in the valley, then we got to go to the
mountaintop.*—Fred Hampton, 1969

The above quote from Fred Hampton, chairman of the Illinois Black
Panther Party and founder of the Rainbow Coalition, a multiracial coalition for socialism, demonstrates the power of solidarity. The metaphor of
people residing in the relative valleys and mountains of social stratification
is powerful. It illustrates two features of solidarity. First, solidarity can
motivate collective action by recognizing that "our plight is the same plight
as the people in the valley." Secondly, it also serves as a way of practicing
politics by acknowledging that "there's work to be done in the valley" before a movement can take on those on the mountaintop.

Solidarity has the status of a buzzword in progressive politics. The
apparent lack of solidarity among contemporary progressives has been
lamented and attributed to various causes of fracturing. Among GAP participants, solidarity was seen as a strategy or a way of building a mass
movement and as an emotional sentiment of empathy and shared humanity. This concept had unique salience in the motivations and practices of
participants of color. It held a sense of connection to marginalized communities and a shared destiny with their members.

This feeling of solidarity was inseparable from their political agendas
and strategies. It was essential to how they approached political life and
why. Their political engagement was shaped by "identifying with members
of a subordinate group, identifying injustices done to that group, opposing
those injuries, and seeing the group as having a shared interest in ending
or diminishing those injustices."[30] Their sense of solidarity drove them
toward pathbreaking strategies to overcome racialized barriers.

Evolution and Engagement

Contentious discussions around inequality and racism are not straightforward pathways to illumination and enlightenment. After all, there is
a certain comfort in maintaining a consistent social identity and set of
beliefs. Disrupting our sense of self and ideas about society's operations
leads to ambiguity and discomfort. However, we might also embrace the
productive conflict of these encounters. Despite being conservative at a
young age, Jake's own experiences growing up had been perforated by the

occasional awareness of his "otherness" as an Asian American in white spaces. As we drove to a meeting of the Whitehall chapter, he told me that while in high school, his brother experienced racist harassment and bullying from white classmates. These experiences combined to spark self-reflection on racial oppression and social change. As Jake pointed out, "We basically evolved now to be where we are today."

Encounters with the church and military had also shaped Jake and Chip's prior conservative mindset. As both were in the military, Jake pointed out that their mentality was "if you're Republican, you're promilitary, so if you're military, you should be Republican." Chip even worked on John McCain's 2008 presidential campaign. He said, "I was with the young Republicans, and yeah, we were like cold calling in Ohio." However, their experiences as Asian American men connected to other people of color in a white-dominated society created tensions they could not rectify with the racial conservatism of the Republican Party. Chip explained,

> I realized I was a libertarian who felt strongly about racial equality. We're both Asian, so being a minority plays a role in that, and so we both grew up in . . . a majority-minority community. And it's like, well, I'm a minority, and a lot of my friends are Black and Hispanic, and I don't like how things are going, and I think, you know, like this is wrong, but I didn't want to be a Republican or a Democrat, and so I was like, "Oh, libertarian is the way to go," and then I realized that um I was a libertarian who had leftist views and didn't know how to consolidate and rectify those views. And then I heard about the GAP, and well, that's how I ended up here.

Nina's narrative about her political and social consciousness also emphasized growth and transformation through participation and exposure. She told me, "The way I feel about politics is that politics is evolutionary, right? Um, that doesn't mean you don't come in with certain stances and with certain ideas, but that does mean that you can be wrong, and you can change your mind, and you can grow, right, with your thought process and your beliefs."

Political evolution requires an openness to the awkwardness and discomfort of spontaneous actions and emergent events. Encounters with interested parties are openings for personal development for all involved. New participants and collaborators gain experiences within grassroots democracy that will aid them in the growth and alteration of their political and social awareness and civic skills. It also enables the inclusion of new perspectives that can radically transform the party and its strategies for the better.

Nina spoke of this perspective in the context of the frustration that many progressive Democrats, attracted to the party by Bernie Sanders, experienced during the 2016 primaries after Hillary Clinton was nominated: "We're getting a real influx from the Democratic Party, you know, and they should, I mean, they should be disappointed. . . . Um, and some people are some, some within the party are fearful of that, that enter, right? Because they're thinking that is pulling the party to the right, kind of like the centrist. . . . Even though I'm very left, that doesn't mean we can't embrace these individuals, right, and do some political education. . . . I don't think it's an either-or situation."

This approach to growing the party demonstrated a sense of pragmatism that saw opportunities for consciousness-raising among political crises and anxieties. This perspective is much less focused on brandishing our political *bona fides* as a progressive or leftist. Instead, it is grounded in the notion that people can grow and change through firsthand engagement in social and political change work. As African American studies scholar Keeanga-Yamahtta Taylor points out, "Liberals become radicals through their own frustrating experiences with the system, but also through becoming engaged with people who became radical before them. So, when radicals who have already come to some important conclusions about the shortcomings of the existing system mock, deride or dismiss those who have not achieved the same level of consciousness, they are helping no one."[31]

At a later conversation, Nina and I discussed personal transformation and political evolution in the context of the limited consciousness of many white GAP participants. She said, "I think me and you, we talked about, the last time, about how oppression is a major issue within the party. . . . And I think that one of the ways to do that is to work on antioppression training and coming and bringing it back to the local level so that we can, we can teach our white counterparts how to interact and engage with people of color, and you know, LGBTQ and women in a more productive way. You know, like learning, teaching them how to do relationship building."

Nina also pointed out that the party could also play a role in the political education in marginalized communities. The party could act as a source of cultural and institutional resources to help remedy political disparities.

But they would have to be willing to change their dominant collective habits. The white participants would have to move outside of their comfort zones and let go of their current control. In this way, Nina connected her own political evolution to her philosophy of community engagement and social change: "It wasn't until . . . I found myself in a situation where I was enlightened and beginning to really take a critical look at these issues, right, that it hit me, you know, that this is a more systemic issue, right? So, what happens in these communities of color that people are so entrenched, right? . . . They're going to continue to be the entrenched, right? . . . Like the saying says, that knowledge is power. And unless that knowledge is put there and people are loving it, and they're being exposed to it, it's not going to be much change, right?"

This insight reflects the central paradox between democracy and oppression and the sense of conflict between how things *are* and how they *should be* that underlies grassroots political action.[32] This form of evolutionary racial politics points toward strategies for political empowerment. The first is to fully validate that racial discrimination occurs at interpersonal, institutional, and systemic levels and persists in the United States. This process includes consciousness-raising practices to generate increased awareness of the structural connections that produce everyday experiences of inequity. This process must also pair with an effort to recognize that deeper engagement and participation in democracy by marginalized groups is vital for transforming interpersonal relationships and institutions.

Spontaneity vs. Structure

Participants of color expressed the merit of showing up and lending support wherever needed as it aligned with the progressive issues and goals outlined in the organization's charters. They saw how actions rooted in solidarity and flexibility would develop authentic and trusting relationships with communities. Nina defined her approach as follows:

> I have this tendency to, in a very spontaneous way, organize action and ask for forgiveness later. And um, there's been many occasions where I had organized actions, protests and rallies and things like that, particularly around racial justice and police brutality. I've come out strong on issues of race, racism, and stuff like that. . . . And as I am organizing and gathering support and interest in public media

and all of that, I will say, "Come on, we gotta be on board. Let's do this. We're going to do this together collectively." And I've managed to organize a lot of events and situations like that where I engaged, you know, got the GAP involved, right, and particularly [with] the Latino community and Black Lives Matter issues.

However, the GAP's routine forms of outreach and engagement favored planning, structure, and control. It centered questions of how the party would benefit directly from a line of action. She told me, "I think that oftentimes, um, GAP members . . . particularly the longer term, uh, members, they don't understand engagement. You know, they don't understand what it is, like everything has to be so analytical to them and so orderly. So, what they'll do is they'll sit around a table, and they plan how they're going to engage. And that's not natural. It doesn't work. It's so—it's very fake. It's very superficial."

In contrast, spontaneous collective action is often timelier and more effective. For example, Nina told me that, after several high-profile instances of police killing Black men back to back, "I quickly, within a three- or four-day period, had organized a protest and rally. . . . I have three or four hundred people out there. And I was able to organize that really quickly, and I didn't sell that as a GAP issue—because it's not. However, when it came time for the GAP to be present, I said, 'Listen, you're going to be there to support.'"

She pointed out that while white GAP participants did come to the rally, "they came out in GAP shirts; they recorded it." It was an attempt to capitalize on a protest to produce visibility for the party. Nina was not convinced that her white counterparts had the ability or even the desire to connect authentically with communities and organizations of color. She clarified, "If they're not co-opting the resistance, right, and they're not co-opting the movement, but instead enhancing it, then that's the better approach." However, "they haven't yet figured out how to do that."

Nina argued that the party should employ a light touch that allowed those most impacted by the issues to lead the way: "There's a difference between, um, organized action and spontaneous action. And of the two, the one that's most effective is a spontaneous action, right? So, you need to let spontaneity, spontaneous behavior, and action happen, and you need to support that, supplement that; we don't need to control, is what I'm saying, to be effective."

She also connected this impulse among white participants to the organizational norm of intensively planning and structuring events and initiatives. She said, "The problem is that they want to have too much structure—too many rules, and they want to control everything. . . . But if you're really going to have any progress or movement, you have to let the people lead. You know, you can't be these, this group of white privileged individuals, kind of giving out orders there and not letting the people that are truly impacted, you know, um, not to step up and take leadership roles and, um, and lead their own causes, you know, and I think that that is a major gap in the party."

Participants of color routinely discussed their work with groups and organizations in communities of color. They stressed that the party should be flexible, sensitive, and responsive to the needs and context of community members rather than attempting to influence and control them for political purposes. As Chip noted during one of our conversations, "It's incumbent upon us to win [other people of color] over and not to say 'Hey, come here—oh, you don't want to come here? Fine.'" As an example, Chip told me the following about his work with a local organization:

> We do, um, either outreach directly to gang members or people who
> have done violent crime. . . . We have a Saturday school program
> where we take donated food and like literally, you might make a
> meal, we provide the kids breakfast, we provide them lunch, and we
> teach them various topics that school might not teach, or we tutor,
> um, English or math or whatever. So I know a lot of people who are
> involved in that program, and it's primarily African American and
> Hispanic, so I had said to Jake, "Hey, here's an opportunity to actually
> get other people of color involved directly and say 'Hey, we want you
> to not only become interwoven fabric of this group but also to take
> a leadership role. We don't want to just be lip service.'" . . . It's like,
> "Hey, what do you think Black people in your city need? Let's set it up,
> let's make it happen. Let's campaign on it."

The white consensus sought to impose order and structure on emotionally charged, energetic movements and moments. It sought to harness that energy and direct it toward the electoral goals of the party while remaining fundamentally in charge. In doing so, it marginalized the knowledge and insights of those communities and problematized them as incompatible with the organization. In contrast, participants of color saw inherent value in supporting and providing a vehicle, a set of resources, and a platform for the people impacted by racial oppression to achieve justice.

Pushing for Progress

Greater inclusion of people of color necessarily meant cultural and structural shifts for the party. Chip, during our conversation, argued that these inevitable changes should be embraced: "They'll say, like, 'Well, we need to bring in—' They'll say, like, low-income people or whatever euphemistic drawing they want to put on it. And they'll say something like, um, 'We have to bring them in slowly because it will change everything too much, or they don't really know what they're doing yet or whatever.' I always think that's absurd because you're not really about it then. *To say you're about diversity and inclusiveness means that some things will change. It will not look like what it looks like now.*" In contrast to the "old guard" of longtime members, he commented, "we're not trying to indoctrinate other people, we're trying to incorporate them, and that's two different things."

He argued that the party should not be seeking out "mindless zombies who just subscribe to your ideas" but rather should be "looking to maybe even change some of your own ideas or hash out ideas against each other." Including new members, particularly people of color and other underrepresented groups, would strengthen the platform and inform the strategies of the party. This vision, however, clashed with its white-dominated hierarchy in collective deliberations. These clashes often resulted in *marginalization, problematization*, and *containment*. Nina pointed out, "White privilege is a major issue, and I think that many of our white counterparts in the party have the inability to self-reflect and the inability to look at themselves and see the error of their ways sometimes and how they can be oppressive and condescending and belittling, and how they themselves engage in power struggle or perpetuate power struggles within the party. They also don't want to concede control and power, and they push back on that quite a bit."

Despite these obstacles, Nina had an admirable track record of pushing the organization toward racial equity. She had been especially effective at helping form coalitions and committees to advance and empower people of color in grassroots progressive politics at the national level. Yet she had much less success in these endeavors at the regional and local levels. Nina stated,

There're some people within our party on a regional level that are obstructionists, and they prevent people of color from coming in and taking power. For example, I'm a regional party leader, but that doesn't mean I have very much power because if I come—if I bring forward any recommendations or proposals, or I have this bird's-eye view, or a different perspective . . . I try to explain to them, "Listen, this is not working." They don't want to hear it because they're very bylaws-driven. It's all about rhetoric. They know how to put forward proposals and policy and the papers and, you know, document things, you know, but they're very limited as far as human nature, and human relationships, and how to deal with people on a racial and cultural level.

Nina prioritized actively recruiting and including people of color so that the party could reflect their interests and insights. Yet she noted, "I bring people of color to the party to stay for a little bit, and then [they] leave. . . . There's been very few people of color who have come to the party and have remained in the long term." At the regional level, she found herself consistently outnumbered by white participants whom she described as "elitist," producing an uphill battle. She argued, "I'm the only person of color sitting at the table with my comrade and a very good friend of mine that I brought into the party. We're the only ones that are sitting at that party with all these individuals going at it with them about what needs to be done, and, in the end, our recommendations are never, very rarely . . . even considered." She decided to focus her energy on "antioppression work" at the national level of grassroots politics, hoping it would trickle down to local groups.

Internal Insurgencies

The practical implications of forcing the party to live up to its potential as a vehicle for racial justice included those with greater racial conscious-ness taking the reins. During our conversation at the diner, Jake told me that they held designs of radically reforming and restructuring the organi-zation from the beginning of his and Chip's participation in their regional chapter. They focused on altering its strategies of outreach and inclusion and prioritizing its racial justice agenda. Jake recalled that these goals were even embedded in their early communications with the leadership. He told me his introduction to their local GAP chapter started when he sent "a really long email . . . laying out what our thoughts were about the party. How to build it. How to grow it." Moreover, he and Chip saw an opportunity to influence the party because their local chapter lacked concrete organization and direction. This opening for energy, structure, and fresh ideas helped them plant a foothold within the organization and work to shape its strategies.

They were not alone in thinking about ways to transform the party from within. Nina sought to connect with other leaders of color within the organization. She told me, "I started taking a look at who the key players are . . . that are people of color like me on the national level. And I was just trying to kind of take a look at how they were interfacing with the party and what they were doing." In particular, she wanted to connect to a longtime and influential Latina leader in the party named Mia, who had recently stepped back from the GAP. She said, "It's really disturbing to me that someone like her couldn't make it in the party." She texted Mia encouragement to lead the effort to get people of color more involved. Mia responded that she was done after working with the party for a decade and being treated as a problem. Reflecting on their exchange, Nina said, "I just think that's a sad commentary, you know? . . . She got to the point of feeling like there was no way up, no moving forward, you know, and that she couldn't use the GAP, where she didn't feel strong enough about the GAP to do that."

A few months later, Nina was at a retreat with colleagues in grassroots progressive politics to do some "soul searching about the party" and decided to reach back out to Mia, this time suggesting "co-opting the party" and starting a movement within the GAP under the mentorship of prominent women of color. In response, Mia told her she hoped activists of color would push them in the right direction: "They don't want women of color leading anything and have made that clear. We tried to do this, but we were stopped at every turn. . . . This has been a decade of me trying. That's enough waste of time for me."

Antiracist activists of color routinely experience burnout. They are forced to educate white peers on issues of racial oppression, deal with their efforts being undermined by whites, make up for white participants that are unwilling to change or act, navigate white fragility, and put up with not receiving credit for ideas and achievements.[33] The organization's white leaders were intolerant of racial stress. The organization's white consensus proved a formidable barrier to even the most capable and accomplished participants of color.

Despite this, an alternative consensus was forming between newer and younger participants and many of the participants of color. Jake told me, "We need to address racism and marginalization of all different groups. . . . It needs to be a systematic redo of our structure." At a recent regional GAP meeting, Jake attended an event to discuss these systematic issues. There, the younger and more racially diverse participants concluded "that we want to take this party over. . . . We wanted to be revolutionary, and we felt that the old guard wasn't capable of being revolutionary. . . . And I was impressed because many of the people that were in attendance were leaders in their own local organizations or on the larger scale."

This incentive for change coalesced around a series of events that several participants highlighted as exemplifying the racialized conflicts and inequalities within the organization. Jake noted, "Some incidents of either racial insensitivity or racism" had taken place, both "at the actual meeting itself" and "reported from back home from certain people of color."

Discussions around generational inequity and ageism were already occurring among his peers at the meeting. He described "struggles within the party to break through this old guard mentality, folks not listening to any of the young people because they're just young." These concerns also became intertwined with concerns about racial discrimination. In a huge setback for the party's racial equity, every Black candidate lost in a recent executive cabinet election for the regional GAP amid allegations about corruption and collusion. This scandal broke just as many Black members met to discuss their struggles and vision. People of color on the cabinet offered immediate solidarity.

They determined that direct action was the best strategy to bring attention to the situation. Jake said, "There was an event for the party at a restaurant. They all marched upon the place, pretty much everyone in solidarity together. It wasn't just members of their assemblies but just people around who heard of what happened and everything and about the struggle that the people of color and the marginalized communities of the party have been going through back home. It was kind of a culmination of all these different factors that went into why they marched. So long story short, they went and basically shut the place down."

The event culminated with a public display of solidarity to highlight persistent issues of exclusion: "Folks stood up and offered their resignations in solidarity with the African American members and all the issues that this party really should be addressing, at least with more vigor and more expedited or faster. It doesn't seem like the folks who are of these communities are really feeling that welcome within this party."

Jake put the events in a broader context. He pointed out, "This party has historically been a white male, white cis male party dominated since its inception. I see it now even more within my own region where there's just literally just white people." He questioned how the election and its aftermath impacted these racial dynamics, stating, "To bring on other folks, the question is by not electing anybody from the African American community . . . [That] raised a lot of issues." Jake said the conversation in the aftermath was, "How can we turn this party around to where folks from these communities feel like they're a) represented and b) welcome?"

Tension was rising to the surface and Jake saw the potential not simply to upend the party's white consensus but also to produce a new, more just one: "Everything else kind of got put on the back burner once this protest occurred, and we're all facing the question of how we move forward. I have a feeling that there is not going to be a simple forgive-and-forget. I don't think there should be a simple forgive-and-forget. I feel like if somebody or some faction is truly toxic to the overall party; then it needs to be addressed. . . . I think it's also a good thing because it's making us address some real issues that the party has been facing."

CONCLUSIONS ON CONSENSUS AND CONFLICT

These stories, perspectives, and strategies highlight the importance of conflict to democratic participation and social change. The racialized tensions and disputes in political actors' accounts provide a source of rearticulation. Engaging with them enables a "redefinition of political interests and identities."[34] Rearticulation, rather than the reproduction of the white consensus, requires a recognition of the reality of racial oppression and the potential of grassroots democracy. In this sense, *democracy must be awkward to be transformative.* For people who experience and resist racial oppression firsthand, the comfort of avoidance is not a viable option.

Participants of color saw that the white consensus advanced a strategy where the purpose of including people of color was to achieve predefined political goals. It was routinely secondary to other concerns, such as maintaining comfort and continuity. But participants of color saw the party as an instrument for racial justice and the political empowerment of communities of color rather than seeing those communities as an instrument for the party.

The participants of color emphasized empowerment over extraction as a means of outreach to marginalized and disenfranchised publics harmed by racial oppression. This insight manifested in practices and an overall ethos prioritizing cultivating greater democratic capacity and political power for these communities. These strategies were grounded in a deeply felt sense of solidarity with communities of color and a critical awareness of the mechanisms of racial oppression and barriers to racially inclusive democracy.

Their political practices advanced by participants of color included the recognition of unresolved tensions, such as those between the goals and strategies of the organization. Alongside this recognition, they practiced productive conflict to resolve those tensions and articulate a new consensus and collective set of plans. Participants of color were at the forefront of efforts to make the party more dynamic and responsive to opportunities for racial justice praxis and solidarity politics to continually realign the organization's ideals, goals, and political practices. This realignment sought to orient the organization toward new collective goals based on the interests and problems faced by marginalized communities.

Conclusion
Pathways to Progressive Political Praxis

Of course, it is possible to maintain many cultural institutions through mindless, unexamined participation in taken-for-granted routines. To the extent that we each do so, we perpetuate realities that have little meaning for us and fail to consider ways we might actively and meaningfully produce alternative realities. But learning about alternative realities teaches ways to grapple with complexity and provides an awareness of other possible scripts. Through critical reflection and analysis, we learn to discern taken-for-granted beliefs and practices; through engaged, mindful participation, we contribute to the ongoing creation of mindful existence.—Jodi O'Brien and Peter E. Kollock, 2001

Democracy requires conflict.

And, like democracy, conflict is *awkward*. It makes us uncomfortable. When we are engaged in conflict, it can feel as though things are unresolved or unsettled. The tension that accompanies conflict holds a great deal of energy that can seem chaotic or frightening. It can motivate harmful actions and dissolve meaningful social relationships. But, with the right conditions and approaches, it can also be a means of creativity, freedom, and positive social change. So, what are those conditions and practices, and how can we bring them about in our democratic participation?

This book looked at the interpretations and practices of the participants of several local chapters of a grassroots progressive political party in the northeastern United States, which I call the Grassroots Action Party (or GAP), in the context of racialized political inequality. An agreement shared among white participants can become the dominant consensus within disproportionately white political organizations such as the GAP. This consensus strengthens as white participants normalize their greater access to symbolic and material resources, in-group solidarity, and social influence. However, *conflict* provides a way of creating new outcomes out of the engagement between opposing interests.

From the outside, our ability to recognize organizational conflict may be obscured by the appearance of a consensus. It gives us the impression of unity and synchronicity. Consensus is a necessary component of an organization. It organizes our understandings and actions. However, in political life, a consensus is often not just a voluntary mutual agreement over strategies and agendas. It is also a product of micropolitics or power struggles over influence within an organization. But the GAP's dominant consensus made its existing power relationships seem inevitable or natural.[1] Hence, many white participants struggled to comprehend the causes and consequences of the party's racial demographics and practices and struggled to imagine, let alone pursue, alternatives. The impact of this type of consensus is potent. Even if we do not believe in or agree with it, this collective understanding of actions, strategies, categories, and arrangements nonetheless influences our social contexts.

Throughout this book, I showed how events and issues seen as unimportant or usual to many white participants in their daily lives were, in fact, parts of larger contradictory social patterns. However, my goal in bringing these tensions to the surface is not to accuse them of hypocrisy. We are all complicated. Social life is rife with paradoxes and ambiguities. Those of us insulated by our relative social position may lack awareness of these contradictions. Whether these forms of ignorance are products of intentional individual action, external social forces, or some combination is debatable. Our awareness, or lack thereof, nonetheless matters greatly. As the psychoanalyst James Hollis writes, "The one question none of us can answer is: *of what are you unconscious*? But that which is unconscious has great power in our lives, may currently be making choices for us, and most certainly has been implicitly constructing the patterns of our personal history."[2] The underlying reasons why we do what we do in social life are notoriously complex and mysterious, even to ourselves.

The true character of our assumptions and impulses and the outcomes they contribute can elude us even as they impact us. So, the purpose of surfacing conflicts and paradoxes is to promote change where inertia and routines produce stagnation. Importantly, we are not fixed. We can be self-aware and imagine ourselves in the perceptions of others.[3] Though they may travel through well-worn paths, our habits are not set in stone. We can reflect. We can change our strategies and practices. Our self-awareness allows us to examine the interplay of our underlying beliefs and routines and how we contribute to larger forms of collective action.

Civic and political participation can change us, especially if we are open to evolving. Our social and political perspectives shift as we encounter new contexts, integrate new information and perspectives, and navigate new dilemmas. In that sense, this case study is not only bounded by space or by my focus on the American Northeast but also, importantly, by time. Indeed, this book may not fully reflect the current state of racial consciousness and political practice among the participants that allowed me to capture a snapshot of the social dynamics within these chapters of the Grassroots Action Party from 2016 to 2017. But more importantly, this snapshot can tell us so much about racial politics, democracy, and everyday life.

In my time with GAP participants, *contradictions* emerged as an important theme. Participants had contradictory accounts of their actions and the actions of others, the purpose of their organization, and the impact of various strategies and routines. Some even expressed contradictory perspectives from one conversation or interaction to the next. Faced with the appearance of contradictions, it may be tempting to conclude that our narratives and views are simply too complex to derive any meaningful conclusions. This conclusion might even make us feel fatalistic about social progress. But these contradictions are instructive and revealing. These incongruities in our ways of making sense of events and experiences are reflections of the "existing contradictions that people grapple with in everyday life."[4] Illuminating, confronting, and struggling through the contradictions of everyday life, especially within a society wrought with social divisions and oppressions, is one of the most productive enterprises in the human experience.

Whether they expressed them directly or implicitly, all the participants developed a set of assumptions, narratives, and understandings about the racial dynamics and characteristics of their communities and organizations that influenced their political actions. White participants' stories, beliefs, and interpretations reflected a lack of in-depth reflection on the structures and processes that produce racial exclusion and segregation. Consider the following quote from Harry, a white participant in the Elkington chapter: "You know, there aren't a whole lot of Black folks in our town. There's a lot of Asian folks, Middle Eastern folks, Southeast

Asians. You know, it's—but not a whole lot of Black folks. So—and that's probably having to do with the cost of the community or what have you, I don't know. I don't know what all those barriers would be. So, I would say I live in . . . a pretty homogenous community in terms of who I bump into and run into and deal with on a day-in, day-out basis."

Despite his insistence that there were "not a whole lot of Black folks," Black people comprised around 5 percent of the population in his town. While that may not seem like an incredibly high component, they comprised the largest nonwhite racial group. Moreover, Harry recognized that his own sense of community was based on those with whom he had regular and routine interactions. He did not question these assumptions, nor did he have a well-developed understanding of the social structures and processes that influenced his racialized sense of community. Despite being limited, Harry's knowledge of his community and its relationship to social divisions and inequalities was not uncommon.

Let us contrast this set of assumptions and narratives with those contained in the following quote from Chip, an Asian American participant in the Whitehall chapter, about an event that highlighted racial inequality in the organization during a racial justice protest:

> Now the table consisted of only white people. Um, now you have a march for racial justice. You're representing, um, the Grassroots Action Party, but you have no minority representation. So, the perception could have been, uh, or would naturally be, you know, at a march for racial justice, where every speaker is a person of color, you have a political party that's largely unknown, um, and it's being represented at a table with no minority representation. So sometimes perception is everything, um, you know, and if folks wrote them off because of that, then—I mean, can we really blame them?

His consideration of how the party was likely perceived demonstrates a greater tendency to engage in perspective-taking and empathy toward communities of color. Even if it led to disappointing conclusions, he considered the party's demographics and efforts in light of racialized political inequality.

In the wake of this event, Chip was active in efforts to raise racial consciousness. He recognized his white compatriots' lack of critical understanding of racial oppression. They did not have a deep awareness of the relationships between processes of racial oppression and everyday political life. Moreover, because they did not grasp this relationship, they could not conceive how it could be addressed within the organization. This was not simply a matter of their thoughts and perceptions but also their choices. Their ignorance also had massive practical implications. By noting how this interaction could have played out differently and for the better, Chip suggested that there was a need for white participants to become more comfortable with their assumptions and worldviews being challenged. They needed to be more willing to productively engage with emerging conflicts and contradictions. They needed to adopt a new approach that built mutual understanding and potential collaborations.

In his communication with fellow participants, he sought to bring racialized contradictions and tensions to light and establish a new set of norms and strategies:

> I said a lack of diversity is an issue surrounding, um, like, white supremacy in the Grassroots Action Party at center stage. Um, and so with regards to white privilege, I said you—you do possess that—as does every other white person. . . . But, um, I kind of drew it like okay, well you could have segued that into—you know, like, "Yeah, I do have privilege, and here is what I am doing to dismantle that, and here is what I am doing to dismantle white supremacy." "Oh. Here is our racial justice platform." "Um, in this section, we talked about this, and we've really been trying to work with an X group, the X group, and the X group." You know, I don't know, there are just ways to go about it, and not everybody is prepared for that. Um, and so there's a lot of *inner education* that needs to be done for our own Grassroots Action Party folks.

Looking at these contradictory perceptions and perspectives reveals the micro-level and everyday challenges to building multiracial coalitions for grassroots progressive movements. It provides us insights about how, in Chip's words, *"inner education"* to gain racial literacy is a critical catalyst to *outer liberation* to achieve racial equality. Participants of color actively grappled with their organization's tensions and limitations. Many concluded that a process of intra-organizational reflection and consciousness-raising would have to precede any shifts in the habits and political strategies of the organization. They had every intention of working toward this goal of raising racial consciousness. The content of communications between members also suggested this imminent change. For example, some white participants began to discuss resources via email about antiracist training intended to identify and address their unconscious participation in maintaining racial oppression. While the outcome of these attempts at education and personal growth among participants is unclear, these issues began to gain wider recognition and attention. Conflict brings about discomforting awareness of contradictions but also provokes productive efforts at building a new organizational consensus out of those contradictions.

CASES, CONVERSATIONS, AND CONCLUSIONS

Until marginalized communities and their allies redefine self-interest, recognize common cause, and find ways to coordinate with one another, large-scale social change will likely remain elusive.
—Jennifer Richeson, 2015

My goal with this book was to find ways to break through the dilemmas and dynamics of grassroots democracy in the context of racialized political inequality. I focused on the experiences and activities of people who occupied space within those dilemmas and dynamics. In other words, though this book is a *case study*, it tells us about much more than this specific case, local chapters of a grassroots progressive political party in the northeastern United States, or even a particular population such as white people, people of color, or grassroots progressive organizers. This case embodies the paradox of contemporary US politics and society found in the coexistence of the ideals of democracy and equality and the realities of racial oppression.[5]

I sought to unearth new understandings of a problematic contemporary situation at the nexus of political and social life that many of us traverse and work to change. Three questions motivated this work in particular: First, what are the challenges of forming multiracial coalitions for progressive social change? Second, how can we, as activists, educators, organizers, or other practitioners, overcome these challenges? And finally, how can we prevent our organizations and political strategies from simply reproducing the racial inequalities and boundaries of our society rather than challenging them? These answers would not come through merely reporting what I did and witnessed during this project. To answer these questions, I put the themes and patterns I observed in my research *in conversation* with each other and other facts and theories. I considered the relationship between large-scale social forces and structures, regional, local, and organizational contexts, and everyday patterns of interpretation and action. In this final chapter, I offer an overview of what I found. I also share some conclusions about racial politics, praxis, and everyday life.

Struggling to Secure a Sense of Self

Chapter 2 emphasized three components that undergirded how GAP participants made meaning of their identities as grassroots progressives: geographic and social contexts; major political and social events; and racial identities, practices, and meanings. Yet these dimensions also revealed the cracks and fissures within the continuity of this collective identity.

GAP participants defined their political sense of self compared to the regional political elite represented by state and local Democratic Party leaders. These claims were bolstered by examples of entrenched barriers to democratic engagement at the local level, cases of controversy and corruption, and articulations of the DNC's hypocrisy and political centrism or conservatism. Dissatisfaction with the policies and strategies of the Democratic Party enabled participants to position their organization as more authentically democratic and egalitarian and make broader critiques of the political system.

For many of us, a concern for the health of democracy drives our engagement in progressive grassroots politics. This concern provides a valued ideal and a point of solidarity. Yet, as we become more active in our participation, we also develop an underlying sense of pessimism toward the current political process in the United States due to its embedded corruption, political inequality, and exclusion of the voices of ordinary people. Similarly, GAP participants expressed awareness of the paradox between the reality of elite domination and the possibility of democracy. This democratic consciousness motivated participants to advocate for radical political and social transformations and develop strategies of political action.

Our reactions to large-scale political events and trends like the 2016 presidential election further mold our sense of self and our understanding of democracy. The election held dire consequences for progressive issues and causes. Yet younger GAP participants who saw themselves as pragmatists found ways to rationalize the results. Some relied on their status as outsiders of the two-party system to downplay the consequences. Others saw the 2016 election as further exemplifying the dysfunction of the US political process. GAP participants who had been in the party for longer and saw themselves as activists used the election and its implications as an opportunity to articulate a commitment to the multifaceted issues and ideals that drove their participation in the first place. One participant even drastically reduced his high-level involvement in leadership positions and scaled back to a rank-and-file member. In contrast, others who had been swayed toward the Democratic Party by the rise of Bernie Sanders as a democratic socialist and potential contender for the nomination found themselves disappointed with Hillary Clinton's primary victory.

Racial meanings and practices served as an additional source of political identity for GAP participants, producing unity and division. Given the racially conservative politics of the Republican Party and the racially centrist politics of the regionally dominant Democratic Party, grassroots progressive political organizations can potentially represent and advance racially progressive practices and policy agendas. Yet not only was the party disproportionately dominated by whites, but the participants also struggled, for numerous reasons, to actualize their commitments to these ideals and outcomes.

The demographics of their organizations and communities, racial ideologies, and everyday actions were also sites for political identity formation and negotiation. GAP participants articulated the relationships between their ideals about racial justice and the makeup and activities of their organization in diverse ways. To explain how the party's racial justice platform failed to translate into greater racial equity and inclusion, some pointed to the dominance of the Democratic Party and the barriers constraining grassroots organizing. This explanation connected to the depiction of political elites as having no real solidarity or empathy for communities of color but using them to advance their causes. Others pointed out that their racially progressive political agenda could help build a multiracial coalition but acknowledged that the party struggled to manifest this possibility fully.

The party's progressive stances on racial justice issues motivated participants of color to remain invested. They saw it as a potential catalyst for altering the racialized practices of the organization and its relationship with surrounding communities. It was an opportunity to align political strategies and solidarities with racially progressive ideals and stated racial justice goals. But these ideals and policy agendas often failed to materialize greater and more substantive inclusion and empowerment of people of color within and through the party. Like the contrast between the ideals of democracy and the reality of political inequality, the gap between the organization's antiracist ideals and its routine practices and their outcomes created tension.

Moreover, it manifested in varied and incoherent articulations of political strategy. Underneath this vague but uniting grassroots progressive political vision were conflicting approaches to political organizing. Participants of color wanted the party to engage in racially conscious efforts at external outreach and internal leadership development to enhance the empowerment and inclusion of communities of color. In comparison, the primarily white majority preferred a more color-blind or passive approach while rationalizing extant forms of inequity and exclusion.

How the participants made sense of relative gains, losses, and challenges in making their racial justice and inclusivity agenda come to fruition further linked racial meanings to grassroots progressive political identity. While the structural blockades faced by grassroots political organizations were well known and acknowledged among almost all participants, participants of color were much more likely to understand, describe, and problematize the specific racialized barriers to political influence and agency endemic to politics and society in the United States. Nonetheless, racial meanings and interpretations of the racial structure stand alongside the impact of regional culture and politics and the ongoing meaning-making of large-scale events and trends as crucial aspects of creating, maintaining, and transforming grassroots progressive political identity. Significantly, it also impacts political strategies.

Conventions and Contradictions

Almost everyone I interacted with in the party agreed that recruiting a racially diverse membership and set of candidates and advancing racially progressive policies was a worthwhile goal and an ideal outcome. On the other hand, its racial demographics remained predominantly white, and significant barriers to achieving these goals often went unacknowledged or unaddressed by white participants. Chapter 3 explored how this tension between ideals and reality was met with *awkwardness* and *discomfort* among white participants.

Chapter 4 uncovered how white participants in the GAP engaged in deliberations, practices, and routine interactions that marginalized people of color from involvement in the party and impacted its political strategies.

I highlighted patterns and trends in white participants' racial consciousness, habits, and relations to social and geographic space. For instance, racialized forms of socialization played a critical role in how they perceived opportunities, problems, and strategies. Many white GAP participants grew up in racially segregated communities (in both social and geographic patterns) that isolated them from repeated and intimate interactions with people of color and prevented opportunities for growing their racial consciousness through engagement with more diverse experiences.

Despite white participants' stated intentions and goals, their sense of self and daily habits reflected their functional relationship to racial oppression. These routine practices have a covert but decisive influence over the distribution of political power and engagement among racial groups. Their tactics and behaviors often focused on navigating or rationalizing but not disrupting the racialized political inequality in their organization and the wider society. Additionally, new habits and strategies that might facilitate these organizational and social transformations were often undermined by an inability to envision and pursue them and a feeling of uneasiness.

Responses from white participants exhibited a lack of serious and profound reflection and engagement with issues of racial oppression and methods of attaining racial justice. They expressed a paralyzing mix of uncertainty or indecision when confronted with the real or imagined task of building multiracial coalitions and empowering communities of color. These patterns reflected, among other things, the constrained racial consciousness they had developed as both a product and a catalyst of living in racially isolated and white-dominated social settings.[6] Moreover, they normalized and universalized these experiences and failed to imagine the connection to centuries of racist policies and practices.

For instance, participants often held unrealistic ideas about the ethnic makeup of their communities and cities. By interrogating why some had downplayed racial diversity in their geographic region, I came to understand the functional purpose of these beliefs. It may have partially derived from misinformation or from extrapolating their social networks. However, it also enabled them to rationalize the whiteness of their organization and familiar social worlds. Their social position in the system of white supremacy thus offered two symbolic resources: a sense that their views of whiteness as normative and universal were legitimate and the ability to maintain distance from experiences and perspectives that would provoke challenges to these assumptions.

Additionally, while these participants had been some of the most well-spoken advocates for progressive politics I had ever engaged with, they had considerable difficulty analyzing and articulating the relationship between systems of racial oppression and their daily lives and political practices. This lack of articulation was a major stumbling block to identifying and discussing practical pathways to achieving racial equity within and through the party. Moreover, several white participants became anxious or wary when I discussed racial justice and inequality in informal conversations and interviews.

Several white participants implied that the onus was not on them but on grassroots progressives of color to find out about the party and try to show up and engage at events and meetings. Participants' relative awareness of the implications of racial oppression for everyday life correlated with the forms of political outreach they advocated and the motivations they cited for their participation. Participants that lacked critical racial consciousness were more likely to express personal and individual incentives for their involvement in grassroots progressive politics, see democratic engagement as a mode of self-actualization, and advocate for strategies that encouraged orthodox political conversion.

There was a routine avoidance of articulating how the collective practices of the party related to racial inequalities and injustices. Many participants expressed support for antiracism and moral outrage at overtly racist events. However, evasion of these issues had become normative behavior. For instance, rather than discussing the practical implications and how the party can practice solidarity and support, participants in organization meetings made light of racial inequalities and power disparities or implied that there were other more critical issues to tackle, such as fundraising, other progressive causes, or upcoming or recent events of note.

Positioning themselves as antiracists often depended on white participants holding abstract moral beliefs about racism. Yet these beliefs were undermined by these participants' social networks, habits, and interpretations of everyday life. They could only imagine the purpose and motivating force behind hypothetical efforts to mobilize and engage people of color or any other underrepresented group as benefiting the organization. The chief goal of such engagement was not to help offset local disparities in political power between social groups but to provide an instrument through which the party could attain power and have more impact. White participants often acted on unspoken racialized assumptions about the residents of various communities, what concerns to prioritize in planning

and strategizing, their image of the ideal participant or most likely sup-
porter, which spaces and people were suitable investments of resources,
or what social and political issues they should prioritize.

These collective habits were also a source of comfort and motivation for
many of the most active veteran participants. White participants often expressed that they liked the GAP because they enjoyed being around others
with whom they felt a sense of shared convictions, friendliness, sociabil-
ity, and ease. However, this reliance on familiarity and agreeableness also
limited the organization's ability to grow and change. White participants
also sought to maintain a sense of continuity and ownership. Accordingly,
some even expressed that avoiding too much rapid inclusion of new participants was preferential, regardless of whether it would help them advance
a racial justice agenda or internal racial equity practices.

An implicit desire for continued ownership or control over the group
had, in effect, limited efforts to include new participants from diverse
backgrounds. Many white participants did not just exhibit a penchant
for maintaining a sense of authority within the organization and their
general approach to new people, contexts, and knowledge. In events that
included new potential participants from underrepresented groups, older
white participants prioritized acts of distinction that demonstrated their
credentials and knowledge base rather than developing new practices,
strategies, and insights.

However, the destruction or alteration of dominant norms, meanings,
and practices does not simply bring about change. It requires the creative act of producing new and better norms, meanings, and practices
or, in this case, new ways of political life. However, the racial politics of
most white GAP participants was a means of self-identification rather
than a wellspring of dynamic action. Because they could not creatively and
productively acknowledge and rethink the contradictions between their
intentions and outcomes, they could not rearticulate their racial politics
and recalibrate themselves toward other possibilities. Consequently, the
social and organizational barriers to the political empowerment of people
of color and the elimination of racialized political inequality through the
party remained intact.

Counternarratives and Critical Consciousness

Despite the overrepresentation and disproportionate influence of white
participants, and even individual chapters of the organization being entirely composed of whites, the GAP was not an all-white organization.

In chapter 4, I highlighted the lived experiences, interpretations, social habits, and political strategies of participants of color in the GAP. Focusing solely on whiteness in political life obscures alternate pathways that could lead to actual grassroots democratic practices and bring about racial equality.

Many expressed the dual challenges of transforming the organization to be more inclusive, equitable, and focused on racial justice goals and changing the broader political system and society. They provided counternarratives that contested the white consensus of the party and shed light on the promise of alternative modes of political praxis and awareness. Participants of color largely agreed that the standard modes of understanding racialized political inequality among the white participants influenced and sometimes even controlled the organization's agenda, political tactics, and collective identity. I refer to this dynamic as the party's *white consensus*.

Participants of color stressed that evolving the party into a medium for racial justice and advancing the interests of communities of color was their strongest motivation for continued participation. They also engaged with conflict as a creative resource rather than something to be outright avoided. Increasing awareness around intrinsic tensions and paradoxes was a potential catalyst for further developing and improving the party and recalibrating its impacts on society. They encouraged greater acknowledgment and consciousness of the limitations and downsides of the party's racial norms and demographics. However, participants of color noted destructive conflict alongside creative and productive engagements. For example, some participants of color ultimately became discouraged by the white consensus, perceived a lack of efficacy within the organization, and retreated to other organizations and modes of political influence.

Participants of color recognized that the party's white consensus reflected an internal set of customs, implicit rules, and assumptions that marginalized and disempowered participants of color. Efforts at growth and outreach were constantly undermined by the pervasive reputation among outsiders as white space. In response, participants of color advocated for the importance of engaging with conflict and tensions to change the party and society. Yet these participants also emphasized that their approach to conflict and change was not aimed at producing greater intraparty divisions around identity groups, escalating conflict for its own sake, or advancing their status. They pointed out that the GAP remained a predominantly white organization due to resistance to the perspectives and suggestions of people of color.

For instance, when considering the prospects of engaging communities of color, many white participants could only envision doing so to convert new participants. Participants of color advocated that the party should build authentic relationships with marginalized racial and ethnic communities by extending backing and empathy for the goals and problems of their residents. Moreover, they saw changes to the conditions of communities rather than party power attainment or personally rising in the party ranks as their most crucial motivating goal. Participants of color had cultivated a more authentic and thought-out disposition towards liberation from racial oppression because of their unambiguous experiences of the harms of these systems.[7]

Participants of color knew that marginalized racial communities held a sense of apt suspicion toward white organizations and institutions that viewed them as instruments in the quest to consolidate power. However, an extractive approach was routinely injected by white participants. The idea of solidarity was essential to participants of color. Their solidarity was based on a felt bond to marginalized communities and a vision of linked fate with their members. Moreover, this deeply felt value of solidarity was intrinsic to their habits and political and personal goals. It directed them to promote and pursue distinct lines of political action that contrasted with the larger collective within the organization. They stressed that the party should be flexible, sensitive, and responsive to the needs and context of community members rather than attempting to influence and control them for political purposes.

Another chief distinction and conflict emerged over the character of the party's engagement with communities in the wake of events or crises. The white consensus was oriented around the imposition of structure and order. These interpretations and practices saw a priority in the current party leadership remaining in charge of engagement efforts to direct the emotional energy brought on by these events toward the political and electoral goals of the party. This approach dismissed impacted communities' passion, resources, and wisdom. It also held the potential to dismiss those communities or issues as fundamentally discordant with the party. In contrast, participants of color realized the intrinsic worth of extending and transforming the party to act as a means for people of color to achieve political equality and combat racial oppression. Additionally, these modes of engagement should arise spontaneously in response to the needs and initiatives of community members.

The practical implications of reckoning with the party's limitations to actualize racial justice suggested affording more influence to those with a broader and more in-depth awareness of racial oppression's social and political impacts. Participants of color possessed distinct abilities to recognize openings and promote practices for organizational and social transformation. Accordingly, participants of color expressed a strong desire to take greater control over the organization. They focused such changes on altering its outreach strategies and inclusion of people of color and the actualization and prioritization of its racial justice agenda. Yet being made solely responsible for the internal work of changing the organization placed an additional burden on participants of color that could potentially lead to burnout without greater support. The narrative that those most worthy of engagement are already most likely to participate due to their social position falls apart in the face of the evidence. It is a losing strategy that reinforces racialized political inequality. Yet the motivating goal of engagement must be about the political empowerment of the communities themselves rather than a specific predetermined political outcome.

AGENCY, ACCURACY, AND ACTION

If we—and now I mean the relatively conscious whites and the relatively conscious blacks, who must, like lovers, insist on, or create, the consciousness of the others—do not falter in our duty now, we may be able, handful that we are, to end the racial nightmare, and achieve our country, and change the history of the world.
—James Baldwin, 1963

Racialized political inequality has been a consistent feature of US society since its inception. The mechanisms producing this form of inequality may have changed over time. But the overall outcome has mainly remained static.[8] The distribution of resources and power has consistently favored those racialized as white. The state and political sphere in the United States is not simply a neutral terrain of racial pluralism and competing interests.[9] Regardless, contestation remains a fundamental aspect of racialized political power dynamics.[10] So, understanding racial politics in the United States requires acknowledging people's agency to contest existing structures of racial oppression.

As sociologist Victor E. Ray points out, "Organizations consolidate re-sources along racial lines in ways that constrain (or enable) human action, seeing organizations as racial structures describes one domain through which racial actors express agency."[11] Our ability to make choices that im-pact outcomes is amplified or muted by the arrangement of resources in society and organizations.[12] Yet agency is not only a product of institu-tional and social structures. It also has subjective components. It is shaped by our internal sense of efficacy or our understanding of our own ability to affect outcomes. Our sense of self and group interests influences it. When it comes to organized efforts at social transformation, our sense of agency is enhanced by the belief that concerted, collective action can change structural conditions and that such changes are not only possible but also liberating and necessary.[13] This sense of possibility and necessity drove the practices of GAP participants of color.

Most white participants expressed a sense of being unable to address the unequal racial dynamics of the party. Some felt that it was not their responsibility. Others felt unable to problematize and address these issues thoroughly. Yet a lack of awareness does not mean a lack of action or ac-tivities. It is not purely passive. Ignorance produces a gap that we fill with other forms of practical knowledge using our agency. Participants all had some explanation for the racial structure and practices of the party, even if they were incomplete or inaccurate. As sociologist Ali Meghji writes, "This creativity is seen in white people constantly finding ways to deploy racialized representations when they are not applicable, and in white peo-ple mutating these representations to make them more acceptable in the relevant interactional setting."[14] In other words, when we act on a set of assumptions, even implicit ones, an act of creativity and imagination is still at work.

We use our agency as we attempt to resolve contradictions. Contra-dictions do not merely exist between racialized groups of people but also between racial meanings and structures. The relationship between racial meanings and structural racism is vital to racial oppression. Power rela-tions play a big part in how we interpret the world and how our society is organized. We strategically use meaning-making practices to perceive and act upon the racial structure. With them, we form and protect a racialized sense of self, rationalize our actions, subvert dominant meanings, and con-sider opportunities for social transformation. We do all this while also nav-igating the racial meanings circulated, amplified, and silenced on a large scale by powerful institutions such as mass media and the political system.

Reconciling the contradictions between dominant narratives, categories, and explanations, and the realities of racial oppression, opens space for racial justice struggles. This is the basic premise of rearticulation. In other words, our collective action and social change efforts are energized by recognizing tensions and contradictions and seeking new ways forward. Through rearticulation, grassroots political organizations can be a vehicle for advancing new strategies, critiques, stories, and habits that tear at the legitimacy of dominant racial meanings.[15]

Seeing the connections and consequences of contradictions requires a certain level of mindful awareness and comfort with conflict. We must identify the racialized impacts of what the monk and peace activist Thich Nhat Hanh calls the "illusion of our separateness."[16] This habituated, institutionalized illusion obscures a holistic view of racial oppression. It naturalizes racialized space and disparities in resources and power.[17] However, sociological research and practice reveal the connections between otherwise separate things. As these illusions evaporate, we have an opportunity to develop new understandings of the connections that become visible. We gain *accuracy* in diagnosing racial inequality and acting in the world accordingly.

As a society, we focus so heavily on political parties' cold and calculated strategies to explain major events and outcomes. So, to benefit readers, I hope to offer a fresh perspective on democracy, racial oppression, and our daily routines. Through my analysis of progressive grassroots organizations and the variety of ways they engage the ongoing impacts of racial oppression, I discovered that consciousness and habits, perhaps even more so than intentional strategies, are drivers of social change and the reproduction of harmful inequalities. Paradoxically, the patterns of our social lives are both durable and dynamic. From a sociological perspective, dominant institutional arrangements and outcomes such as inequality persist across time and space. From a historical perspective, we can see social systems as impermanent and conducive to change.

Habits and Harms

So much of our discussions of political life focus on the intentional and rational strategies people use to achieve their goals. However, our somewhat irrational and semiconscious habits shape political outcomes. Our social habits are the patterned sets of actions we take and assumptions we make, day in and day out, without much thought. Habits are not bad in and of themselves. The habitual nature of social life and interactions is not some fundamental human failing. It is a pragmatic element of social life. What matters is the causes and consequences of our habits. In this sense, focusing on the *racial habits* we engage in during our democratic engagement helps us understand and challenge the racialized inequalities that characterize political life in the United States.

Observing and analyzing the daily experiences and practices of grassroots progressives reveals the centrality of habits in the relationship between social and political life. The rise and growth of progressive grassroots organizations and actors signal emergent forms of racialized collective action through this political movement. In other words, grassroots progressives make up a racial project within the larger sphere of racial politics.[18] Sociologists Michael Omi and Howard Winant define racial projects as "attempts to both shape the ways in which social structures are racially signified and the ways that racial meanings are embedded in social structures."[19] However, studying racial projects by focusing on *attempts* rather than practices suggests a narrow focus on purely tactical and rational forms of action. These assumptions would lead us to treat our collective action as something inherently strategic and intentional. We miss out on a part of the story when we see the organizations and movements that make up racialized collective action as almost anthropomorphic vehicles for goal attainment.

On the other hand, the concept of racial projects focuses on *outcomes* and categorizes antiracist and racist projects based on their impacts on the racial order. Outcome-oriented research can demonstrate meaningful relationships but often fails to show how outcomes are produced, sustained, and changed. Rationalistic and outcome-oriented approaches to racial politics reveal important things but obscure others. Seeing the relationship between movements and organizations and racialized political inequality requires looking at social processes in their immediate real-life context. So, in this book, I sought to expand our understanding of racial projects by looking at micro-decisions in collective action and the implicit communication and habitual social actions that undergird social and political life.

By only focusing on what people say they want to do or naming the immense consequences of a particular movement or organization, we forget a crucial aspect of racialization and oppression—that it is an ongoing social process. The linchpin of our collective political action is the routine, patterned, habitual social actions amid our political engagement in a racially stratified society. Seeing this dimension requires a structurally informed interactionist approach to democratic engagement. I have sought to cultivate such an approach in this book. I encourage scholars and practitioners to continue to build on this foundation. In other words, drawing on the GAP participant Walter's realization about his habits of racial silence in chapter 4, we need to pay attention to the "invisible etiquette" that governs everyday life, even in people's political participation.

While I have brought to light the consequences of specific racial habits, habits in and of themselves are not harmful in political life; many benefits of habituation and routinization in political organizations and collective action exist. In a sense, participants must have some consensus about recursive actions for collective political entities to function. It ingrains the organizational identity into the everyday life of participants. It also maintains the movement and encourages continued engagement. Habits become crystalized and grounded in individual identity and meaning making them about the self while also holding the potential of impacting social arrangements. Throughout this study, I identified ways that habits grounded in community and solidarity can transform individuals, organizations, and society. Moreover, habituation motivates emotional and energetic investment, particularly from dominant group members who want to express their ideals and characteristics through political actions.

However, I also identified the limitations of habits. I highlighted some downsides of forms of dominant group habituation by paying attention to conflicts about recursive actions between white participants and participants of color. First, I found a negative relationship between the habits of the dominant group and the need to be dynamic in the face of new challenges and opportunities, rearticulate new strategies, and cultivate new rituals and routines. Relatedly, these dominant habits render organizations less able to be responsive to real human communities that face the dire consequences of social and political problems rather than abstract ideals. Moreover, the dominant group consensus about collective and organizational habits reduces their willingness to embrace contradictions and conflict as a source of growth because it threatens individual identity and meaning-making practices. In other words, dominant group members tend to use grassroots progressive politics to define themselves as a certain kind of person. Instead, those in that category need to critically reflect on the practical implications of our habits and routines for issues like racialized political inequality. This critical introspection and the ability to act on it is a matter of realizing our agency.

ACTIVATING AGENCY

Our actions are shaped by the *structure* of external social constraints and the *agency* we use to make individual choices.[20] The context of racial oppression is crucial for understanding the interplay between structure and agency in modern society. The social system, meso-level organizations, the interaction order, and our agency are all deeply racialized.[21] As sociologist Ali Meghji writes, "Without bringing agency into the equation, we are left in a situation whereby the social-structure perfectly mirrors itself in the interactional order, with little room for individual creativity or maneuver."[22] Racial oppression operates through structure *and* agency to constrict power and resources among elite whites and obliterate social freedom for the masses.

Moreover, there is a crucial difference between *agency* and *responsibility*. That difference is a matter of power. Reversing the course of racist social reproduction requires maximizing marginalized groups' agency. We must create and embed new practices and arrangements that support efforts at self-definition and self-direction for people of color. This task is daunting, taken at face value. But it can also be rendered as something more pragmatic. Grassroots political organizations can grow the sense of responsibility of dominant groups and the sense of agency of marginalized groups through habituating five practices: *leveling, listening, accountability, discomfort*, and *deep reflection*. Ultimately, these practices enable a more accurate vision of the relationship between racial oppression and everyday social actions to emerge.

Leveling describes practices ensuring social hierarchies and inequalities do not form within groups. These can be explicit rules, implicit norms, ingrained habits, or other social mechanisms. In the context of a political organization, leveling explicitly needs to center on not reproducing external social inequalities within the internal dynamics of the collective and the organizational structure. Leveling practices were already taking place in the GAP. For instance, rules to ensure gender parity, such as having multiple leaders and officers, at least one of whom is not male, were instituted in some of the chapters. Yet leveling practices that sought to eradicate the impact of external racial inequalities within the party were essentially nonexistent.

Developing effective leveling practices for diminishing racialized political inequality requires *listening* to the experiences and perspectives of people of color. Instituting the process of listening and making it a part of our routine allows for essential insights to come into view. It produces a more concrete understanding of the barriers to equality, empathy for the experiences these barriers create, and a greater feeling of mutual solidarity and trust. From listening, dominant group members also learn to rethink their *accountability* and to practice political actions in service of communities rather than in service of a moral ideal or personal value.

To realize these three dimensions, everyone in the organization, especially dominant group members, must cultivate a greater tolerance for *discomfort*. Changing our everyday social patterns and sense of self can be quite unsettling even as it is necessary. Finally, effectively transforming political organizations requires *deep reflection* on the causes and consequences of current practices grounded in the understandings gained from listening.

Overt, institutionalized, and intentional forms of excluding people of color from exercising the vote and other political and civil rights and participating in decision-making persist. Racialized barriers remain even if they have different names and mechanics than in the past. Movements that take up the cause of bringing about more significant inclusion in democracy and combating these forms of oppression are always actively engaged in the work of social change and justice. Grassroots parties are one such important vehicle for racial justice in society. Yet, within grassroots political organizations that take on progressive goals, benevolent intentions are rendered meaningless when they become paired with collective habits formed without adequate racial consciousness and literacy.

Racial justice and grassroots political organizations are a logical fit. After all, racial justice cannot be achieved without mass participation in democracy. Racial justice is only realized when we consider the interests and perspectives of all human beings through the strengthening of democracy.[23] Democracy helps people get together and collectively produce a vision of justice through participation and deliberation. The democratic enterprise is not about merely telling people their interests, the just or fair outcomes of political contestations, or the correct sets of actions to take.

It helps people bring forth their own insights, wisdom, and perspectives so that an organic vision of a more fair and equal society, and the steps to create that society, can emerge. Democracy means employing engagement as a remedy for ignorance.

Racial oppression produces estrangement, alienation, and social division between people. It takes intentionality to break down the stereotypes and assumptions that maintain racial hierarchies. Inclusive participation in democracy is a mechanism to unite people divided by inequity. This requires actively working to dismantle the misunderstandings that prevent people from collectively finding new ways to solve problems and improve communities. Democratic spaces that not only include but empower socially marginalized groups help fulfill W. E. B. Du Bois's vision of social progress: "The history of the world is the history of the discovery of the common humanity of human beings among steadily-increasing circles of men."[24] Yet there is an inherent potential for discomfort and conflict that comes with inclusion and democratic enfranchisement.

The process of individual and social transformation is necessarily uncomfortable. It unsettles the present state of things. We often derive our sense of comfort and security from the idea that we can depend upon things to remain a certain way. However, an equitable democracy is one in which temporary discomfort, uncertainty, or *awkwardness* does not prevent us from fully acknowledging and addressing the full humanity of each other. The outcome of an inclusive and equitable democracy that gives voice to the understandings and experiences of excluded groups is a more empathetic, nourishing, and just social context for everyone involved. Comfort and discomfort are racialized. For people of color, experiencing racial discrimination and controlling images is necessarily uncomfortable. Moreover, racial disparities in social power dictate whose comfort matters in the definition of the situation.[25] Yet white grassroots progressives can and should use their agency to engage in discomfort and resolve the contradictions—between their practices and intentions and their strategies and outcomes.

Research Appendix
Poking and Prying with a Purpose

Research is formalized curiosity. It is poking and prying with a purpose.
—Zora Neale Hurston, 1942

Researching democracy is also awkward.

I began this study with a curiosity about the possibilities and limitations of grassroots democracy in a society structured by racial oppression. I was motivated to better understand these issues to advance democratic participation. I determined that the Grassroots Action Party (GAP), a progressive grassroots political organization with regional chapters in the northeastern United States, would be an excellent well from which to quench my thirst for deeper understanding.

Through proposals, planning, feedback from colleagues and mentors, and early encounters, I developed a loose idea of what I would do and why. But it all felt very speculative. It was difficult to imagine myself doing any of these things and even harder to picture what would come of them. So I did what I suspect many ethnographers do, whether they admit it or not. I continued to show up, take notes, ask questions, pay attention, and see what happened.

Ethnographic research is less about frantically searching for patterns in the social world and more about having the patience and curiosity to let them appear over time. Up-close, on-the-ground participation and observation can be challenging and tedious. Some of the most trying elements include gaining and sustaining access to events at inconvenient times or locations; noticing and recording relevant social patterns unfolding throughout the field site; and navigating the fine line between social interactions and research practices.[1] The monotony and trials of this approach, however, enable it to reveal what would otherwise remain obscured.

I finally felt that this study was revealing answers when I could anticipate how respondents would answer my questions. I also began to identify similar patterns occurring among multiple chapters of the organization. Some of these moments felt surreal. Two of the local chapters of the GAP faced contestations over dissatisfaction with their organization's name during the same week. At another point, in interviews only one day apart, participants of color from differing regional chapters expressed a desire to implement some training or education to raise the racial consciousness of their white compatriots. During the final month of this study, things happening in the field felt oddly predictable and repetitive.

This book draws on a case study using three forms of qualitative data: (1) participant observation, (2) semistructured interviews, and (3) documents retrieved from the field. My overarching goal was to record and identify patterns and variations in the meanings and practices of the participants of regional chapters of this grassroots political organization. The study focuses on specific sites and groups of people as the "case." The case reflects its context, such as the demographic and political dynamics in the northeastern United States. However, I focused on the patterns and relationships among participants' discourse and action within the case. Rather than seeking to generalize about a population, I aimed to produce insights useful for analysts and practitioners.

ETHNOGRAPHY AND EXPLORATION

Today, the ethnographer knows she does not have much understanding of her own world, whether that world is referred to in terms of the absence of culture under contemporary conditions, the continuously unfolding contemporary, the great transformation, or with one of the current terms for the mysteries of the present situation.
—David A. Westbrook, 2008

I tried to spend as much time with the participants as possible and joined their activities when feasible. This intensive engagement helped me produce a sensitivity toward "the meanings that the people under study attribute to their social and political reality."[2] Throughout my time in the field, I interacted with participants at political events such as door-to-door campaigning, meals, informal social gatherings, fundraisers, protests, and standing outside with candidate signs during elections. As both a participant and an observer, my goal was to understand how people understood and reacted to the critical situation of racialized political inequality in their grassroots democratic practices.

Matters of Methodology

Research is replete with practical challenges. I observed the meetings and activities of the participants and took notes on their statements and actions. I used the notes feature on my iPhone as a discreet method of recording observations. This technique also facilitated the transfer of my field notes to my computer so that I could flesh them out as more detailed memos. Sometimes, for various reasons, I could not record notes while in the field. I recorded voice memos on my phone as I drove long distances home from meetings and events to avoid losing the details and impressions etched in my mind. Capturing and retaining as many vivid descriptions as possible of the events that unfolded was an ongoing challenge. Every time I returned home from the field, I would engage in a "brain dump," forgoing all other activities and social contact until I had typed out as much relevant information as possible from my encounter.

Access was another practical matter. I faced a relatively smooth transition into the political and social world of the GAP chapters. I began my contact in the field site by attending a large regional meeting held by the Grassroots Action Party and networking with participants. I expanded my field site to include interviews with the participants of six regional subsections of the organization. I focused my participant observation on the meetings and organizational events of three regional subgroups spanning three states. At meetings, I introduced myself to the attendees. During this introduction and subsequent conversations, I explained that I was both a participant in grassroots politics and a sociologist interested in understanding democracy and social inequality. I announced that, as a sociologist, I was studying the experiences and stories of people who participate in progressive grassroots politics.

However, this study was nearly inclusive of multiple parties. At a large gathering of progressive activists sponsored by the GAP, another grassroots progressive party had set up a table for recruitment. I introduced myself and asked about their interest in my project. A few weeks later, I met with a few participants at a coffee shop. They were intrigued but expressed three major concerns. First, they worried that I would misunderstand the organization if I approached it as an identity-based social movement rather than a party engaged in revolutionary political struggle. Second, they were afraid that I would record and write about their strategies and inner culture in a way that could be taken out of context. Finally, one of the participants who had a background in social science had investigated my previous research on race and racism. They were anxious that I would advance a narrative that grassroots progressives are just white men who don't engage with racial oppression or people of color.

They offered to participate in interviews but not ethnographic observations if I offered participants coauthorship or the ability to proofread manuscripts.[3] I told them that while I understood, ultimately, the work would reflect on myself rather than the organization's reputation, and that I just wanted to understand how grassroots progressives deal with challenges in organizing, including racial inequality. All I could promise was anonymity and a commitment to telling the story from my perspective and drawing insights and conclusions based on my reading of the narratives and actions of others. They agreed to discuss it further and get back to me. Two months later, I received an email asking if I had rethought whether I would give them the final say over any publications from the project. I respectfully declined.

Deciding where and when to be in contact with participants and the field was another problem. I had a plethora of obligations weighing down on me simultaneously. But "immersion in a community, a cohort, a locale, or a cluster of related subject positions," as much as was logistically possible, was a guiding principle.[4] On average, I spent between two and ten hours with participants per week. I attended two to four monthly organization meetings alongside additional informal and structured socializing with participants. Data collection often involved extensive traveling and tight scheduling.

By engaging in the daily lives of participants rather than just organizational events, my project "expands . . . how we understand the boundaries of the 'political.'"[5] I spent time with participants in more informal settings— coffee shops, diners, bookstores, libraries, ice cream shops, and at their homes. By participating in their dilemmas, conflicts, successes, and downfalls, I could better take on their perspectives. It allowed me to see how people act in various settings. It enabled me to ask questions grounded in my actual participation and observations. Moreover, spending time with GAP participants outside of the traditional spaces bounded by the organization helped me develop a higher level of rapport and interpersonal comfort.

Finally, what a researcher does with their findings is another practical matter. Rather than building toward grand and potentially abstract theories about how society operates, I wanted to develop "a 'pragmatics' that would assess knowledge claims in terms of context, purposes, and consequences."[6] Drawing heavily on this pragmatist approach to sociology provided two benefits. First, it enabled me to develop dynamic and flexible interpretations of situations that reflected the uniqueness of each interaction and the broader context of racialized political inequality. Second, it allowed me to focus on identifying the consequences of a set of social actions. Intending to provide readers with actionable and practical knowledge, I endeavored to "ethically or politically assess potential consequences" of actions and interactions.[7]

The Case Is Crucial

In this book I set out to resolve a paradox: the persistence of normalized whiteness and racial inequities within organizations dedicated to racial equity, political empowerment of people of color, and grassroots democracy. This case study helped me gain "a recognition and an understanding of where the case differs from what is normal or expected."[8] This paradox represented the unexplained and unexpected effects of social systems on participants' everyday lives. Using knowledge of broader historical, social, and political patterns, processes, and trends, I contextualized the interpretations and understandings of those within this case study. Through placing the findings within the context of broader social forces and outcomes, I was able to "juxtapose what people say they are up to against what they actually do."[9] I uncovered participants' logic, worldviews, habits, and assumptions, to not only understand their everyday lives but to analyze them in relation to broader political and societal circumstances.

While I found relevant frameworks and theories, none conclusively explained the patterns and processes I observed in the field. Working through emergent tensions and synthesizing previously disparate conceptions of the social world proved fruitful. This approach allowed me to derive new explanations for the patterns in my data that advanced established theories and generated knowledge useful for political praxis and social change.

The Situation Is the Subject

This book is based on a case study. Perhaps more importantly, though, what is this study a case *of*?[10] The subject of this study is *grassroots democratic participation within a racially stratified and politically unequal society*. Rather than simply describing a group of grassroots progressives, I wanted to understand the social and political situation that participants in grassroots progressive political organizations find themselves in and attempt to navigate and impact. Attention to social groups and their reflection of social structures was crucial to understanding how the broader social context of racial oppression and inequality shaped actions and interactions.

Racial consciousness was not simply manifest in people's descriptions, evaluations, and articulations of issues and events but also in practices reflecting their knowledge about what to do to achieve a goal or actualize an ideal. So I approached the difference between white participants' stated goals and the fruits of their actions as a "tension point."[11] It exposed the spaces wherein "practitioners no longer know what to do, so that the acts, gestures, discourses that up until then had seemed to go without saying become problematic."[12]

As I regarded my study's subject as the situation, I considered contact with participants and the field as *encounters*.[13] Within these encounters, I interrogated silences, avoidances, or discomfiture. I paid attention to the spaces during interviews where participants became silent, paused, or became less articulate, and I paid attention to the topics on which they could speak in nuanced, confident, and clear ways; asking about a range of their experiences with issues and topics allowed for comparing and observing which issues elicited various levels of social literacy, articulateness, and awareness from respondents.

Rituals, Routines, and Reproduction

I focused on rituals in participants' political and social activities, especially during meetings and events. I also noticed patterned social interactions that became routine. Paying close attention to rituals and routines revealed participants' social habits. Social habits connect the ritualistic underpinnings of everyday life to the taken-for-granted and practical knowledge that people use to navigate their social environment. Within meetings and events, shared taken-for-granted assumptions about how things are and how they are done provided the participants with a sense of morality and collective norms. It attuned them to a sense of correct forms of action and speech, and, in a broader sense, what *should* happen.

Rituals and routines are distinct. For instance, *rituals* are ceremonial and symbolic. They are connected to meaning-making and the signification of the moral, transcendent, or collective.[14] In contrast, *routines* emerge when the social order is routinized. In this sense, people engage in specific sequences of action due to a sense of procedure that provides security and familiarity.[15] Because they induce order, structure, and patterns in everyday social life, rituals and routines play a significant role in social reproduction—how the social structure is made and remade.

Rituals and routines that I saw within interactions in the field often signified larger social structures or reproduced structural outcomes. Through rituals as simple as the structure of meetings, the situation and its meaning were amplified in social significance and participants' affective response. The consequences and effects of these rituals shaped proceeding social interactions and situations. Routines and rituals demonstrate how a structurally bound interaction order nonetheless constrained GAP members' seemingly spontaneous or strategic actions.

Rituals and routines are mechanisms of *reproduction*. Revealing them helps us better understand racialized outcomes like the implicit exclusion of people of color or the avoidance of deliberations and strategies that center on racial justice. I focus on social reproduction, not merely for explaining this sustained state of relations and inequalities, but so that by highlighting relevant mechanisms, we can imagine and practice alternatives.

One reproduction mechanism highlighted in the study through participants' narratives and recursive practices is racial consciousness. Consciousness is not simply a vehicle for transmitting our prior knowledge and context into the present. Our consciousness of social problems such as racial oppression can be raised and cultivated in ways that cut to the core of our everyday habits. Revealing the underlying barriers to this transformation is crucial for new possibilities of thought and action.

INTERVIEWS AND INTERACTIONS

There are no observers of internal events of thought and feeling except those to whom they occur.—Robert Stuart Weiss, 1994

Throughout the study, I conducted forty-three semistructured interviews. I positioned myself as an outsider with a strong interest in learning about the issues inherent in participation in progressive grassroots politics. I interviewed participants in multiple iterations throughout the project to gauge their interpretations and reactions to events in the field and within society. I asked about their life histories and the situations and choices that brought them to their current situation. I asked about their experiences, thoughts, and feelings concerning racial and political issues and, importantly, how they act or don't act on those thoughts, feelings, and experiences. I also asked how they make sense of the tactics and characteristics of their organization.

I used semi-structured interview questions to gain a set of comparative answers to specific questions of concern around their motivations for participating in the GAP, their perceptions of the purpose and structure of the organization, and their perceptions of various political events and issues. Some interviews were informal and nondirective "to encourage the interviewee to talk about a given topic with a minimum of direct questioning or guidance" and "elicit 'spontaneous' accounts."[16] Even unstructured moments of informal conversation allowed participants to recount experiences or articulate their viewpoint.

I put these narratives, descriptions, and beliefs in dialogue with other information. I considered the positionality of the speaker, the patterned interactions I observed, and the historical and structural context. I looked at the experiences and sentiments they discussed to understand their political identities, social networks, social consciousness, daily habits, and thoughts on strategies and organizational matters.

Storytelling and Social Structures

Focusing on personal narratives allowed me to uncover features of the everyday lives and social locations of grassroots progressives that were "more legible from an insider's view."[17] I collected "retrospective first-person account[s] of the evolution of an individual life over time and in social context."[18] I asked participants about their memories and interpretations of experiences. These stories helped me to peer into their subjective experiences and sense of self.

I focused on how participants accounted for their awareness of various social and political issues and the decisions and contexts that shaped their political participation. Asking participants to tell me about their impressions of events and issues allowed for the "documentation of the lifelong consequences of transformative experiences" and the "revelation of details of everyday life that prove only in retrospect to be salient."[19] These personal accounts told me how events and stories were significant to participants rather than how they actually happened.

Recording and analyzing divergent narratives about the same events and issues from differing social positions helped me break through the notion that "grassroots progressives" was a monolith to see racialized differences in consciousness, strategies, habits, and experiences. Asking for people of color within the GAP to share personal stories of their experiences in grassroots politics became "a source of counternarratives to undermine misleading generalizations."[20] As the social scientists Mary Jo Maynes, Jennifer L. Pierce, and Barbara Laslett argue, "the circulation of politicized identities are always matters of contest; personal narratives can be valuable documents of such contestation."[21] Through contestation, "the stories of outgroups attempt to subvert [the] reality" constructed by dominant groups.[22] This approach revealed tensions and ambiguities underlying the seeming consensus presented by the organization's stated goals, political platforms, and outward-facing documents.

Questions about events that had racialized implications, such as interracial interactions, accusations of bias, the conflict between racial group members, or efforts to address and discuss racial issues, were fruitful. Semi-structured but conversational interviews with people of color enabled them to express "the seemingly 'small' or 'trivial' but stressful or humiliating events of everyday life" and "verbalize intuitively felt racism."[23]

Getting participants to share their life stories became crucial when understanding the relationship between racial consciousness, racial habits, and political strategies. It provided participants a space to articulate their sense of what they do, why, and how. When asking them to account for how their own previous experiences accounted for their awareness of racial oppression, these answers helped provide context to the patterned collective actions of their organization that maintained racial homogeneity. In interpreting the life stories of participants, I treated them "as both unique and as connected to social and cultural worlds and relationships that affect their life chances."[24] I paid close attention to how the personal stories referenced public storylines, used common narrative structures, and reflected a specific time, space, and way of selecting and organizing events and details.[25]

Through the combination of participant observation data and interview data, they emerge as both narrators who author personal narratives about their own lives through their voice and from their subject position and, simultaneously, social beings who act and interact in the world. These are *ontological narratives*, "the stories that social actors use to make sense of— indeed, to act in—their lives."[26] Such narratives "define who we are; this, in turn, can be a precondition for knowing what to do."[27] Approaching my participants as narrators and social actors helped me merge field notes and interview data to depict a larger picture of the situation.

The People Are Participants

Throughout this book, I refer to the people within this study as "participants." What I mean by using this language is that people are both social agents and personal storytellers. The term "participant" does not refer to participation in this study. Instead, I am referring to the sociological concept of "participants," which refers to the social actors within an organization. In the sociology of organizations, participants are "those individuals who, in return for a variety of inducements, make contributions to the organization."[28] They are a crucial component of organizations, as "it is their energy, their conformity, their disobedience that constitutes and shapes the structure of the organization."[29] Referring to the people who participate in the GAP exclusively as "members" or only referring to the collective or organization as an actor could obscure the vital role of people's actions in the social processes that I aim to describe.

Indeed, "without participation, there is no social structure, no organization."[30] So, I center the narratives and activities of participants because they "are the instruments of both continuity—the reproduction of structure—and change—the production of novelty and innovation."[31]

Participation links the people, the organization, and the broader social situation. It has three essential features: (1) an active mode of engagement with the social world, (2) a mode of representation in the civic life and political system of a society, and (3) a form of social and political praxis. Focusing on people's dynamic, agentive, and creative participation in political life enabled me to examine the actions of participants rather than merely describing a set of fixed and prearranged statuses or roles. Yet participation in political life is not simply sporadic and spontaneous. It is also characterized by discernable and stable rituals and routines that lead to the reproduction of social states and outcomes over space and time.

POWER AND POSITIONALITY

Qualitative research considers the positionality of both the researcher and the researched as core aspects of inquiry to understand how knowledge and experience are situated, co-constructed, and historically and socially located. This methodological expectation for reflexivity does

not just allow for richer data, but also requires researchers to consider
power within and surrounding the research process and to employ an
ethic of care for their subjects and for the overall work of qualitative
research.—Jennifer A. Reich, 2021

Undergoing any form of social research, especially research on people's political lives, is full of difficult decisions relating to the researcher's social position and power. Throughout my time in the field, I strove to examine and process my interests and intentions as both a researcher and a civically engaged person. Civically engaged research can be a double-edged sword. On the positive end, caring about the problem I investigated was a source of resilience and commitment. My concern for the consequences of political inequality and racial oppression gave me a sense of purpose. This engagement motivated my study beyond the abstract goal of knowledge production or career aspirations.

However, studying and understanding something you have no personal stake in is perhaps cognitively and emotionally easier. Because these issues were not merely a source of fascination but a source of social suffering, I also had to remain aware of my biases, interests, and concerns so that they did not color my understanding of what was happening, how it was happening, and why it was happening. Locating myself in relation to GAP participants, examining the impacts of my social location and relationships with those I encountered in the field, and considering my training, analytical frame, and epistemological and political orientations were intrinsic aspects of this study.

My relationship with what I experienced in the field deserved careful and conscious attention. As an advocate for social progress and democracy, my thoughts and feelings about the political system in the United States mirror many of the statements made by my participants. Given that I focused on an organization primarily white and upper-middle class, I also hailed from a similar racial and social class background as many participants. Due to the familiarity and resonance of these perspectives and social positions, I had to find ways to make them strange. In my personal and academic life, I have spent time learning the history, sociology, and politics of whiteness, masculinity, and middle-classness, rendering them objects of inquiry. I have also engaged in a decades-long process of employing this knowledge to contextualize and understand my own lived experience and identity.

Making these familiar stories, people, and situations strange required constant reflection on my knowledge, social position, and worldview throughout this study's data collection, analysis, and writing phases. Allowing for a sense of complexity was an extremely crucial tool in allowing for ambivalence and the ability to develop my interpretation of what was going on beyond reducing things into pre-existing binary debates. My fieldwork, analysis, and writing did not simply entail encounters with participants and their social world but a series of confrontations with the inherent awkwardness of the situation.

Awareness through Awkwardness

While much of the phenomena I observed during my study centered on how people avoid tension and fail to engage with contradictions, I realized early on that I had no choice but to face them. So, I kept a journal where I worked through "productive tensions."[32] Writing was an important way of processing my data, thoughts, and feelings. I wrote through the contradictions, tensions, and the meaning of my political engagement.

By answering the analytical questions of how and why things happened in my case study, I developed my answers to more fundamentally pragmatic questions about how political praxis can combat racial injustice. We live in a society wherein politics is spoken of in terms of flashpoint events and tactics for achieving victory. Yet, through this study, I became more acutely aware of how rituals and routines, assumptions and ways of thinking, and underlying conflicts matter as much as grand strategies and significant events. Perhaps more than anything, this project drove me toward public and pragmatic sociological endeavors to improve how people think about and engage in civic and political life.

By analyzing and describing actual events, I ran the risk of misunderstanding and misrepresenting the people who were a part of this project. This concern was at the front of my mind. Rather than identifying good and bad actors, I focused on what people did and how it contributed to specific outcomes. Ultimately, my goal was to help anyone who engages with my work to understand the more extensive social processes beyond the scope of individual actors. Observing and analyzing the micro- and meso-levels of social interactions and organizations in ways that produced insights into the macro reality of racialized political inequality was sometimes a perplexing endeavor. Even if fraught with challenges, ethnography is not only a series of awkward moments but a series of awkward moments with a purpose.

I spent a long time grappling with positionality and insider/outsider status. It was one thing to think about how I accessed and encountered people, but it was another thing to write about them. Writing about them meant thinking about my background, position in society, relationships with the people I would encounter, and how I would present myself and write myself into the text. Because the researcher/author is essentially the protagonist, ethnographic writing requires a delicate touch. In describing what happened, I also presented how and why things happened. Attributing causality and motivations in my writing and analysis was another awkward challenge. Among social scientists, there remains intense disagreement over whether analysis of motivations is even possible. I focused on using the patterns and processes I observed to intuit causality and relatedness where possible. I attempted to suggest alternative explanations and then considered how the explanations fit in with other patterns I noticed in the field.

Noticing, for instance, that white participants tended not to have clear and articulate narratives about how they could address the impacts of racial inequality and discrimination on their organization could have been explained by several factors. So, this observation was not recorded and analyzed in isolation. I sought to explore these possibilities in subsequent encounters in the field and interviews. Moreover, this pattern fits into a larger set of themes about white participants' lack of awareness and reluctance to acknowledge and openly discuss racial oppression and its implications.

Insider/Interlocutor (or Outsider/Observer)

A question often posed to ethnographers is whether they are an *insider* or *outsider* to the field.[33] It matters whether a researcher holds social categories in common with research participants. Despite the limitations of this binary, these statuses affected what I observed and interrogated. Relational categories like whether I counted as "one of us" shaped how participants perceived and treated me. I had to discern how to present my views on political issues best and understand the GAP's social and political stances.[34]

In/outgroup distinctions also map onto power relations. The position of the researcher or *observer* inherently placed me in a position of power to record, select, and interpret the words and practices of participants. This power to define others with authority is connected to structural inequalities. Social scientific research that does not acknowledge this issue can obscure the problems it seeks to illuminate. Systems of oppression have routinely been normalized, naturalized, hidden, and facilitated through the production of academic and scientific knowledge.

Given these genuine dangers, I reflected on how my social position as a white middle-class male influenced what I noticed and perceived, how I interpreted what I perceived, and the social performances of participants in both naturalistic observations and interviews. I practiced interpretive reflexivity and reflected on the relationship between social position, relations in the field, and my interpretive processes.[35] Throughout the text, I shared how I came to conclusions based on my observations, including "reality tests" where I engaged in "trying out interpretations of everyday action."[36] In this sense, I saw myself as an *interlocutor*, someone who was asking questions and probing to find answers.

Reflexivity, solidarity, empathy, and conscious awareness of the social fact of oppression and its implications were tools for attempting an emancipatory project that challenges racial subjugation in the face of my dominant social position. My social consciousness and racial literacy resulted in specific felt relations with the GAP participants I encountered. Aligning oneself with a particular subgroup within an organization under study can prevent access to other groups and facilitate distrust. Negotiating relationships and interactions with participants already embedded in a dynamic web of social relations strategically was challenging but fruitful. I found anthropologist and author Zora Neale Hurston's distinction between "skinfolk" and "kinfolk" helpful in reflecting on the influence of my commitments in my fieldwork.[37] I came to view many of the white participants as "skinfolk." I used the assumption of white solidarity and my own experiences as a white person to render their understanding of the world more accessible and legible. Other participants, white and of color, felt more like "kinfolk" in terms of practical solidarity and a shared awareness and confrontation with racial oppression and white supremacy.

Reflecting on Race, Reactions, and Regionality

Belonging to dominant social groups provided me with access to racialized, classed, and gendered social dynamics in the field. I interrogated my whiteness and masculinity as sites of power and unearned advantage that created potential ignorance or misconceptions. I asked myself how my self-presentation shaped my access and how others responded. I explicitly considered how things might have gone differently if I had held other social identities. Ongoing conversations with colleagues, friends, and collaborators, particularly people of color, were crucial throughout the research process in attuning, as best as possible, my awareness of how my social position shaped my observations and conclusions.

My tastes and preferences presented barriers and resources for navigating the field in both anticipated and unanticipated ways. I correctly anticipated that my political views, vegetarianism, dedication to healthy eating, social consciousness, and social awkwardness would influence my interactions. I also had a decent knowledge of history and political systems but less knowledge of local politics. I did not expect the level to which region mattered and quickly realized that I would need to grapple with issues of regionality. I am from the Midwest but had lived in the northeastern United States for three years before my study. I was aware of the region's norms and quirks. But I still held this awareness from an outsider's perspective.

So, to sum up, what was my position in the field and relation to participants and even my research topic? As much as the insider/outsider dichotomy is helpful, I felt somewhere between a partial insider and a sympathetic outsider throughout my time in the field. I used this mix of positions and relations to my advantage by remaining conscious of these dynamics. In a nutshell, I presented myself as curious, interested in shared causes, and empathetic, yet willing to notice things and ask questions that encouraged participants to articulate things that some would have otherwise preferred not to discuss.

Notes

Introduction

1. Bonilla-Silva, *Racism without Racists.*
2. Mills, *Sociological Imagination.*
3. Lewis, "'What Group?,'" 627.
4. Albert and Whetton, "Organizational Identity."
5. This was not the first time that animal rights advocates had made such comparisons. Major animal rights organizations such as PETA and smaller groups have spurred outrage and controversy through their use of images of the lynchings, chattel slavery, and genocide of people of color as an analog to animal mistreatment. See Melissa Harris-Perry, "Michael Vick, Racial History and Animal Rights," *The Nation*, December 30, 2010, https://www.thenation.com /article/archive/michael-vick-racial-history-and-animal-rights/.
6. Harris-Perry, "Michael Vick."
7. Martin, *Empowering.*
8. Wingfield, "Are Some Emotions"; Durr and Wingfield, "Keep Your."
9. S. Collins, "Black Mobility."
10. Kanter, *Men and Women*; S. Collins, "Black Mobility."
11. Alexander, *New Jim Crow.*
12. Katznelson, *When Affirmative Action.*
13. Mendelberg and Oleski, "Race and Public Deliberation"; Hawkesworth, "Congressional Enactments"; Perrin, *Citizen Speak*; Mendelberg, Karpowitz, and Oliphant, "Gender Inequality."
14. Doane, "What Is Racism?"; Bonilla-Silva, *Racism without Racists.*
15. Du Bois, *Darkwater*, 110.
16. Willner, "Micro-Politics"; Mudge and Chen, "Political Parties."
17. Bonilla-Silva, "Rethinking Racism," 469.
18. Essed, *Understanding Everyday Racism*, 38.
19. Thomas, "Affect"; Bonilla-Silva, "Feeling Race."
20. Thomas, "Affect."
21. Ahmed, *Cultural Politics.*
22. Ahmed, "Phenomenology of Whiteness."
23. Mark Carrigan, "The Sociology of Awkwardness" (blog post), MarkCarrigan.net, December 9, 2013, https://markcarrigan.net/2013/12/09 /the-sociology-of-awkwardness/.
24. Scheff, "Ubiquity of Hidden Shame."
25. James Baldwin, "As Much Truth as One Can Bear: To Speak Out about the World as It Is, Says James Baldwin, Is the Writer's Job," *New York Times*, January 14, 1962.

26. J. Clegg, "Stranger Situations"; Wherry, Seefeldt, and Alvarez, "To Lend or Not."

27. Goffman, "Embarrassment."

28. Lizardo and Collett, "Embarrassment"; Du Bois, *Souls of Black Folk*.

29. Lizardo and Collett, "Embarrassment."

30. J. Clegg, "Importance of Feeling Awkward."

31. Scheff, "Ubiquity of Hidden Shame."

32. Shelton, West, and Trail, "Concerns."

33. Kotsko, *Awkwardness*; Reeser, "Producing Awkwardness."

34. Ahmed, *Cultural Politics*; Ioanide, *Emotional Politics*.

35. Kotsko, *Awkwardness*, 7.

36. Ahmed, "Phenomenology of Whiteness"; Combs, *Bodies out of Place*.

37. Ahmed, "Phenomenology of Whiteness," 159.

38. Zembylas, "Affect, Race, and White."

39. Picca and Feagin, *Two-Faced Racism*; Bonilla-Silva, *Racism without Racists*.

40. Tilly, *Democracy*.

41. Schlozman, Verba, and Brady, *Unheavenly Chorus*; Verba, Burns, and Schlozman, "Knowing and Caring"; Fullerton and Stern, "Racial Differences"; Logan, Darrah, and Oh, "Impact of Race."

42. Dubrow, "Political Inequality"; Laurison, Brown, and Rastogi, "Voting Intersections."

43. Berman, *Give Us the Ballot*; C. Anderson, *One Person, No Vote*.

44. Einstein, Palmer, and Glick, "Racial Disparities."

45. Einstein, Palmer, and Glick, "Racial Disparities."

46. Beecher Field, *Town Hall Meetings*.

47. Haney López, *Dog Whistle Politics*.

48. Mudge and Chen, "Political Parties," 232.

49. Hughey, "We've Been Framed!"; Oliver, "Ethnic Dimensions."

50. Mudge and Chen, "Political Parties."

51. Hutchings and Valentino, "Centrality of Race."

52. Willner, "Micro-Politics."

53. Perrin, *American Democracy*, 49.

54. Eastwood, "Role of Ideas."

55. Weber, "Social Psychology," 280.

56. Perrin, *American Democracy*.

57. Du Bois, *Darkwater*; Tilly, *Democracy*; Derber, *Welcome to the Revolution*.

58. Martin, *Empowering Progressive Third Parties*.

59. Jeffery M. Jones, "Support for Third U.S. Political Party Up to 63%," Gallup, October 4, 2023, https://news.gallup.com/poll/512135/support-third -political-party.aspx.

60. Jeffery M. Jones, "Independent Party ID Tied for High; Democratic ID at New Low," Gallup, January 12, 2024, https://news.gallup.com/poll/548459 /independent-party-tied-high-democratic-new-low.aspx.

61. A. P. Joyce, "#DemExit: Are Progressives Really Abandoning the Democratic Party?" *Mic*, February 27, 2017, www.mic.com/articles/169820 /dem-exit-are-progressives-really-abandoning-the-democratic-party.

62. Fraser, *Old Is Dying*.

63. Mouffe, *For a Left Populism*; Fraser, *Old Is Dying*.

64. Derber, *Welcome to the Revolution*; George Monbiot, "America's New Revolutionaries Show How the Left Can Win," *The Guardian*, July 11, 2018, https://www.theguardian.com/commentisfree/2018/jul/11/america -left-alexandria-ocasio-cortez-new-york-primary; Katrina vanden Heuvel, "Progressive Insurgents Are Propelling Democrats into the Future," *Washington Post*, July 10, 2018, www.washingtonpost.com.

65. "'The Old Order Is Disappearing': How Progressive Grassroots Movements Are Sweeping the U.K. & U.S.," *Democracy Now!*, July 12, 2018, https://www .democracynow.org/2018/7/12/the_old_order_is_disappearing_how.

66. "'Old Order Is Disappearing.'"

67. Joe Garofoli, "Progressive Working Families Party Lands in California, and Is Targeting Moderate Democrats," *San Francisco Chronicle*, January 14, 2022, www.sfchronicle.com/bayarea/article/Progressive-Working-Families -Party-lands-in-16770927.php.

68. Jessica Yarvin, "Is Socialism in the United States Having a Moment?" *PBS NewsHour* (website), March 27, 2017, www.pbs.org/newshour/politics /socialism-united-states-moment.

69. Patrick Strickland, "More Americans Joining Socialist Groups under Trump." *Al Jazeera* (website), February 9, 2017, www.aljazeera.com /features/2017/2/9/more-americans-joining-socialist-groups-under-trump; Yarvin, "Is Socialism."

70. Morgan Gstalter, "Democratic Socialists of America See Membership Spike after Ocasio-Cortez Win," *The Hill*, June 28, 2018, https://thehill.com /blogs/blog-briefing-room/news/394679-democratic-socialists-of-america -see-membership-spike-after/.

71. Strickland, "More Americans Joining."

72. Derber, *Welcome to the Revolution*, xvii.

73. Shafer, "Republicans and Democrats," 342.

74. Du Bois, *Black Reconstruction in America*; Blauner, *Racial Oppression in America*; Bonilla-Silva, *White Supremacy*; Feagin, *Systemic Racism*; Bracey, "Toward a Critical Race."

75. Blauner, *Racial Oppression in America*; P. Collins, *Black Feminist Thought*; Feagin, *Systemic Racism*.

76. Mills, "White Supremacy"; Tilly, *Democracy*; Bracey, "Toward a Critical Race"; Rosino, "Boundaries and Barriers."

77. Mills, "White Ignorance"; Mueller, "Producing Colorblindness"; Bonilla-Silva, *Racism without Racists*.

78. Essed, *Understanding Everyday Racism*; P. Collins, *Black Feminist Thought*; Bonilla-Silva, *Racism without Racists*.

79. Roithmayr, *Reproducing Racism*, 4–5.

80. Weber, "Politics as a Vocation."

81. Davis, *Women, Culture, and Politics*, 14.

82. Addams, *Democracy and Social Ethics*; Eliasoph, *Politics of Volunteering*.

83. Nagda, "Breaking Barriers"; Sorenson, "Road to Empathy."

84. Stout, *Blessed Are the Organized*, xiii.

85. Bonilla-Silva, *Racism without Racists*, 15.

86. Picca and Feagin, *Two-Faced Racism*, 83.

87. Gidley, "Note on the Awkwardness," 529.

88. Gidley, "Note on the Awkwardness," 529.

89. O'Brien and Kollock, *Production of Reality*, 58.

90. See Hughey, Embrick, and Doane, "Paving the Way," 1352.

91. Goffman, "'Interaction Order.'"

92. Rosino, "Dramaturgical Domination."

93. Carrigan, "Sociology of Awkwardness."

94. Omi and Winant, *Racial Formation*.

95. Meghji, "Activating Controlling Images."

96. Pfeffer, *Power in Organizations*, 7.

Chapter One

1. Shefter, *Political Parties*; Cox, *History of Third Parties*.

2. Lichterman, *The Search for Political Community*.

3. Giddens, *Modernity and Self-Identity*.

4. Morris, "Reflections on Social."

5. Thomas E. Patterson, "News Coverage of the 2016 Presidential Primaries: Horse Race Reporting Has Consequences," Shorenstein Center on Media, Politics, and Public Policy (website), July 11, 2016, https://shorensteincenter.org /news-coverage-2016-presidential-primaries/.

6. Zoizner, "Consequences."

7. Scott, *Organizations*.

8. Perrin, *Citizen Speak*; Woodly, *Reckoning*.

9. Woodly, *Reckoning*.

10. While grassroots parties are often regarded as "voices for change"—see, e.g., Cox, *History of Third Parties*, 111—they can also represent reactive or regressive stances on social and political issues, such as the white backlash represented by George Wallace's Independent Party—see Hughey, "White Backlash." Here, I focus explicitly on groups whose platforms claim to advance racial justice rather than subvert it.

11. Cox, *History of Third Parties*.

12. Gillespie, *Challengers to Duopoly*.

13. For instance, Eldridge Cleaver of the Black Panther Party ran for president in 1968 under the Peace and Freedom Party, garnering over a hundred thousand votes in 20 states—see Ali, *In the Balance*.

14. Ali, *In the Balance*; Walton, Puckett, and Deskins, *African American Electorate*; McAdam and Kloos, *Deeply Divided*.

15. Walton, Puckett, and Deskins, *African American Electorate*.

16. Marquez and Espino, "Mexican American Support."

17. Josue Estrada, "Raza Unida Party Chapters 1970–1974," Mapping American Social Movements Project, Civil Rights and Labor History Consortium, University of Washington, accessed June 11, 2024, https://depts .washington.edu/moves/Raza_Unida_map.shtml.

18. Marquez and Espino, "Mexican American Support."

19. Dittmer, *Local People*.

20. Dittmer, *Local People*; Payne, *I've Got the Light*.

21. Dittmer, *Local People*; Payne, *I've Got the Light*.

22. McAdam and Kloos, *Deeply Divided*.

23. Hughey and Parks, *Wrongs of the Right*; McAdam and Kloos, *Deeply Divided*.

24. Hughey and Parks, *Wrongs of the Right*; McAdam and Kloos, *Deeply Divided*; Hughey, "White Backlash."

25. Hughey and Parks, *Wrongs of the Right*; McAdam and Kloos, *Deeply Divided*.

26. Hajnal and Troustine, "Race and Class Inequality."

27. Hajnal and Troustine, "Race and Class Inequality."

28. Tilly, *Democracy*, 119.

29. Cox, *History of Third Parties*; Bibby and Maisel, *Dilemmas in American Politics*; Martin, *Empowering Progressive Third Parties*.

30. Jacobs, Cook, and Carpini, *Talking Together*; Walsh, *Talking about Politics*.

31. Cox, *History of Third Parties*, 111.

32. Bachrach and Botwinick, *Power and Empowerment*.

33. Bachrach and Botwinick, *Power and Empowerment*, 10.

34. Woodly, *Reckoning*.

35. Importantly, racial categories do not link to biological or innate human characteristics—see, e.g., Obasogie, *Blinded by Sight*; Graves, *Emperor's New Clothes*. They influence social reality. Yet, paradoxically, they are still collective fabrications. European elites formally developed and legally sanctioned the category "white" in the seventeenth century—see Allen, *Invention*. Through the actions of powerful actors and the support of nonelites who came to be recognized as "white," the meaning of "whiteness" as something that provided people with rights to resources and freedoms became enshrined in laws, institutions, and social norms over the next few centuries—see, e.g., Coates, "Law and the Cultural"; Gossett, *Race*; Rosino, "Dramaturgical Domination."

36. Frankenberg, *White Women*.

37. Bonilla-Silva, *White Supremacy*; Mills, "White Supremacy."

38. Mills, "White Supremacy," 40.

39. Allen, *Invention*; Roediger, *Wages of Whiteness*; Glenn, *Unequal Freedom*; Feagin, *Systemic Racism*.

40. Du Bois, *Black Reconstruction*; Roediger, *Wages of Whiteness*.

41. Du Bois, *Black Reconstruction*; Roediger, *Wages of Whiteness*.

42. Lewis, "'What Group?,'" 626.

43. Marx, *Class Struggles*; Lukács, *History and Class Consciousness*.

44. Twine, *White Side*. "Racial consciousness" is often discussed among scholars as merely the recognition of group cultural and ethnic differences and/or the perceived interests of one's own group—see, e.g., Banton, *Ethnic and Racial Consciousness*. The term has also been appropriated by white nationalists to rationalize that those classified as white should continue to assert their dominant interests upon society. In contrast, I theorize racial consciousness as a form of critical consciousness focused on the historical and social processes that produce and maintain white supremacy and how that system produces harmful conditions, social suffering, and dehumanization.

45. Du Bois, *Souls of Black Folk*.

46. Mills, "White Ignorance"; Mueller, "Producing Colorblindness."

47. Rosino, "Dramaturgical Domination."

48. Du Bois, *Souls of Black Folk*.

49. Savory, "Rending of the Veil," 334.

50. Du Bois, *Souls of Black Folk*; Rawls, "'Race' as an Interaction."

51. Rawls, "'Race' as an Interaction"; Farough, "Social Geographies."

52. Mills, *Sociological Imagination*, 5.

53. Mansbridge, "Making of Oppositional Consciousness," 5.

54. Rosino, "Dramaturgical Domination."

55. Winant, *New Politics of Race*, 29.

56. Winant, *New Politics of Race*, 29.

57. Rosino, "Dramaturgical Domination"; Meghji, "Activating Controlling Images."

58. Du Bois, *Souls of Black Folk*; E. Anderson, "White Space"; Bonilla-Silva, *Racism without Racists*.

59. Du Bois, *Souls of Black Folk*; E. Anderson, "White Space," 2015.

60. Rosino, "Boundaries and Barriers."

61. Twine, *White Side*.

62. Carter, Picca, and Murray, "Racialization in Public," 142.

63. Diaquoi, "Symbols in the Strange."

64. Hagerman, "White Families and Race"; Carter, Picca, and Murray, "Racialization in Public"; Underhill, "Parenting during Ferguson."

65. Hagerman, "Reproducing and Reworking," 69.

66. Christian Cosseru, "Mind in Indian Buddhist Philosophy," *Stanford Encyclopedia of Philosophy* (online), edited by N. Edward, Spring 2017, https://plato.stanford.edu/archives/spr2017/entries/mind-indian-buddhism/.

67. Outlaw, *Critical Social Theory*.

68. Lewis, "'What Group?,'" 626.

69. Mansbridge and Morris, *Oppositional Consciousness*.

70. Mansbridge, "Making of Oppositional Consciousness," 4.

71. Mansbridge, "Making of Oppositional Consciousness," 5.

72. "Quick Facts: Puerto Rico," US Census Bureau (website), accessed 2018, www.census.gov/quickfacts/fact/table/PR/PST045218.

73. Gonzalez-Sobrino, "Puerto Rico's Politics," 81.

74. Glaude, *Democracy in Black*.

75. Rosino and Hughey, "War on Drugs."

76. Lewis, *Race in the Schoolyard*; Hughey, *White Bound*.

77. Bonilla-Silva, *Racism without Racists*.

78. Bonilla-Silva, *Racism without Racists*.

79. Bourdieu, *Distinction*.

80. Mayorga-Gallo, *Behind the White*, 22.

81. Bourdieu, *Distinction*.

82. Bonilla-Silva, Goar, and Embrick, "When Whites Flock Together," 248.

83. The concept of white habitus—see Bonilla-Silva, *Racism without Racists*—focuses on how whites represent and perceive the racialized social world around them. However, habitus is not only about tastes, feeling, emotions, and perceptions but also about social practices—see Bourdieu, *Outline of a Theory*.

84. Many scholars of race and racism note that although whites as a group are fractured by other group memberships, they all benefit from the racialized social system. See Bonilla-Silva, *Racism without Racists*, proposing that racism is rational for whites—in contradiction to the irrationality often afforded to racism; see, e.g., Blauner, *Racial Oppression in America*. This approach provides insights into how white people articulate rationalizations for racialized social interactions and structures. Yet it assumes that social action functions in a purely calculated and instrumental manner. It suggests that people inherently pursue rational means of maximizing their benefits from social situations and arrangements. However, social actions are not inherently rational—see Weber, *Protestant Ethic*. They only appear as such in the light of rationalization.

85. Bonilla-Silva, "What Makes Systemic Racism."

86. Sullivan, *Revealing Whiteness*, 21.

87. MacMullan, *Fly Wheel of Society*, 250.

88. Du Bois, *Dusk of Dawn*, 86. See also Perry, *More Beautiful*, 33: "There is a danger in the language of unconsciousness, even as researchers pursue such work with great skill and integrity. For the nonacademic or nonsocial scientist who adopts the language of unconscious bias, there may be an inclination to identify all bias as unconscious rather than to connect the very conscious and present discourses about people of color to unconsciously biased practices."

89. Bonilla-Silva, *Racism without Racists*.

90. Hughey, Embrick, and Doane, "Paving the Way."

91. Glaude, *Democracy in Black*, 56.

92. Glaude, *Democracy in Black*, 56.

93. Rosino, "Dramaturgical Domination."

94. Goffman, "Interaction Order."

95. Hart, *Cultural Dilemmas*, 4.
96. Hart, *Cultural Dilemmas*, 4.
97. Blee, *Democracy in the Making*.
98. Bachrach and Botwinick, *Power and Empowerment*; Hildreth, "Word and Deed."
99. Addams, *Democracy and Social Ethics*.
100. Eliasoph, *Politics of Volunteering*.
101. Eliasoph, *Politics of Volunteering*.
102. Blee, *Democracy in the Making*.
103. Blee, *Democracy in the Making*.
104. Hart, *Cultural Dilemmas*; Blee, *Democracy in the Making*.
105. Blee, *Democracy in the Making*.
106. Lipsitz, *How Racism Takes Place*, 6.
107. Logan, "Persistence of Segregation," 166.
108. Logan, "Persistence of Segregation," 164.
109. Lichterman, *Search for Political Community*.
110. P. Collins, "New Politics of Community."
111. Haynes, *Red Lines, Black Spaces*, 150.
112. Haynes, *Red Lines, Black Spaces*, 152.
113. Sigelman et al., "Making Contact?"; McPherson, Smith-Lovin, and Cook, "Birds of a Feather"; DiPrete et al., "Segregation in Social Networks"; Quillian and Campbell, "Beyond Black and White."
114. Krysan and Crowder, *Cycles of Segregation*, 12.
115. Moore, *Reproducing Racism*; Anderson, "White Space."
116. Farough, "Social Geographies," 244.
117. Moore, *Reproducing Racism*; Anderson, "White Space."
118. Bracey and Moore, "'Race Tests.'"
119. Dwyer and Jones, "White Sociospatial Epistemology," 212.
120. Dwyer and Jones, "White Sociospatial Epistemology," 212.
121. Alegria, "Constructing Racial Difference," 255.
122. Vanderbeck, "Inner-City Children," 214.
123. Lewis, "What Group?," 636.
124. Du Bois, *Darkwater*, 69.
125. Hart, *Cultural Dilemmas*, 15.
126. Hildreth, "Word and Deed," 269.
127. Hildreth, "Word and Deed," 269.

Chapter Two

1. "Public Opinion on Abortion," Pew Research Center, accessed on June 30, 2018, www.pewforum.org/fact-sheet/public-opinion-on-abortion/; "Democrats Far More Supportive than Republicans of Federal Spending for Scientific Research," Pew Research Center, May 1, 2017, www.pewresearch.org/fact-tank/2017/05/01/democrats-far-more-supportive-than-republicans-of-federal-spending-for-scientific-research/; Pew Research Center, "Most Americans Say Trump's Election Has Led to Worse Race Relations in the U.S.," press release,

December 19, 2017, https://assets.pewresearch.org/wp-content/uploads
/sites/5/2017/12/19140928/12-19-2017-race-relations-release.pdf.

2. Miller and Connover, "Red and Blue States."

3. American Psychological Association, *Stress in America*.

4. Ioanide, *Emotional Politics of Racism*; Bonilla-Silva, "Feeling Race."

5. Collins, Mandel, and Schywiola, "Political Identity."

6. Hall, "Work of Representation."

7. Walsh, *Talking about Politics*, 33.

8. Feinberg et al., "Political Reference Point," 8.

9. Z. Robinson, *This Ain't Chicago*.

10. Z. Robinson, *This Ain't Chicago*, 13.

11. Bryan, *Real Democracy*.

12. "How Red or Blue Is Your State?," *The Hill*, October 24, 2014,
http://thehill.com/blogs/ballot-box/house-races/221721-how-red-or-blue-is
-your-state.

13. "How Red or Blue."

14. "2016 Presidential Election Results," *New York Times*, August 9, 2017,
www.nytimes.com/elections/results/president; "Presidential Results," CNN,
accessed May 15, 2021, www.cnn.com/election/2020/results/president.

15. Frank, *Listen, Liberal*.

16. Braunstein, *Prophets and Patriots*, 10.

17. Andrew Prokop, "Why the Electoral College Is the Absolute Worst,
Explained," *Vox*, December 19, 2016, www.vox.com/policy-and
-politics/2016/11/7/12315574/electoral-college-explained-presidential
-elections-2016.

18. Stout, *Blessed Are the Organized*, xv.

19. Kraus, "Community Struggles," 238.

20. Kraus, "Community Struggles," 238.

21. Gramsci, *Selections*.

22. Walsh, *Talking about Politics*; Feinberg et al., "Political Reference Point."

23. Feinberg et al., "Political Reference Point."

24. Parlett, *Demonizing a President*.

25. Here I am drawing loosely on Pierre Bourdieu's work on multiple forms of
capital—see Bourdieu, *Distinction*.

26. Hunt, *Screening*, 130.

27. Albert and Whetton, "Organizational Identity."

28. American Psychological Association, *Stress in America*, 1.

29. Jennifer Sweeton, "Post-Election Stress Disorder in Women" (blog post),
accessed July 11, 2024, https://www.jennifersweeton.com/post-election-stress
-disorder-in-women/; Derber, *Welcome*.

30. Derber, *Welcome*.

31. Hooghe and Dassonville, "Explaining the Trump Vote," 1.

32. Knowles and Tropp, "Racial and Economic Context"; Schaffner,
Macwilliams, and Nteta, "Understanding White Polarization"; Major, Blodorn,
and Blascovich, "Threat of Increasing Diversity."

33. Walsh, *Talking about Politics*.
34. "Most Americans Say," Pew Research Center.
35. See Rosino, *Debating the Drug War*.
36. Heidemann, "Overcoming Uncertainty," 93.
37. Omi and Winant, *Racial Formation*.
38. Moghaddam and Harré, "Words, Conflicts," 2.
39. Kinder and Sanders, *Divided by Color*, 66.
40. Kinder and Sanders, *Divided by Color*; Haney López, *Dog Whistle Politics*.
41. Derber, *Welcome to the Revolution*, 57.

Chapter Three
1. Bonilla-Silva, "Rethinking Racism," 469.
2. Warren, *Fire in the Heart*, 150.
3. Jackson, "White Space, White Self"; Moore, *Reproducing Racism*; E. Anderson, "White Space."
4. Lewis, "'What Group?'" 627.
5. Roithmayr, *Reproducing Racism*, 5.
6. Baldwin, *Fire Next Time*, 8.
7. Gallagher, "'Blacks, Jews, Gays.'"
8. It has been fruitful and humbling to acknowledge that, despite my own sociological and practical knowledge about racial oppression, my own experiences of comfort and discomfort are still shaped by the racialized interaction order.
9. Meghji, "Activating Controlling Images."
10. Frankenberg, *White Women, Race Matters*, 68.
11. Whites often express incoherent statements about racial issues when speaking publicly—see, e.g., Picca and Feagin, *Two-Faced Racism*; Bonilla-Silva, *Racism without Racists*.
12. Bell and Hartmann, "Diversity in Everyday Discourse"; Mayorga-Gallo, "White-Centering Logic."
13. This dynamic mirrors racial outsourcing in other fields like business and health care—see, e.g., Wingfield, *Flatlining*.
14. Lichterman, *Search for Political Community*.
15. See Winchester, "Converting to Continuity."
16. Frankenberg, *White Women, Race Matters*; Twine, *White Side*; Mueller, "Producing Colorblindness"; Bonilla-Silva, *Racism without Racists*.
17. Twine, *White Side*.
18. Tracey Jan, "Redlining Was Banned 50 Years Ago. It's Still Hurting Minorities Today," *Washington Post*, January 28, 2019, www.washingtonpost.com/news/wonk/wp/2018/03/28/redlining-was-banned-50-years-ago-its-still-hurting-minorities-today/.
19. Rosino, "Boundaries and Barriers," 947.
20. Frankenberg, *White Women, Race Matters*.

21. Lewis, "'What Group?'"; Doane, "Contested Terrain"; Steinberg, *Race Relations*; Mueller, "Producing Colorblindness."

22. Picca and Feagin, *Two-Faced Racism.*

23. MacMullan, *Habits of Whiteness*, 171.

24. Rosino, "Dramaturgical Domination."

25. Lewis, *Race in the Schoolyard.*

26. Mueller, "Producing Colorblindness."

27. See, e.g., Lewis, *Race in the Schoolyard*; Doane, "Contested Terrain"; Steinberg, *Race Relations*; Mueller, "Producing Colorblindness."

28. Melissa Hillman, "Privilege Is What Allows Sanders Supporters to Say They'll 'Never' Vote for Clinton," *Quartz*, March 22, 2016, https://qz.com /644985/privilege-is-what-allows-sanders-supporters-to-say-theyll-never -vote-for-clinton/; Robert Chappell, "Third Party Voting Is the Height of White Privilege," *Madison365*, October 5, 2016, https://madison365.com/third-party -vote-height-white-privilege/; Michael Arcenaux, "Bernie Sanders or Bust? That's a Stance Based on Privilege," *The Guardian*, March 7, 2016, www .theguardian.com/commentisfree/2016/mar/07/democratic -vote-hillary-clinton-election-2016-bernie-sanders.

29. See DiAngelo, *White Fragility*, for a similar, albeit overly psychological and individualistic, accounting of racial stress and whiteness in diversity training sessions.

30. Sears and Henry, "Origins of Symbolic Racism," 259.

31. Entman and Rojecki, *Black Image.*

32. Lewis, "'What Group?'"

33. Hughey, *White Bound.*

34. Munn, "One Friend Rule."

35. Bonilla-Silva, *Racism without Racists.*

36. Munn, "One Friend Rule," 16.

37. Young, "Justice, Inclusion," 156.

38. Young, "Justice, Inclusion," 156.

39. Young, "Justice, Inclusion," 156.

40. Moghaddam and Harré, "Words, Conflicts," 2.

41. Harré et al., "Recent Advances."

42. Lakoff, *Don't Think*; Lakoff, *Political Mind.*

43. See Bourdieu, *Distinction.*

44. Omi and Winant, *Racial Formation*, 2nd ed., 90.

45. Omi and Winant, *Racial Formation*, 2nd ed.

46. Leon, Cedric, and Tuğal, "Political Articulation."

Chapter Four

1. Delgado, "Storytelling for Oppositionists"; Solórzano and Yosso, "Critical Race Methodology."

2. Delgado, "Storytelling for Oppositionists," 2415.

3. Delgado, "Storytelling for Oppositionists"; Feagin, *White Racial Frame*.

4. In this chapter, I highlight the experiences of one participant in particular: Nina. Nina is a Latina who had an active presence in her local chapter of the GAP as well as regional and national domains of grassroots progressive politics. Her numerous and varied experiences with the party, her candor about her personal experiences and awareness of racial oppression, and her history of antiracist and grassroots activism made my conversations with her particularly revealing and insightful.

5. Scott, *Organizations*, 27.

6. Scott, *Organizations*.

7. Ray, "Theory of Racialized Organizations."

8. Omi and Winant, *Racial Formation*, 2nd ed.; Ray, "Theory of Racialized Organizations."

9. Kellett and Dalton, *Managing Conflict*.

10. Kellett and Dalton, *Managing Conflict*.

11. Kellett and Dalton, *Managing Conflict*.

12. P. Collins, "Learning from the Outsider."

13. P. Collins, "Learning from the Outsider."

14. Ray, "Theory of Racialized Organizations," 42.

15. Bonilla-Silva, "From Bi-Racial to Tri-Racial."

16. Lipset, *Consensus and Conflict*, 3.

17. Essed, *Understanding Everyday Racism*, 38.

18. Essed, *Understanding Everyday Racism*.

19. Essed, *Understanding Everyday Racism*; Bonilla-Silva, *Racism without Racists*.

20. Taylor, *From #BlackLivesMatter*, 216.

21. C. Robinson, *Black Marxism*.

22. As scholars of racial capitalism have demonstrated, racial oppression produced social alienation and a sense of group interests vital to capitalist domination. Colonialism and imperialism were primary means for capitalists to amass the labor and resources that comprise the legs upon which capitalism stands—see, e.g., Du Bois, *Black Reconstruction in America*; Robinson, *Black Marxism*; Melamed, "Racial Capitalism."

23. Carmichael and Hamilton, *Black Power*, 86.

24. Vera and Gordon, *Screen Saviors*; Fitzgerald, "White Savior"; M. Hughey, *White Savior Film*; Schultz, "*Glory Road* (2006)"; Belcher, "There Is No"; Harrington, "Is Quentin Tarantino"; Murphy and Harris, "White Innocence"; Maurantonio, "'Reason to Hope?'"

25. Hughey, *White Savior Film*; Cann and McCloskey, "Poverty Pimpin' Project"; Bex and Craps, "Humanitarianism, Testimony"; Bandyopadhyay, "Volunteer Tourism."

26. Garcia Bedolla and Michelson, *Mobilizing Inclusion*.

27. Hajnal and Troustine, "Race and Class Inequality."

28. Hajnal and Troustine, "Race and Class Inequality," 149.

29. La Due Lake and Huckfeldt, "Social Capital."

30. Mansbridge, "Making of Oppositional Consciousness," 5.

31. Keeanga-Yamahtta Taylor, "Don't Deride Liberals Who Attended the Women's March—Recruit Them to Radical Politics," *In These Times*, January 23, 2017, https://inthesetimes.com/article/womens-march-donald-trump-protest-radical-politics-socialism.

32. See, e.g., Hope and Jagers, "Role of Sociopolitical Attitudes," 460; the authors find that "acknowledging systemic inequity promotes civic engagement among Black youth."

33. Gorski and Erakat, "Racism, Whiteness."

34. Omi and Winant, *Racial Formation*, 3rd ed., 163.

Conclusion

1. The dynamics I identified and described throughout this book in many ways resemble the concept of *cultural hegemony*—see Gramsci, *Selections from the Prison*—albeit at the meso-level of an organization. Under conditions of cultural hegemony, dominant groups hold influence over cultural narratives and representations. These narratives and representations depict the interests of the dominant group as ideal and define their social position and perspective as standard—see Lears, "Concept of Cultural Hegemony."

2. Hollis, *Finding Meaning*, 8.

3. Mead, *Mind, Self, and Society*.

4. Sølvberg and Jarness, "Assessing Contradictions," 192.

5. Case studies have both an object and a subject. This is a crucial distinction that bears repeating. The *object* is the case in a strictly technical sense: the participants in several local chapters of a grassroots progressive organization in the northeastern United States. But there is an equally important matter—this book's *subject*—see, e.g. Becker, "Cases, Causes, Conjunctures"; G. Thomas, "Typology for the Case." The subject tells us what it is a case *of*. The subject of this book is *grassroots democratic participation within a racially stratified and politically unequal society*.

6. Bonilla-Silva and Embrick, "'Every Place Has.'"

7. Morris and Braine, "Social Movements and Oppositional."

8. Seamster and Ray, "Against Teleology."

9. Bracey, "Toward a Critical Race."

10. Rosino, "Boundaries and Barriers."

11. Ray, "Theory of Racialized Organizations," 35.

12. Ray, "Theory of Racialized Organizations."

13. Mansbridge, "Making of Oppositional Consciousness."

14. Meghji, "Activating Controlling Images," 230.

15. Scholars continue to engage in heated debates about whether racial progress resulting from rearticulation by collective struggles such as the civil rights movement is a forgone conclusion—see, e.g., Omi and Winant, *Racial Formation*; Bracey, "Toward a Critical Race." Of course, the history of the United

States is riven with patterned racist retrenchment and backlash following the achievements of organized movements for racial justice—see C. Anderson, *White Rage*. However, the purpose of racial rearticulation is to identify strategies and conditions relating to racial justice rather than to make predictions or even to engage in large-scale causal analysis.

16. Quoted in Loy, *Ecobuddhism*, 98.

17. See also Jones, *New Social Face*, on "institutionalized delusion" and Williams, Owens, and Syedullah, *Radical Dharma*, on racial oppression, spirituality, and human freedom. I am indebted to this intersection of Buddhist philosophy and critical theories of society and racial inequality for my understanding of the role of consciousness, solidarity, and delusions in this study.

18. Omi and Winant, *Racial Formation*, 3rd ed.

19. Omi and Winant, *Racial Formation*, 3rd ed., 125.

20. Giddens, "Problems of Action."

21. Bonilla-Silva, "Rethinking Racism"; Rosino, "Dramaturgical Domination"; Ray, "Theory of Racialized Organizations"; Meghji, *Racialized Social System*.

22. Meghji, "Activating Controlling Images," 231.

23. Du Bois, *Darkwater*.

24. Du Bois, *Darkwater*, 557.

25. Rosino, "Dramaturgical Domination."

Appendix

1. See, e.g., Baiocchi and Connor, "The Ethnos in the Polis," 141, who argue "political ethnography allows the researcher to bring up the mundane details that can affect politics, providing a 'thick description' where one was missing." Thick description is a style of observation and writing that transcends "mere fact and surface appearances" to reveal "detail, context, emotion, and the webs of social relationships that join persons to one another"—see, Denzin, *Interpretive Interactionism*, 83.

2. Schatz, "Ethnographic Immersion," 5.

3. Having read various qualitative studies on marginalized group members— see, e.g., Duneier, *Sidewalk.*; Gurr, *Reproductive Justice*—I was aware of this approach.

4. Kubik, "Ethnography of Politics," 5.

5. Kubik, "Ethnography of Politics," 10.

6. Seidman, "Pragmatism and Sociology."

7. Seidman, "Pragmatism and Sociology," 757.

8. G. Thomas, "Doing Case Study," 581.

9. Burawoy, *Ethnography Unbound*, 2.

10. A case study indicates selecting a subject and object of inquiry rather than a specific research method or methodology—see, e.g., G. Thomas, "Typology." In this case, the object is the case itself, the participants of several regional chapters of a grassroots progressive political party in the northeastern United

States. I also developed a set of insights and narratives that can be placed in the contexts of other cases and theories. The case itself is the *object*, but the question of importance is instead the *subject* of the case—see, e.g., Becker, "Cases, Causes, Conjunctures"; G. Thomas, "Typology."

11. Flyvbjerg, "Why Mass Media Matter," 100.

12. Foucault, as quoted in J. Miller, *Passion of Michael Foucault*; Clegg, Flyvbjerg, and Haugaard, "Reflections on Phronetic."

13. From this analytical frame, I sought to describe and understand the patterns that took place within gatherings that involved GAP participants (including informal conversations) rather than the organization or group itself— see Goffman, *Encounters*. In other words, my fieldwork comprised of producing encounters in which I could observe grassroots democratic participation via everyday social settings.

14. Durkheim, *Elementary Forms*; R. Collins, *Interaction Ritual Chains*.

15. Giddens, *Modernity and Self-Identity*.

16. Essed, *Understanding Everyday Racism*, 68.

17. Maynes, Pierce, and Laslett, *Telling Stories*, 6.

18. Maynes, Pierce, and Laslett, *Telling Stories*, 4.

19. Maynes, Pierce, and Laslett, *Telling Stories*, 6.

20. Maynes, Pierce, and Laslett, *Telling Stories*, 9.

21. Maynes, Pierce, and Laslett, *Telling Stories*, 9.

22. Delgado, "Storytelling for Oppositionists," 2413.

23. Essed, *Understanding Everyday Racism*, 81.

24. Maynes, Pierce, and Laslett, *Telling Stories*, 10.

25. Somers, "Narrative Constitution."

26. Somers, "Narrative Constitution," 618.

27. Somers, "Narrative Constitution," 618.

28. Scott, *Organizations*, 19.

29. Scott, *Organizations*.

30. Scott, *Organizations*, 20.

31. Scott, *Organizations*, 20.

32. Chapkis, "Productive Tensions."

33. Emerson, *Contemporary Field Research*.

34. On one hand, questions or incredulity revealed the rationalizations that participants held for their stances and actions. But this approach risked participants becoming closed or guarded. Indeed, many times participants tried to set boundaries or became defensive within such interactions, particularly around issues regarded as contentious such as racism. While positioning myself as a fellow "true believer" was generative of greater access and rapport, it limited the range of conversations and social logic that I could reveal.

35. Lichterman, "Interpretive Reflexivity."

36. Lichterman, "Interpretive Reflexivity," 39.

37. Hurston, *Dust Tracks*; Williams, "Skinfolk, Not Kinfolk."

Bibliography

Newspapers, Magazines, and News Websites

Al Jazeera   New York Times
American Prospect PBS NewsHour
CNN   Quartz
The Guardian   San Francisco Chronicle
The Hill   Truthout
In These Times   Vox
Madison365   Washington Post
The Nation

Books, Journal Articles, and Dissertations

Addams, Jane. *Democracy and Social Ethics*. New York: Macmillan, 1902.

Ahmed, Sara. *The Cultural Politics of Emotion*. Edinburgh, Scotland: Edinburgh University Press, 2004.

———. "A Phenomenology of Whiteness." *Feminist Theory* 8, no. 2 (2007): 149–68.

Albert, S., and D. A. Whetton. "Organizational Identity." *Research in Organizational Behavior* 7 (1985): 263–95.

Alegria, Sharla. "Constructing Racial Difference through Group Talk: An Analysis of White Focus Groups' Discussion of Racial Profiling." *Ethnic and Racial Studies* 37, no. 2 (2012): 241–60.

Alexander, Michelle. *The New Jim Crow: Mass Incarceration in the Age of Colorblindness*. New York: New Press, 2010.

Ali, Omar H. *In the Balance of Power: Independent Black Politics and Third-Party Movements in the United States*. Athens: Ohio University Press, 2008.

Allen, Theodore W. *The Invention of the White Race*. Vol. 2, *The Origin of Racial Oppression in Anglo-America*. New York: Verso, 1997.

American Psychological Association. *Stress in America: The State of Our Nation*. Washington, DC: American Psychological Association, 2017.

Anderson, Carol. *One Person, No Vote: How Voter Suppression Is Destroying Our Democracy*. New York: Bloomsbury, 2018.

———. *White Rage: The Unspoken Truth of Our Racial Divide*. New York: Bloomsbury Publishing Plc, 2017.

Anderson, Elijah. "The White Space." *Sociology of Race and Ethnicity* 1, no. 1 (2015): 10–21.

Bachrach, Peter, and Aryeh Botwinick. *Power and Empowerment: A Radical Theory of Participatory Democracy*. Philadelphia: Temple University Press, 1992.

Baiocchi, Gianpaolo, and Brian T. Connor. "The Ethnos in the Polis: Political Ethnography as a Mode of Inquiry." *Sociology Compass* 2, no. 1 (2008): 139–55.

Baldwin, James. *The Fire Next Time.* New York: Dial, 1963.

Bandyopadhyay, Ranjan. "Volunteer Tourism and 'The White Man's Burden': Globalization of Suffering, White Savior Complex, Religion and Modernity." *Journal of Sustainable Tourism* 27, no. 3 (2019): 327–43. https://doi.org /10.1080/09669582.2019.1578361.

Banton, Michael. *Ethnic and Racial Consciousness.* New York: Routledge, 1997.

Becker, Howard S. "Cases, Causes. Conjunctures. Stories and Imagery." In *Case Study Method,* ed. Roger Gomm, Martyn Hammersley, and Peter Foster, 223–33. London: Sage, 1992.

Beecher Field, Jonathan. *Town Hall Meetings and the Death of Deliberation.* Minneapolis: University of Minnesota Press, 2019.

Belcher, Christina. "There Is No Such Thing as a Post-Racial Prison: Neoliberal Multiculturalism and the White Savior Complex on *Orange Is the New Black.*" *Television and New Media* 17, no. 6 (2016): 491–503.

Bell, Joyce M., and Douglas Hartmann. "Diversity in Everyday Discourse: The Cultural Ambiguities of 'Happy Talk.'" *American Sociological Review* 71, no. 2 (2007): 895–914.

Berger, Peter L., and Thomas Luckmann. *The Social Construction of Reality: A Treatise in the Sociology of Knowledge.* New York: Penguin, 1966.

Berman, Ari. *Give Us the Ballot: The Modern Struggle for Voting Rights in America.* New York: Picador, 2015.

Bex, Sean, and Stef Craps. "Humanitarianism, Testimony, and the White Savior Industrial Complex: What Is the What versus Kony 2012." *Cultural Critique* 92 (2016): 32–56.

Bibby, John F., and Sandy L. Maisel. *Dilemmas in American Politics: Two Parties—Or More?: The American Party System.* Boulder, CO: Westview Press, 2002.

Blauner, Robert. *Racial Oppression in America.* New York: HarperCollins, 1972.

Blee, Katherine. *Democracy in the Making: How Activist Groups Form.* New York: Oxford University Press, 2012.

Bonilla-Silva, Eduardo. "Feeling Race: The Racial Economy of Emotions." *American Sociological Review* 84, no. 1 (2019): 1–25.

———. "From Bi-Racial to Tri-Racial: Towards a New System of Racial Stratification in the USA." *Ethnic and Racial Studies* 27, no. 6 (2006): 931–50.

———. *Racism without Racists: Color-Blind Racism and the Persistence of Racial Inequality in America.* 6th ed. Lanham, MD: Rowman & Littlefield, 2021.

———. "Rethinking Racism: Toward a Structural Interpretation." *American Sociological Review* 62, no. 3 (1997): 465. https://doi.org/10.2307/2657316.

———. "What Makes Systemic Racism Systemic?" *Sociological Inquiry* 91, no. 3 (2021): 513–33.

———. *White Supremacy and Racism in the Post–Civil Rights Era*. Boulder, CO: Lynne Rienner, 2001.

Bonilla-Silva, Eduardo, and David G. Embrick. "'Every Place Has a Ghetto . . .': The Significance of Whites' Social and Residential Segregation." *Symbolic Interaction* 30, no. 3 (2007): 323–45.

Bonilla-Silva, Eduardo, Carla Goar, and David G. Embrick. "When Whites Flock Together: The Social Psychology of White Habitus." *Critical Sociology* 32, no. 2–3 (March 2006): 229–53. https://doi.org/10.1163/156916306777835268.

Bourdieu, Pierre. *Distinction: A Social Critique of the Judgement of Taste*. Cambridge, MA: Harvard University Press, 1984.

———. *Outline of a Theory of Practice*. Translated by Richard Nice. New York: Cambridge University Press, 1995.

Bracey, Glenn E. "Toward a Critical Race Theory of State." *Critical Sociology* 41, no. 3 (May 2015): 553–72. https://doi.org/10.1177/0896920513504600.

Bracey, Glenn, and Wendy Leo Moore. "'Race Tests': Racial Boundary Maintenance in White Evangelical Churches." *Sociological Inquiry* 87, no. 2 (2017): 282–302.

Braunstein, Ruth. *Prophets and Patriots: Faith in Democracy across the Political Divide*. Berkeley: University of California Press, 2017.

Bryan, Frank M. *Real Democracy: The New England Town Meeting and How It Works*. Chicago: University of Chicago Press, 2003.

Burawoy, Michael. *Ethnography Unbound*. Berkeley: University of California Press, 1991.

Cann, Collete N., and Erin McCloskey. "The Poverty Pimpin' Project: How Whiteness Profits from Black and Brown Bodies in Community Service Programs." *Race Ethnicity and Education* 20, no. 1 (2017): 72–86.

Carmichael, Stokely, and Charles V. Hamilton. *Black Power: The Politics of Liberation in America*. Toronto: Vintage, 1967.

Carter, Shannon K., Leslie H. Picca, and Brittany N. Murray. "Racialization in Public and Private: Memories of First Racial Experiences." *Race and Social Problems* 4, nos. 3–4 (2012): 133–43.

Chambers, Samuel A. "Working on the Democratic Imagination and the Limits of Deliberative Democracy." *Political Research Quarterly* 58, no. 4 (2005): 619–23.

Chapkis, Wendy. "Productive Tensions: Ethnographic Engagement, Complexity, and Contradiction." *Journal of Contemporary Ethnography* 39, no. 5 (2010): 483–97.

Clair, Matthew, and Jeffrey S. Denis. "Racism, Sociology Of." In *International Encyclopedia of the Social and Behavioral Sciences*, 2nd ed., ed. James D. Wright, 857–63. Vol. 19. Waltham, MA: Elsevier, 2015.

Clegg, Joshua. "Stranger Situations: Examining a Self-Regulatory Model of Socially Awkward Encounters." *Group Processes and Intergroup Relations* 15, no. 6 (2012): 693–712.

———. "The Importance of Feeling Awkward: A Dialogical Narrative Phenomenology of Socially Awkward Situations." *Qualitative Research in Psychology* 9, no. 3 (2012): 262–78.

Clegg, Stewart, Bent Flyvbjerg, and Mark Haugaard. "Reflections on Phronetic Social Science: A Dialogue between Stewart Clegg, Bent Flyvbjerg and Mark Haugaard." *Journal of Political Power* 7, no. 2 (2014): 275–306.

Coates, Rodney D. "Law and the Cultural Production of Race and Racialized Systems of Oppression: Early American Court Cases." *American Behavioral Scientist* 47, no. 3 (2003): 329–51.

Collins, Patricia Hill. *Black Feminist Thought: Knowledge, Consciousness, and the Politics of Empowerment.* 2nd ed. New York: Routledge, 2000.

———. "Learning from the Outsider Within: The Sociological Significance of Black Feminist Thought." *Social Problems* 33, no. 6 (1986): 14–32.

———. "The New Politics of Community." *American Sociological Review* 75, no. 1 (2010): 7–30.

Collins, Randal. *Interaction Ritual Chains.* Princeton, NJ: Princeton University Press, 2005.

Collins, Robert, David R. Mandel, and Sarah S. Schywiola. "Political Identity over Personal Impact: Early U.S. Reactions to the COVID-19 Pandemic." *Frontiers in Psychology* 12 (2021). https://doi.org/10.3389/fpsyg.2021.607639.

Collins, Sharon M. "Black Mobility in White Corporations: Up the Corporate Ladder but out on a Limb." *Social Problems* 44, no. 1 (1997): 55–77.

Combs, Barbara Harris. *Bodies out of Place: Theorizing Anti-Blackness in U.S. Society.* Athens: University of Georgia Press, 2022.

Cox, Vicki. *The History of Third Parties.* New York: Chelsea House, 2007.

Davis, Angela Y. *Women, Culture, and Politics.* New York: Vintage, 1990.

Delgado, Richard. "Storytelling for Oppositionists and Others: A Plea for Narrative." *Michigan Law Review* 87, no. 8 (1989): 2411–41.

Denzin, Norman K. *Interpretive Interactionism.* Thousand Oaks, CA: Sage, 1989.

Derber, Charles. *Welcome to the Revolution: Universalizing Resistance for Social Justice and Democracy in Perilous Times.* New York: Routledge, 2017.

DiAngelo, Robin. *White Fragility: Why It's So Hard for White People to Talk about Racism.* New York: Beacon, 2018.

Diaquoi, Raygine. "Symbols in the Strange Fruit Seeds: What 'The Talk' Black Parents Have with Their Sons Tells Us about Racism." *Harvard Educational Review* 87, no. 4 (2017).

DiPrete, Thomas A., Andrew Gelman, Tyler McCormick, Julien Teitler, and Tian Zheng. "Segregation in Social Networks Based on Acquaintanceship and Trust." *American Journal of Sociology* 116, no. 4 (2011): 1234–83.

Dittmer, John. *Local People: The Struggle for Civil Rights in Mississippi.* Urbana: University of Illinois Press, 1994.

Doane, Ashley W., Jr. "Contested Terrain: Negotiating Racial Understandings in Public Discourse." *Humanity and Society* 27, no. 4 (2003): 554–75.

———. "What Is Racism? Racial Discourse and Racial Politics." *Critical Sociology* 32, no. 2–3 (2006): 255–74.

Du Bois, W. E. B. *Black Reconstruction in America*. New York: The Free Press, 1935.

———. *Darkwater: Voices from within the Veil*. New York: Harcourt, Brace, 1920.

———. *Dusk of Dawn: An Essay toward an Autobiography of a Race Concept*. New York: Oxford University Press, 2007.

———. *The Souls of Black Folk*. Chicago: A. C. McLurg, 1908.

Dubrow, Joshua Kjerulf. "Political Inequality Is International, Interdisciplinary, and Intersectional." *Sociology Compass* 9, no. 6 (2015): 477–86.

Duneier, Mitchell. *Sidewalk*. New York: MacMillan, 1999.

Durkheim, Emile. *The Elementary Forms of Religious Life*. Translated by Karen E. Fields. New York: Free Press, 1912.

Durr, Marlese, and Adia M. Harvey Wingfield. "Keep Your 'N' in Check: African American Women and the Interactive Effects of Etiquette and Emotional Labor." *Critical Sociology* 37, no. 5 (2011): 557–71.

Dwyer, Owen J., and John Paul Jones III. "White Sociospatial Epistemology." *Social and Cultural Geography* 1, no. 2 (2000): 209–22.

Eastwood, Jonathon. "The Role of Ideas in Weber's Theory of Interests." *Critical Review* 17, nos. 1–2 (2005): 89–100.

Einstein, Katherine Levine, Maxwell Palmer, and David Glick. *Racial Disparities in Housing Politics: Evidence from Administrative Data*. Initiative on Cities, Boston University, 2018. https://maxwellpalmer.com/research/racial _disparities_in_housing_politics.pdf.

Eliasoph, Nina. *The Politics of Volunteering*. Malden, MA: Polity Press, 2013.

Emerson, Robert M. *Contemporary Field Research: Perspectives and Formulations*. 2nd ed. Salem, WI: Waveland Press, 2001.

Entman, Robert, and Andrew Rojecki. *The Black Image in the White Mind: Media and Race in America*. Chicago: University of Chicago Press, 2001.

Essed, Philomena. *Understanding Everyday Racism: An Interdisciplinary Theory*. Newbury Park, CA: Sage, 1991.

Farough, Steven D. "The Social Geographies of White Masculinities." *Critical Sociology* 30, no. 2 (2004): 241–64.

Feagin, Joe R. *Systemic Racism: A Theory of Oppression*. New York: Routledge, 2006.

———. *The White Racial Frame: Centuries of Racial Framing and Counter-Framing*. 3rd ed. New York: Routledge, 2020.

Feinberg, Matthew, Alexa M. Tullett, Zachary Mensch, William Hart, and Sara Gottlieb. "The Political Reference Point: How Geography Shapes Political Identity." *PLOSone* 12, no. 2 (2017).

Fitzgerald, Michael Ray. "The White Savior and His Junior Partner: The Lone Ranger and Tonto on Cold War Television (1949–1957)." *Journal of Popular Culture* 46, no. 1 (2013): 79–108.

Flyvbjerg, Bent. "Why Mass Media Matter and How to Work with Them: Phronesis and Megaprojects." In *Real Social Science: Applied Phronesis*, edited by B. Flyvbjerg, T. Landman, and S. Schram, 95–121. Cambridge, UK: Cambridge University Press, 2012.

Frank, Thomas. *Listen, Liberal; or, Whatever Happened to the Party of the People?* New York: Picador, 2016.

Frankenberg, Ruth. *White Women, Race Matters: The Social Construction of Whiteness*. Minneapolis: University of Minnesota Press, 1993.

Fraser, Nancy. *The Old Is Dying and the New Cannot Be Born*. Brooklyn, NY: Verso, 2019.

Fullerton, Andrew S., and Michael J. Stern. "Racial Differences in the Gender Gap in Political Participation in the American South, 1592–2004." *Social Science History* 37, no. 2 (2013): 145–76.

Gallagher, Charles A. "'Blacks, Jews, Gays and Immigrants Are Taking Over': How the Use of Polling Data Can Distort Reality and Perpetuate Inequality among Immigrants." *Ethnic and Racial Studies* 37, no. 5 (2014): 731–37.

Garcia Bedolla, Lisa, and Melissa R. Michelson. *Mobilizing Inclusion: Transforming the Electorate through Get-Out-the-Vote Campaigns*. New Haven, CT: Yale University Press, 2012.

Giddens, Anthony. *Modernity and Self-Identity: Self and Society in the Late Modern Age*. Stanford, CA: Stanford University Press, 1991.

———. "Problems of Action and Structure." In *The Giddens Reader*, edited by Philip Cassell, 88–175. Stanford, CA: Stanford University Press, 1993.

Gidley, Ben. "A Note on the Awkwardness of the Ethnographer." *Sociological Review* 57, no. 3 (2009): 526–29.

Gillespie, David J. *Challengers to Duopoly: Why Third Parties Matter in American Two-Party Politics*. Columbia: University of South Carolina Press, 2012.

Glaude, Eddie S. *Democracy in Black: How Race Still Enslaves the American Soul*. New York: Crown Publishers, 2016.

Glenn, Evelyn Nakano. *Unequal Freedom: How Race and Gender Shaped American Citizenship and Labor*. Cambridge, MA: Harvard University Press, 2002.

Goffman, Erving. "Embarrassment and Social Organization." *American Journal of Sociology* 62, no. 3 (1956): 246–71. https://www.jstor.org/stable/2772920.

Goffman, Erving. *Encounters: Two Studies in the Sociology of Interactions*. Indianapolis, IN: Bobbs-Merrill, 1961.

———. "The Interaction Order: American Sociological Association, 1982 Presidential Address." *American Sociological Review* 48, no. 1 (1983): 1–17.

Gonzalez-Sobrino, Bianca. "Puerto Rico's Politics of Exclusion." *Contexts* 17, no. 1 (2018): 80–81.

Gorski, Paul C., and Noura Erakat. "Racism, Whiteness, and Burnout in Antiracism Movements: How White Racial Justice Activists Elevate Burnout in Racial Justice Activists of Color in the United States." *Ethnicities* 19, no. 5 (2019): 784–808. https://doi.org/10.1177/1468796819833871.

Gossett, Thomas F. *Race: The History of an Idea in America.* New York: Oxford University Press, 1965.

Gramsci, Antonio. *Selections from the Prison Notebooks.* New York: International Publishers, 1929.

Graves, Joseph L. *The Emperor's New Clothes: Biological Theories of Race at the Millennium.* New Brunswick, NJ: Rutgers University Press, 2001.

Gurr, Barb. *Reproductive Justice: The Politics of Health Care for Native American Women.* New Brunswick, NJ: Rutgers University Press, 2014.

Hagerman, Margaret Ann. "Reproducing and Reworking Colorblind Racial Ideology: Acknowledging Children's Agency in the White Habitus." *Sociology of Race and Ethnicity* 2, no. 1 (2016): 71.

———. "White Families and Race: Colour-Blind and Colour-Conscious Approaches to White Racial Socialization." *Ethnic and Racial Studies* 37, no. 14 (2014): 2598–2614.

Hajnal, Zoltan, and Jessica L. Troustine. "Race and Class Inequality in Local Politics." In *The Double Bind: The Politics of Racial and Class Inequalities in the Americas,* edited by Juliet Hooker and Alvin B. Tillery Jr., 139–56. Washington, DC: American Political Science Association, 2016.

Hall, Stuart. "The Work of Representation." In *Representation: Cultural Representations and Signifying Practices,* edited by Stuart Hall, 13–74. London: Sage, 1997.

Hampton, Fred. "Power Anywhere Where There's People." Speech. Olivet Church, Chicago, 1969. Transcript printed in a pamphlet by the Illinois chapter of the Black Panther Party. Marxists Internet Archive. https://www.marxists.org/archive/hampton/1969/misc/power-anywhere-where-theres-people.htm.

Haney López, Ian F. *Dog Whistle Politics: How Coded Racial Appeals Have Reinvented Racism and Wrecked the Middle Class.* Oxford, UK: Oxford University Press, 2014.

Harré, Rom, Fathali M. Moghaddam, Tracey Pilkerton Cairnie, Daniel Rothba, and Steven R. Sabat. "Recent Advances in Positioning Theory." *Theory and Psychology* 19, no. 1 (2009): 5–31.

Harrington, Andrew. "Is Quentin Tarantino Calvin Candie?: The Essence of Exploitation in *Django Unchained.*" *Black Camera* 7, no. 2 (2016): 79–87.

Hart, Stephen. *Cultural Dilemmas of Progressive Politics: Styles of Engagement among Grassroots Activists.* Chicago: University of Chicago Press, 2001.

Hawkesworth, Mary. "Congressional Enactments of Race-Gender: Toward a Theory of Raced-Gendered Institutions." *American Political Science Review* 97, no. 4 (2003): 529–50.

Haynes, Bruce D. *Red Lines, Black Spaces*. New Haven, CT: Yale University Press, 2001.

Heidemann, Kai. "Overcoming Uncertainty: Agency, Stance, and the Rise of Collective Action in Times of Crisis." *Sociological Focus* 51, no. 2 (n.d.): 79–96. https://doi.org/10.1080/00380237.2017.1370938.

Hildreth, R.W. "Word and Deed: A Deweyan Integration of Deliberative and Participatory Democracy." *New Political Science* 34, no. 3 (2012): 295–320.

Hollis, James. *Finding Meaning in the Second Half of Life*. New York: Gotham Books, 2006.

Hooghe, Marc, and Ruth Dassonville. "Explaining the Trump Vote: The Effect of Racist Resentment and Anti-Immigrant Sentiments." *PS: Political Science and Politics*, April 12, 2018. https://doi.org/10.1017/S1049096518000367.

Hope, Elan C., and Robert J. Jagers. "The Role of Sociopolitical Attitudes and Civic Education in the Civic Engagement of Black Youth." *Journal of Research on Adolescence* 24, no. 3 (2014): 460–70.

Hughey, David G., Embrick, Matthew W., and Ashley "Woody" Doane. "Paving the Way for Future Race Research: Exploring the Racial Mechanisms within a Color-Blind, Racialized Social System." *American Behavioral Scientist* 59, no. 11 (2015): 1347–57.

Hughey, Matthew W. "We've Been Framed! A Focus on Identity and Interaction for a Better Vision of Racialized Social Movements." *Sociology of Race and Ethnicity* 1, no. 1 (January 2015): 137–52. https://doi.org/10.1177/2332649214557334.

———. "White Backlash in the 'Post-Racial' United States." *Ethnic and Racial Studies Review* 37, no. 5 (2014): 721–30.

———. *White Bound: Nationalists, Antiracists, and the Shared Meanings of Race*. Stanford, CA: Stanford University Press, 2012.

———. *The White Savior Film: Content, Critics, and Consumption*. Philadelphia: Temple University Press, 2014.

Hughey, Matthew W., and Gregory S. Parks. *Wrongs of the Right: Language, Race, and the Republican Party in the Age of Obama*. New York: New York University Press, 2014.

Hunt, Darnel M. *Screening the Los Angeles "Riots": Race, Seeing, and Resistance*. New York: Cambridge University Press, 1997.

Hurston, Zora Neale. *Dust Tracks on a Road: A Memoir*. Philadelphia: J. B. Lippincott, 1942.

Hutchings, Vincent L., and Nicholas A. Valentino. "The Centrality of Race in American Politics." *Annual Review of Political Science* 7 (2004): 383–408. https://doi.org/10.1146/annurev.polisci.7.012003.104859.

Ioanide, Paula. *The Emotional Politics of Racism: How Feelings Trump Facts in an Era of Colorblindness*. Stanford, CA: Stanford University Press, 2015.

Jackson, Ronald L. "White Space, White Self: Mapping Discursive Inequity into the Self." *Quarterly Journal of Speech* 85, no. 1 (1999): 38–54.

Jacobs, Lawrence R., Fay Lomax Cook, and Michael X. Delli Carpini. *Talking Together: Public Deliberation and Political Participation in America*. Chicago: University of Chicago Press, 2009.

Jones, Ken. *The New Social Face of Buddhism: An Alternate Sociopolitical Perspective.* Boston: Wisdom Publishers, 2003.

Kanter, Rosabeth Moss. *Men and Women of the Corporation.* New York: Basic, 1977.

Katznelson, Ira. *When Affirmative Action Was White: An Untold History of Racial Inequality in Twentieth-Century America.* New York: W. W. Norton, 2005.

Kellett, Petter M., and Diana G. Dalton. *Managing Conflict in a Negotiated World: A Narrative Approach to Achieving Dialogue and Change.* Thousand Oaks, CA: Sage Publications, 2001.

Kinder, Donald R., and Lynn M. Sanders. *Divided by Color: Racial Politics and Democratic Ideals.* Chicago: University of Chicago Press, 1996.

Knowles, Eric D., and Linda R. Tropp. "The Racial and Economic Context of Trump Support: Evidence for Threat, Identity, and Contact Effects in the 2016 Presidential Election." *Social Psychological and Personality Science,* 2018. https://doi.org/10.1177/1948550618759326.

Kotsko, Adam. *Awkwardness: An Essay.* New York: Zer0 Books, 2010.

Kraus, Celene. "Community Struggles and the Shaping of Democratic Consciousness." *Sociological Forum* 4, no. 2 (1989): 227–39.

Krysan, Maria, and Kyle Crowder. *Cycles of Segregation: Social Processes and Residential Stratification.* New York: Russell Sage Foundation, 2017.

Kubik, Jan. "Ethnography of Politics: Foundations, Applications, Prospects." In *Political Ethnography: What Immersion Contributes to the Study of Power,* edited by Edward Schatz, 25–52. Chicago: University of Chicago Press, 2009.

La Due Lake, Ronald, and Robert Huckfeldt. "Social Capital, Social Networks, and Political Participation." *Political Psychology* 19, no. 3 (2002): 567–84.

Lakoff, George. *Don't Think of an Elephant: Know Your Values and Frame the Debate.* White River Junction, VT: Chelsea Green, 2004.

———. *The Political Mind: A Cognitive Scientist's Guide to Your Brain and Its Politics.* Westminster, UK: Penguin Books, 2009.

Laurison, Daniel, Hana Brown, and Ankit Rastogi. "Voting Intersections: Race, Class, and Participation in Presidential Elections in the United States 2008–2016." *Sociological Perspectives* 65, no. 4 (2022): 768–89.

Lears, T. J. Jackson. "The Concept of Cultural Hegemony: Problems and Possibilities." *American Historical Review* 90, no. 3 (1985): 567–93.

Leon, Cedric de, Manali Desai, and Cihuan Tuğal. "Political Articulation: The Structured Creativity of Parties." In *Building Blocs: How Parties Organize Society,* edited by C. Leon, M. Desai, and C. Tuğal, 1–36. Stanford, CA: Stanford University Press, 2015.

Lewis, Amanda E. *Race in the Schoolyard: Negotiating the Color Line in Classrooms and Communities.* New Brunswick, NJ: Rutgers University Press, 2003.

———. "'What Group?' Studying Whites and Whiteness in the Era of 'Color-Blindness.'" *Sociological Theory* 22, no. 4 (December 2004): 623–46. https://doi.org/10.1111/j.0735-2751.2004.00237.x.

Lichterman, Paul. "Interpretive Reflexivity in Ethnography." *Ethnography* 18, no. 1 (2017): 35–45.

———. *The Search for Political Community: American Activists Reinventing Commitment*. Cambridge, UK: Cambridge University Press, 1996.

Lipset, Seymore Martin. *Consensus and Conflict: Essays in Political Sociology*. New Brunswick, NJ: Transaction Publishers, 1990.

Lipsitz, George. *How Racism Takes Place*. Philadelphia: Temple University Press, 2011.

Lizardo, Omar, and Jessica L. Collett. "Embarrassment and Social Organization: A Multiple Identities Model." *Social Forces* 92, no. 1 (2013). http://www.jstor .org/stable/43287528.

Logan, John R. "The Persistence of Segregation in the 21st Century Central Metropolis." *City and Community* 12, no. 2 (2013): 160–68.

Logan, John R., Jennifer Darrah, and Sookhe Oh. "The Impact of Race and Ethnicity, Immigrant and Political Context on Participation in American Electoral Politics." *Social Forces* 90, no. 3 (2012): 993–1022.

Loy, David R. *Ecobuddhism: Buddhist Teachings for the Ecological Crisis*. Somerville, MA: Wisdom Publishers, 2018.

Lukács, György. *History and Class Consciousness: Studies in Marxist Dialectics*. Boston, MA: MIT Press, 1972.

MacMullan, Terrance. "The Fly Wheel of Society: Habit and Social Meliorism in the Pragmatist Tradition." In *A History of Habit: From Aristotle to Bourdieu*, edited by Tom Sparrow and Adam Hutchison, 229–53. New York: Lexington Books, 2013.

———. *Habits of Whiteness: A Pragmatist Reconstruction*. Bloomington: Indiana University Press, 2009.

Major, Brenda, Alison Blodorn, and Gregory Major Blascovich. "The Threat of Increasing Diversity: Why Many White Americans Support Trump in the 2016 Presidential Election." *Group Processes and Intergroup Relations* 21, no. 6 (2018): 931–40.

Mansbridge, Jane. "The Making of Oppositional Consciousness." In *Oppositional Consciousness: The Subjective Roots of Social Protest*, edited by Jane Mansbridge and Aldon Morris, 1–19. Chicago: University of Chicago Press, 2001.

Mansbridge, Jane, and Aldon Morris, eds. *Oppositional Consciousness: The Subjective Roots of Social Protest*. Chicago: University of Chicago Press, 2001.

Marquez, Benjamin, and Rodolfo Espino. "Mexican American Support for Third Parties: The Case of La Raza Unida." *Ethnic and Racial Studies* 33, no. 2 (2010): 290–312.

Martin, Jonathan H., ed. *Empowering Progressive Third Parties in the United States: Defeating Duopoly, Advancing Democracy*. New York: Routledge, 2015.

Marx, Karl. *Class Struggles in France, 1848-1850*. New York: International Publishers, 1850.

Maurantonio, Nicole. "'Reason to Hope?' The White Savior Myth and Progress in 'Post-Racial' America." *Journalism and Mass Communication Quarterly* 94, no. 4 (2017): 1130–45.

Maynes, Mary Jo, Jennifer L. Pierce, and Barbara Laslett. *Telling Stories: The Use of Personal Narratives in the Social Sciences and History*. Ithaca, NY: Cornell University Press, 2012.

Mayorga-Gallo, Sarah. *Behind the White Picket Fence: Power and Privilege in a Multiethnic Neighborhood*. Chapel Hill: University of North Carolina Press, 2014.

———. "The White-Centering Logic of Diversity Ideology." *American Behavioral Scientist* 63, no. 13 (2019): 1789–1809. https://doi.org /10.1177/0002764219842619.

McAdam, Doug, and Karina Kloos. *Deeply Divided: Racial Politics and Social Movements in Postwar American Society*. New York: Oxford University Press, 2014.

McPherson, Miller, Lynn Smith-Lovin, and James M. Cook. "Birds of a Feather: Homophily in Social Networks." *Annual Review of Sociology* 27 (2001): 415–44.

Mead, George Herbert. *Mind, Self, and Society from the Standpoint of a Social Behaviorist*. Chicago: University of Chicago Press, 1934.

Meghji, Ali. "Activating Controlling Images in the Racialized Interaction Order: Black Middle-Class Interactions and the Creativity of Racist Action." *Symbolic Interaction* 42, no. 2 (2019): 229–49.

———. *The Racialized Social System*. Cambridge, UK: Polity Press, 2022.

Melamed, Jodi. "Racial Capitalism." *Critical Ethnic Studies* 1, no. 1 (2015): 76–85.

Mendelberg, Tali, Christopher F. Karpowitz, and Baxter J. Oliphant. "Gender Inequality in Deliberation: Unpacking the Black Box of Interaction." *Perspectives on Politics* 12, no. 1 (2014): 18–19.

Mendelberg, Tali, and John Oleski. "Race and Public Deliberation." *Political Communication* 17 (2000): 169–91.

Miller, James. *The Passion of Michael Foucault*. New York: Simon and Schuster, 1993.

Miller, Patrick R., and Pamela Johnson Connover. "Red and Blue States of Mind: Partisan Hostility and Voting in the United States." *Political Research Quarterly* 68, no. 2 (2015): 225–39.

Mills, Charles W. "White Ignorance." In *Race and Epistemologies of Ignorance*, edited by S. Sullivan and N. Tuana, 11–38. Albany: State University of New York Press, 2007.

———. "White Supremacy as a Sociopolitical System." In *White Out: The Continuing Significance of Racism*, edited by Ashley W. Doane Jr. and Eduardo Bonilla-Silva, 35–48. New York: Routledge, 2003.

Mills, C. Wright. *The Sociological Imagination*. New York: Oxford University Press, 1959.

Moghaddam, Fathali M., and Rom Harré. "Words, Conflicts and Political Processes." In *Words of Conflict, Words of War: How the Language We Use in Political Processes Sparks Fighting*, edited by F. Moghaddam and R. Harré, 1–30. Santa Barbara, CA: Praeger, 2010.

Moore, Wendy Leo. *Reproducing Racism: White Space, Elite Law Schools, and Racial Inequality*. Lanham, MD: Rowman & Littlefield, 2007.

Morris, Aldon. "Reflections on Social Movement Theory: Criticisms and Proposals." *Contemporary Sociology* 29, no. 3 (2000): 445–54.

Morris, Aldon, and Naomi Braine. "Social Movements and Oppositional Consciousness." In *Oppositional Consciousness: The Subjective Roots of Social Protest*, edited by Jane Mansbridge and Aldon Morris, 20–37. Chicago: University of Chicago Press, 2001.

Mouffe, Chantal. *For a Left Populism*. Brooklyn, NY: Verso, 2018.

Mudge, Anthony L., and Anthony S. Chen. "Political Parties and the Sociological Imagination: Past, Present, and Future Directions." *Annual Review of Sociology* 40, no. 305 (2014): 330.

Mueller, Jennifer C. "Producing Colorblindness: Everyday Mechanisms of White Ignorance." *Social Problems* 64, no. 2 (2017): 219–38.

Munn, Christopher W. "One Friend Rule: Race and Social Capital in an Interracial Network." *Social Problems* 65, no. 4 (2017): 473–90. https://doi.org/10.1093/socpro/spx020.

Murphy, Mollie K., and Tina M. Harris. "White Innocence and Black Subservience: The Rhetoric of White Heroism in *The Help*." *Howard Journal of Communications* 29, no. 1 (2018): 49–62.

Nagda, Biren (Ratnesh) A. "Breaking Barriers, Crossing Borders, Building Bridges: Communication Processes in Intergroup Dialogues." *Journal of Social Issues* 62, no. 3 (2006): 553–76.

Obasogie, Osagie. *Blinded by Sight: Seeing Race through the Eyes of the Blind*. Stanford, CA: Stanford University Press, 2013.

O'Brien, Jodi, and Peter Kollock. *The Production of Reality: Essays and Readings on Social Interaction*. 3rd ed. Thousand Oaks, CA: Pine Forge Press, 2001.

Oliver, Pamela. "The Ethnic Dimensions in Social Movements." *Mobilization: An International Quarterly* 22, no. 4 (2017): 395–416.

Omi, Michael, and Howard Winant. *Racial Formation in the United States: From the 1960s to the 1990s*. 2nd ed. New York: Routledge, 1994.

——. *Racial Formation in the United States*. 3rd ed. New York: Routledge, 2015.

Outlaw, Lucius, Jr. *Critical Social Theory in the Interests of Black Folk*. Lanham, MD: Rowman and Littlefield, 2005.

Parlett, Martin. *Demonizing a President: The Foreignization of Barack Obama*. Denver, CO: Praeger, 2014.

Payne, Charles. *I've Got the Light of Freedom: The Organizing Tradition and the Mississippi Freedom Struggle*. Berkeley: University of California Press, 1995.

Perrin, Andrew J. *American Democracy: From Tocqueville to Townhalls to Twitter*. New York: Polity Press, 2014.

———. *Citizen Speak: The Democratic Imagination in American Life*. Chicago: University of Chicago Press, 2006.

Perry, Imani. *More Beautiful and More Terrible: The Embrace and Transcendence of Racial Inequality in the United States*. New York: New York University Press, 2011.

Pfeffer, Jeffrey. *Power in Organizations*. Lanham, MD: Pittman Publishing, 1981.

Picca, Leslie H., and Joe R. Feagin. *Two-Faced Racism: Whites in the Backstage and Frontstage*. New York: Routledge, 2007.

Quillian, Lincoln, and Mary E. Campbell. "Beyond Black and White: The Present and Future of Multiracial Friendship Segregation." *American Sociological Review* 68, no. 4 (2003): 540–66.

Rawls, Anne Warfield. "'Race' as an Interaction Order Phenomenon: W. E. B. Du Bois's 'Double Consciousness' Revisited." *Sociological Theory* 18, no. 2 (2000): 241–74.

Ray, Victor. "A Theory of Racialized Organizations." *American Sociological Review* 84, no. 1 (February 2019): 26–53. https://doi.org/10.1177/0003122418822335.

Reeser, Todd W. "Producing Awkwardness: Affective Labour and Masculinity in Popular Culture." *Mosaic: An Interdisciplinary Critical Journal* 50, no. 4 (2017): 51–68.

Reich, Jennifer A. "Power, Positionality, and the Ethic of Care in Qualitative Research." *Qualitative Sociology* 44 (2021): 575–81.

Robinson, Cedric J. *Black Marxism: The Making of the Black Radical Tradition*. Chapel Hill: University of North Carolina Press, 1983.

Robinson, Zandria F. *This Ain't Chicago: Race, Class, and Regional Identity in the Post-Soul South*. Chapel Hill: University of North Carolina Press, 2014.

Roediger, David R. *The Wages of Whiteness: Race and the Making of the American Working Class*. London: Verso, 1991.

Roithmayr, Daria. *Reproducing Racism: How Everyday Choices Lock In White Advantage*. New York: New York University Press, 2014.

Rosino, Michael L. "Boundaries and Barriers: Racialized Dynamics of Political Power." *Sociology Compass* 10, no. 10 (2016): 939–51.

———. *Debating the Drug War: Race, Politics, and the Media*. New York: Routledge, 2021.

———. "Dramaturgical Domination: The Genesis and Evolution of the Racialized Interaction Order." *Humanity and Society* 41, no. 2 (May 2017): 158–81. https://doi.org/10.1177/0160597615623042.

Rosino, Michael L., and Matthew W. Hughey. "The War on Drugs, Racial Meanings, and Structural Racism: A Holistic and Reproductive Approach." *American Journal of Economics and Sociology* 77, no. 3–4 (2018): 849–92.

Savory, Jerold J. "The Rending of the Veil in W. E. B. Du Bois's *The Souls of Black Folk*." *CLA Journal* 15, no. 3 (1972): 334–37.

Schaffner, Brian F., Matthew Macwilliams, and Tatishe Nteta. "Understanding White Polarization in the 2016 Vote for President: The Sobering Role of Racism and Sexism." *Political Science Quarterly* 133, no. 1 (2018): 9–34.

Schatz, Edward. "Ethnographic Immersion and the Study of Politics." In *Political Ethnography: What Immersion Contributes to the Study of Power*, edited by Edward Schatz, 1–22. Chicago: University of Chicago Press, 2009.

Scheff, Thomas. "The Ubiquity of Hidden Shame in Modernity." *Cultural Sociology* 8, no. 2 (2014): 129–41. https://doi.org/10.1177/1749975513507244.

Schlozman, Kay Lehman, Sidney Verba, and Henry E. Brady. *The Unheavenly Chorus: Unequal Political Voice and the Broken Promise of American Democracy*. Princeton, NJ: Princeton University Press, 2012.

Schultz, Jaime. "*Glory Road* (2006) and the White Savior Historical Sport Film." *Journal of Popular Film and Television* 42, no. 4 (2014): 205–13.

Scott, W. Richard. *Organizations: Rational, Natural, and Open Systems*. Upper Saddle River, NJ: Prentice Hall, 1998.

Seamster, Louise, and Victor Ray. "Against Teleology in the Study of Race: Toward the Abolition of the Progress Paradigm." *Sociological Theory* 36, no. 4 (2018): 315–42.

Sears, David O., and P. J. Henry. "The Origins of Symbolic Racism." *Journal of Personality and Social Psychology* 85, no. 2 (2003): 275.

Seidman, Steven. "Pragmatism and Sociology: A Response to Clough, Denzin and Richardson." *Sociological Quarterly* 37, no. 4 (1996): 753–59.

Shafer, Byron. "Republicans and Democrats as Social Types; or, Notes toward an Ethnography of the Political Parties." *Journal of American Studies* 20, no. 3 (1986): 341–54.

Shefter, Martin. *Political Parties and the State: The American Historical Experience*. Princeton, NJ: Princeton University Press, 1994.

Shelton, J. Nicole, Tessa V. West, and Thomas E. Trail. "Concerns about Appearing Prejudiced: Implications for Anxiety during Daily Interracial Interactions." *Group Processes and Intergroup Relations* 13, no. 3 (2010): 329–44.

Sigelman, Lee, Timothy Bledsoe, Susan Welch, and Michael W. Combs. "Making Contact? Black-White Social Interaction in an Urban Setting." *American Journal of Sociology* 101, no. 5 (1996): 1306–32.

Solórzano, Daniel G., and Tara J. Yosso. "Critical Race Methodology: Counter-Storytelling as an Analytical Framework for Education Research." *Qualitative Inquiry* 8, no. 2 (2002): 23–44.

Sølvberg, Lisa, and Vegard Jarness. "Assessing Contradictions: Methodological Challenges when Mapping Symbolic Boundaries." *Cultural Sociology* 13, no. 2 (2019): 178–97. https://doi.org/10.1177/1749975518819907.

Somers, Margaret R. "The Narrative Constitution of Identity: A Relational and Network Approach." *Theory and Society* 23, no. 5 (1994): 605–49.

Sorenson, Nicholas. "The Road to Empathy: Dialogic Pathways for Engaging Diversity and Improving Intergroup Relations." PhD dissertation, Department of Psychology, University of Michigan, 2010.

Steinberg, Stephen. *Race Relations: A Critique*. Stanford, CA: Stanford University Press, 2007.

Stout, Jeffrey. *Blessed Are the Organized: Grassroots Democracy in America*. Princeton, NJ: Princeton University Press, 2010.

Sullivan, Shannon. *Revealing Whiteness: The Unconscious Habits of Racial Privilege*. Bloomington: Indiana University Press, 2006.

Taylor, Keeanga-Yamahtta. *From #BlackLivesMatter to Black Liberation*. Chicago, IL: Haymarket, 2016.

Thomas, Gary. "Doing Case Study: Abduction, Not Induction, Phronesis Not Theory." *Qualitative Inquiry* 16, no. 7 (2010): 575–82.

———. "A Typology for the Case Study in Social Science Following a Review of Definition, Discourse, and Structure." *Qualitative Inquiry* 17, no. 6 (2011): 511–21.

Thomas, James M. "Affect and the Sociology of Race: A Program for Critical Inquiry." *Ethnicities* 14, no. 1 (February 2014): 72–90. https://doi.org/10.1177/1468796813497003.

Tilly, Charles. *Democracy*. Cambridge, UK: Cambridge University Press, 2007.

Twine, France Winddance. *A White Side of Black Britain: Interracial Intimacy and Racial Literacy*. Durham, NC: Duke University Press, 2010.

Underhill, Megan R. "Parenting during Ferguson: Making Sense of White Parents' Silence." *Ethnic and Racial Studies* 41, no. 11 (2018): 1934–51.

Vanderbeck, Robert M. "Inner-City Children, Country Summers: Narrating American Childhood and the Geographies of Whiteness." *Environment and Planning A* 40 (2008): 1132–50.

Vera, Hernan, and Andrew Gordon. *Screen Saviors: Hollywood Fictions of Whiteness*. Lanham, MD: Rowman and Littlefield, 2003.

Verba, Sidney, Nancy Burns, and Kay Lehman Schlozman. "Knowing and Caring about Politics: Gender and Political Engagement." *Journal of Politics* 58, no. 4 (1997): 1051–72.

Walsh, Katherine Cramer. *Talking about Politics: Informal Groups and Social Identity in American Life*. Chicago: University of Chicago Press, 2004.

Walton, Hanes, Jr., Sherman C. Puckett, and Donald R. Deskins Jr. *The African American Electorate: A Statistical History*. Thousand Oaks, CA: CQ Press, 2012.

Warren, Mark R. *Fire in the Heart: How White Activists Embrace Racial Justice*. New York: Oxford University Press, 2010.

Weber, Max. "Class, Status, Party." In *From Max Weber: Essays in Sociology*, edited by H. H. Gerth and C. Wright Mills, 180–195. New York: Oxford University Press, 1946.

———. "Politics as a Vocation." In *From Max Weber: Essays in Sociology*, edited by H. H. Gerth and C. Wright Mills, 77–128. New York: Oxford University Press, 1946.

———. *The Protestant Ethic and the Spirit of Capitalism*. Translated by Talcott Parsons. Boston, MA: Unwin Hyman, 1905.

———. "The Social Psychology of World Religions." In *From Max Weber: Essays in Sociology*, edited by H. H. Gerth and C. Wright Mills, 267–301. New York: Oxford University Press, 1946.

Westbrook, David A. *Navigators of the Contemporary: Why Ethnography Matters*. Chicago: University of Chicago Press, 2008.

Wherry, Frederick, Kristin Seefeldt, and Anthony Alvarez. "To Lend or Not to Lend to Friends and Kin: Awkwardness, Obfuscation, and Negative Reciprocity." *Social Forces* 98, no. 2 (2019): 753–93. https://doi.org/10.1093/sf/soy127.

Williams, Brackette F. "Skinfolk, Not Kinfolk: Comparative Reflections on the Identity of Participant-Observation in Two Field Situations." In *Feminist Dilemmas in Fieldwork*, edited by Diane L. Wolf, 72–95. New York: Routledge, 1996.

williams, Rev. angel Kyodo, Lama Rod Owens, and Jasmine Syedullah. *Radical Dharma: Talking Race, Love, and Liberation*. Berkeley: North Atlantic Books, 2016.

Willner, Roland. "Micro-Politics: An Underestimated Field of Qualitative Research in Political Science." *German Policy Studies* 7, no. 3 (2011): 155–85.

Winant, Howard. *The New Politics of Race: Globalism, Difference, Justice*. Minneapolis: University of Minnesota Press, 2004.

Winchester, Daniel. "Converting to Continuity: Temporality and Self in Eastern Orthodox Conversion Narratives." *Journal for the Scientific Study of Religion* 54, no. 3 (2015): 439–60.

Wingfield, Adia Harvey. "Are Some Emotions Marked 'Whites Only'? Racialized Feeling Rules in Professional Workplaces." *Social Problems* 57, no. 2 (2010): 251–68.

———. *Flatlining: Race, Work, and Health Care in the New Economy*. Berkeley: University of California Press, 2019.

Woodly, Deva R. *Reckoning: Black Lives Matter and the Democratic Necessity of Social Movements*. New York: Oxford University Press, 2022.

Young, Iris Marion. "Justice, Inclusion and Deliberative Democracy." In *Deliberative Politics: Essays on Democracy and Disagreement*, edited by S. Macedo, 151–58. New York: Oxford University Press, 1999.

Zembylas, Michalinos. "Affect, Race, and White Discomfort in Schooling: Decolonial Strategies for 'Pedagogies of Discomfort.'" *Ethics and Education* 13, no. 1 (2018): 86–104.

Zoizner, Alon. "The Consequences of Strategic News Coverage for Democracy: A Meta-Analysis." *Communication Research* 48, no. 1 (2021): 3–25. https://doi.org/10.1177/0093650218808691.

Index

accountability, 22, 94, 158

Addams, Jane, 46

agency: lack of, 50, 123; and racial consciousness, 37, 152–53; and responsibility, 157–59

Alegria, Sharla, 49

Alexander, Michelle, 8, 94

American Psychological Association, 63

animal rights advocacy, 4–5, 177n5

antiracism, 134–35, 148–49; commitment to, 100–101

authority, white, 106–8

author's experiences, 3–10

author's methodology, 1–2, 11–12, 17, 23–24, 25–26, 143–44; access to GAP, 163–65; case study method, 165–66; ethnographic research, 161–67; interview techniques, 167–70; journal-keeping, 172; lived experiences, 16–17; outcome-oriented research, 155–56; "participants," status of, 170; power and positionality, 170–75; routines vs. rituals, 166–67

avoidance, of racial issues, 94. *See also* racial silence/reticence

awareness (racial consciousness), 35–43

awkwardness: acceptance of, 127–28; and awareness, of researcher, 172–73; and conflict, 138–39; discomfort, tolerance of, 158; goals/visions translated to procedures, 29–31; and racialized interactions, 12–14, 24–25; as social phenomenon, 14; and transformative democracy, 136–37. *See also* conflict; discomfort

Baldwin, James, 87, 152

Berger, Peter L., 103

Biden, Joe, 55

Black community: American South and Democratic Party, 32; race as defining characteristic, 47–48

Black Lives Matter movement, 7–8, 10, 75, 101

Black Panther Party, 41, 126

Bonilla-Silva, Eduardo, 23, 44

"bottom-up" participation. *See* grassroots organizations

Bourdieu, Pierre, 43

Braunstein, Ruth, 55

Brown, Michael, 8

capitalism: capitalist domination, 188n22; critiques of, 120

Carmichael, Stokely, 121

Carrigan, Mark, 12

case study methodology, 165–66, 189n5, 190n10. *See also* author's methodology

Chambers, Samuel A., 84

Chavez, Cesar, 4

Clair, Matthew, 70

class consciousness, 35, 117, 120

Clinton, Hillary, 18, 55, 64, 98, 128, 145

collective habits, 44, 46, 104, 129, 149, 158

Collins, Patricia Hill, 47, 114

conflict: avoidance of, 109–10; awkwardness of, 138–39; concealed by consensus, 113–18; destructive, 114; productive, 113. *See also* awkwardness; discomfort

www.ingramcontent.com/pod-product-compliance
Lightning Source LLC
Chambersburg PA
CBHW020531270326
41927CB00006B/536